Leadership through the Lens

Leadership through the Lens

Interrogating Production, Presentation, and Power

Creshema R. Murray

LEXINGTON BOOKS
Lanham • Boulder • New York • London

Published by Lexington Books
An imprint of The Rowman & Littlefield Publishing Group, Inc.
4501 Forbes Boulevard, Suite 200, Lanham, Maryland 20706
www.rowman.com

Unit A, Whitacre Mews, 26-34 Stannary Street, London SE11 4AB

British Library Cataloguing in Publication Information Available

Library of Congress Cataloging-in-Publication Data Available

ISBN 978-1-4985-6151-8 (cloth : alk. paper)
ISBN 978-1-4985-6152-5 (electronic)

∞™ The paper used in this publication meets the minimum requirements of American National Standard for Information Sciences—Permanence of Paper for Printed Library Materials, ANSI/NISO Z39.48-1992.

Printed in the United States of America

For my great-grandparents, Mosely and Janie Murray, for showing me how to be a leader.

For my mother, Chandra Murray Tarver, for always cheering, encouraging, and supporting me throughout my leadership endeavors.

For my sister, Shay Tarver, for listening while I lead

Contents

Preface

Creshema R. Murray

This book explores and examines the production, performance, power, and presentation of leadership culture through television. Television is a key medium of education and socialization; transferring multiple images and messages through news programs, scripted and unscripted reality television, dramas, and situational comedies. We use television as a gateway to understand difference, reify social encounters, and learn how to perform life. When I first began working on this project, it was out of the desire to appreciate the manner in which television has shaped the way I understand life, in particular the way that I understand the organizational functions of life. As an organizational communication scholar, educated in a critical, cultural, and rhetorical school, I have always had aspirations to analyze the power of mediated organizational encounters. Through this book, it is my hope for readers to consider the way we view leaders, leadership, and leadership practices.

Why *Leadership Through the Lens*? Television, as a cultural forum, provides a variety of tools impacting our understanding of perceptions and expectations of what leading is and how it is done. There are numerous examples of how we document leadership theories and explore leadership practices; however, there was not a text available to document the complex, yet simple relationship between television production, viewership, and the personal performance of leadership.

Through this book, it is my intent that scholars in communication studies, leadership studies, and media studies will engage in dialogue about the importance of using a variety of televised experiences to teach and study leaders and leadership. This book is broken into three sections: production, presentation, and power. The first section, Production of Knowledge, approaches leadership through the guise that televised portrayals of leadership are directly impacted by the people behind the lens. The stories that we see are a direct result of what the people in charge of the lens; creators, writers, and producers, want viewers to see. The second section, Presentation of Identity, explores the role race, age, gender, and the body play in our understanding of leadership practices. This section provides stories illustrating how these identity constructs impact the different ways in which we see leadership practices unfold. Each chapter in this section presents the multiple intersections of identity as key tools in exploring the differences in the way leadership is performed based on differences. The final section, Power of Opportunity, evaluates the power given to television viewers regarding their understanding of how leaders function. This section assesses leadership from a cultural lens of examining how leaders navigate their work space, develop relationships, and understand the ways in which these individuals function in the work world. There is no one right way to lead and this section expresses how workplace relationships control how leaders view their role and power in organizations.

I have learned so much about life, society, and culture throughout my years in front of the television lens. As a loyal viewer of television, I have found myself to be an avid scholar of what takes place behind the lens; critiquing the messages, observing the meanings, and understanding how these images impact my life. It is my hope that this text is used as a vessel to value organizational life, identify cultural differences, recognize social issues, and appreciate the role that television plays in our understanding of leadership.

Part I

PRODUCTION OF KNOWLEDGE

Chapter 1

Leadership Lessons Hiding in Plain Sight

Teaching Leadership Through Television

Gail T. Fairhurst and Joseph M. Deye[1]

It has become commonplace to observe that Millennials are quite different than previous generations. They are more diverse demographically, appear less trusting of others, and need more stimulation in their personal, professional, and academic lives (Drake, 2014; Murray, 2011; Varallo, 2008). Millennials are also heavy consumers of pop culture, whose media and technology intakes constitute "an important part of who they are as individuals" (Considine, et al., 2009, p 475). As students, they want to be actively engaged in order to make relevant connections between classroom material and their own lives (McGlynn, 2005). Often the engagement and stimulation they desire, even *require*, manifests itself in a heavy use of multimedia experiences. As such, Millennials appear to be transforming the classroom experience in ways we have not seen before.

We have responded by incorporating numerous televised (and other media) examples in the teaching of a 4000-level course in leadership communication at our university. Television has become an important tool for teaching leadership because of its frequent portrayals in scripted and unscripted workplace and political settings (e.g., Michael Scott in *The Office;* Hillary Clinton and Donald Trump as 2016 U.S. presidential candidates with 24/7 news coverage and mock portrayals by Kate McKinnon and Alec Baldwin, respectively, on *Saturday Night Live*; CEOs' frequent appearances before the U.S. Congress, and so on).

In teaching leadership communication, we have incorporated these and other media examples to stimulate and heighten the personal connection that Millennials want from the classroom experience. Indeed, televised content has become a ubiquitous pedagogical tool across many courses in social science curriculums. But does it come at a cost? What leadership lessons are hiding in plain sight when we confront the strengths and the weaknesses of television as a pedagogical tool?

In this chapter, we will discuss the merits and flaws of several of our television examples. Importantly, we will also discuss the collateral learning of this pedagogical approach that is, content aside, *how* are students learning? For example, does television normalize white male bodies as leaders to the exclusion of women and people of color? Does it put an inordinate focus on individuals over the collective efforts required to affect large-scale change? Does it valorize them by doing so or does it degrade their performances in damned-if-you, damned-if you-don't circumstances?

While John Dewey (1963) first raised the notion of collateral learning, Neil Postman (1985) took this a step further by observing the ways in which teaching and entertainment have become inseparable in the television era. As this trend has only continued with Millennials (and, perhaps, heightened), we are also obliged to ask, how do we remain reflexive about television as an epistemology, and what do we communicate to students of leadership communication in this regard? Our chapter will thus address how to confront television's potentially distorting effects.

LEADERSHIP LESSONS IN TELEVISED CONTEXTS

As indicated, we have responded to the challenge put forth by the Millennial generation by incorporating televised portrayals of leadership communication through news reports, commentaries, dramatic presentations, satire, and other forms of humor. However, John Dewey (1938, 1998: 49–50) cautions the following: "Perhaps the greatest of all pedagogical fallacies is the notion that a person learns only the particular things he [*sic*] is studying at the time. Collateral learning in the way of formation of enduring attitudes, of like and dislikes, may be and often is much more important than the (intended lesson) ... the most important attitude that can be formed is that of desire to go on learning. If the impetus in this direction is weakened instead of being intensified, something much more than mere lack of preparation takes place. The pupil is actually robbed of native capacities which otherwise would enable him to cope with the circumstances that he meets in the course of life."

Following Dewey, without a strong appreciation for collateral learning—the outcomes of which should reinforce a continuous learning mindset—not only are students' perspectives narrowed, but ultimately so are their coping abilities. To wit, we can preach that diversity and inclusion are important values for leadership of multicultural societies, but if our examples of successful leadership focus too heavily on white males, of what value is the diversity lesson?

Historically, the Western (read, American) prototype of leadership has indeed favored the white, middle class male as a heroic figure who, by force of nature or will, bent the environment to his vision of it (Nkomo, 1988; 1992; Yukl, 1999). Not only was leadership gendered, raced, and classed, it was disembodied, psychologized, and valorized for individual foresight above collective accomplishment (Collinson & Hearn, 1996; Denis, Langley, & Sergi, 2012; Fairhurst, 2007). Whether conditions have changed appreciably in contemporary organizations is a matter of debate.

For example, there are certainly more women in leadership roles than when Rosabeth Moss Kanter (1977) wrote her groundbreaking book on gender and tokenism, *Men and Women of the Corporation,* which marked the first time women entered the workforce in larger numbers in other than "pink collar" positions. Yet, despite much stronger numbers (Eagly, Johannesen-Schmidt, & Engen, 2003), they remain a minority, particularly at higher levels, compared to their male counterparts (Eagly, 2007). The same can also be said for African Americans and other ethnic or religious minorities who struggle with the so-called glass ceiling (Parker, 2005).

However, the roots of gender's effect on leadership grow much deeper than an initial look at the numbers would suggest. This is because masculinity discourses continue to dominate what it means to be a leader (e.g., a strong, take charge use of language, an orientation to power and authority, eschewal of soft forms of power, and so on), so much so that women readily adopt these discourses as they assume managerial roles (Collinson & Hearn, 1996; Lin & Cheng, 2007; Ragins, 1991) and often experience role conflict as a result (Eagly & Karau, 2002; Heilman, 2001). The study or promotion of such practices begs the question of alternative ways of leading in which struggles over meaning, identity, and difference surface and resolve in ways that do not (re)produce masculine privilege (Aschraft & Mumby, 2004)—and, by implication, white, middle class privilege (Parker, 2005).

Related to issues of gender and race is the body. On the one hand, Sinclair (2005) argued that leadership establishes itself, in part, through a hierarchy of body masculinities in which leaders are depicted as defying their bodies (e.g., think Gandhi's fasting or Enron executive Jeff Skilling's extreme motocross racing with his executive team). At the same time, leadership behavior in the management literature is very nearly bodiless that is, lacking *any* focus on the body (Collinson & Hearn, 1996; Kerfoot & Knights, 1996; Sinclair, 1998): "If one is male, powerful and senior, then one is more likely to be portrayed as bodiless—and this is precisely the point" (Sinclair, 2005:390). The naturalization of the white male as the embodiment of leadership thus begs the question of alternative body possibilities vis-à-vis issues of gender, sexuality, skin color, or disability.

Finally, the psychologizing of leadership and its valorization is related. Fairhurst (2007) described the dominance of leadership psychology throughout its history vis-à-vis an almost exclusive focus on the individual and cognitive in lieu of the social and cultural. Each lens has its own set of questions for which it is ideally suited—and one should not be used to study the other. Indeed, studying the social and cultural aspects of leadership by focusing on individual perceptions in surveys and seven point scales (historically, the default way to study leadership) predisposed scholars to individualist and heroic models of leadership where agency is easy to exaggerate. Studying social interaction, by contrast, displays the ways in which leadership may shift and distribute itself in the sequentialized patterns of control and control sharing that emerge (Fairhurst, 2007; Fairhurst & Connaughton, 2014; Fairhurst, Green & Courtright, 1995).

Denis et al. (2012) envelope the above argument as one of four streams of research that entertains leadership as a plural phenomenon: 1) sharing leadership in teams, 2) pooling leadership at the top of the organization, 3) spreading leadership across boundaries over time, and 4) producing (multiple) forms of leadership in social interaction. This more relational, distributed, and collective view of leadership is a relatively recent (research) phenomenon, but a necessary counterweight to individual and heroic models, which do not easily explain the increasingly wicked problems leaders face in complex societies that require collaborative responses (Grint, 2005; Sheep, Fairhurst, & Khazanchi, 2017).

Based on the above judgments about the leadership literature, a set of value commitments form the foundation for the course—and the criteria for selecting televised portrayals for classroom presentation with collateral learning in mind. They include a commitment to challenge: 1) the dominance of cognitive views of leadership to focus on its relational, embodied, and collective aspects; 2) a romanticized view of leadership as individualist, heroic, white, and masculine in favor of more realist and diverse portrayals; and 3) power as a neutral resource with one that is interest-laden, ideological, disciplinary, and both positive and negative. All three commitments are intended to shape the learning, including collateral learning, around leadership communication, which we seek to make clear in the following course examples (see also the Appendix for a summary).

SELECTION OF TELEVISED PORTRAYALS
FOR CLASSROOM PRESENTATION

What is Leadership?

The course opens by showing students a number of televised portrayals of leadership, which are designed to get them thinking about the complexity of leadership and the difficulties involved in defining it. These vary according to what is newsworthy at the moment, but a sampling might include the following:

1. A *Saturday Night Live* clip in which the actress, Kate McKinnon, plays Mary Barra, CEO of General Motors, testifying before Congress and dodging answers, to great comedic effect, about GM's failure to recall millions of small cars over a catastrophic safety defect. This 2014 skit shows a white female as a CEO, but one who is using the power of apology and ambiguity to skirt taking full responsibility. The clip problematizes whether issues of ethics and morality are necessary to define leadership.
2. The 2016 presidential campaign clips of Donald Trump insulting women, the disabled, Mexicans, veterans, journalists, and others. Although these clips would have dashed the campaigns of most other candidates, many in the American electorate deemed Trump "authentic" for making these politically offensive remarks. They thus problematize how the issue of authenticity figures in defining leadership.
3. A clip from a TED talk entitled, "Leadership Lessons from the Dancing Guy," shows a young male dancing at a music festival. He begins to attract a crowd only when a second person engages the "dancing guy." This clip presents leadership as over glorified and first followers as the "real" leaders. We thus problematize the role of attribution and whether leadership exists without followers in defining leadership.
4. A clip from a televised news conference of Thane Maynard, Director of the Cincinnati Zoo, who justifies the shooting of the lowland gorilla, Harambe, when a young boy climbed into his enclosure in 2016. This clip showcases the role of leaders during crisis management, a moment of high drama, compared to the more mundane aspects of the job.

Based on a selection of these portrayals, which we vary by gender, age, race, nationality, and setting, students must decide, "What is leadership?" Typically, it makes for a thought-provoking discussion.

Moving Beyond Leadership Psychology

We begin the course in earnest with a relatively brief, two-lecture acknowledgment of the contributions of leadership psychology. We review such theories as trait approaches, style approaches, situational leadership theory, leader-member exchange, transformational and charismatic leadership, as well as servant leadership, to name a few. Two movie portrayals (subsequently televised) demonstrate these theories, as well as a supplemental TED talk and audio recording.

First, we present the movie trailer from *Patton,* which is a 1970 American biographical war film about General George S. Patton during World War II (starring George C. Scott). The trailer showcases a military leader demonstrating a style approach to leadership, specifically, an autocratic style and the ways in which Scott, the actor, positions his body to show dominance, confidence, and hyper-masculinity. Moreover, it shows how theories historically rooted in the psychology of leadership emphasize the individual with a strong inner motor, where "power relations are unproblematic and ... white male leaders are the people in charge who create visions, make decisions, and transmit orders, while followers are an undifferentiated collective who carry out orders from 'above'" (Collinson & Tourish, 2015, p. 585). Finally, the trailer demonstrates the Hollywood myth-making machinery that turns ordinary individuals into heroes.

Second, Itay Talgam's TED talk on the world's great orchestra conductors is an excellent follow-up to demonstrate the role of the body, sans *any* spoken words, in creating leadership styles. During orchestra performances, Talgam contrasts body positions and movements that invite and respond to orchestra members versus dictate and control their performances. It thus serves as a nice counterpoint to the *Patton* clip vis-à-vis the role of the body.

Third, clips from the movie, *Sister Act,* show the African American actress, Whoopi Goldberg, playing a lounge singer hiding in a convent, unexpectedly leading and transforming a choir. "Sister Mary Clarence," as she is called, demonstrates charismatic leadership theory as she takes the choir to new heights by the force of her personality, immediately attracting a new and younger crowd into the church and later winning an invitation to perform at the Vatican. The focus is on the individual, a trait view of leadership, undifferentiated followers, and unproblematized power, which we highlight for students.

Fourth, to counter the light-hearted, unrealistic *Sister Act* portrayal of charismatic leadership, we play portions of the Jonestown Death Tape. It is an audio recording, available on the Internet, made on November 18, 1978, at the Peoples Temple compound in Jonestown, Guyana. It was made just before and during the mass suicide and murder of over 900 members of the cult started by Jim Jones. It demonstrates the dark side of charisma, this time, with very real consequences.

To summarize, the introduction to leadership psychology is done with examples that vary by gender, race, social class, and nationality with collateral learning along these dimensions in mind. Students also see leadership cast repeatedly vis-à-vis having a strong inner motor; however, this psychological lens is acknowledged, but never denigrated as incorrect or without merit. Like all lenses, it has its strengths and its blind spots. The latter sets the stage for a more communicative and relational view of leadership, which problematizes issues of communication, power, and followership.

The Power of Framing

We introduce *The Power of Framing: Challenging the Language of Leadership* (Fairhurst, 2011; hereafter *TPOF*), the main textbook for the course, at this point. *TPOF* focuses on leadership as a co-constructed relational process, grounded in a meaning-centered view of human communication (e.g., leadership emerges when the uncertainty, confusion, and undecidability of "the situation here and now" opens it up for interpretation and provides an opportunity for the more verbally skilled to emerge as leaders, p. 7). Its treatment of power focuses on the role of discourse in both enabling communication and disciplining social actors to its ways. Discourse also interacts with one's mental models that, in turn, shape core framing tasks. Finally, chapters within this book also emphasize developing a heightened sensitivity to language, priming to control one's spontaneous communication, emotions and emotional contagion, ethics and moral positioning, and finally, a deep understanding of context (Fairhurst, 2011). Several televised videos support the presentation of *TPOF's* content.

For example, in the first chapter, two CEOs are presented as poor examples of leadership framing. Both are white males, but they appear to differ in social class. Bob Murray, a former miner with a rough appearance and delivery, was the president and CEO of Crandall Canyon Mines.[2] In two televised news conferences in 2007, he contradicted (what he putatively knew to be) the facts by categorically denying that his company's practice of "retreat mining" caused the underground explosion that killed six workers and three members of a rescue team. In addition, at a time when he was supposed to be addressing the needs of the miners' families, he used the first news conference to speak at length about Americans' need for the coal mining industry. It was widely regarded as an insensitive, off-putting performance.

In close succession to this example, we present the case of the extremely well-spoken Tony Hayward, the British CEO of British Petroleum. He unceremoniously lost his job when he went yachting during the height of 2010 Gulf Oil crisis, triggered by the explosion of the Deep Water oilrig. Shortly thereafter, he told a television reporter, "We're sorry for the massive disruption it's caused to their lives. There's no one who wants this thing over more than I do. I'd like my life back." Like Bob Murray, Hayward's performance was greatly out of touch with the demands of the moment. Their appearance contrasts an American blue collar CEO with a British upper class CEO, both struggling mightily to relate to their audiences.

To help students understand the difference between discourses (i.e., sociohistorical systems of thought that also function as linguistic tool bags), mental models (i.e., deeply held images of how the world works), and core framing tasks (i.e., communication goals of the moment), we present an episode of (the American television show) *The Office*, entitled "Diversity Day." We ask students to analyze it for these key concepts. In this episode, Michael Scott is the leader of the office who tries and fails to teach diversity by invoking stereotypes of nearly every major social category (e.g., gender, race, religion, nationality). The humor is designed for laughter at, not with, these stereotyped portrayals. We follow this up with a real-life audiotape of a police rescue of an injured officer in which students are given the same assignment; however, this rescue is the first to introduce an example of collective and distributed leadership.

To underscore issues of context, language, priming, emotions, and the tension between individual and collective leadership, we present a 2003, ABC news special on the 40th anniversary of Martin Luther King's *I Have a Dream Speech*. This documentary does a particularly good job of communicating the deep racial divides in America at the time, which provides necessary context for the speech for Millennials for whom this is often lacking. It showcases Dr. King's great concern for crafting the right language, the role that priming (parts of his speech) at previous venues played, and how emotional contagion played a huge role in the eventual performance of the speech. Finally, because the documentary interviews many other members of the American civil rights movement at the time, it provides an opportunity for students to understand the collective leadership of this movement without diminishing Dr. King's contributions.

To address ethics and the role of moral positioning in framing, we presented Oprah Winfrey's 2013 televised interview of Lance Armstrong, the American who for many years was the leader of the U.S. Postal Service professional cycling team and a seven-time winner of the Tour de France. Upon being found guilty of blood doping, he was forced to give back his titles in 2012. His televised interview details the bullying tactics he used as the leader of the team, although his nonverbals during the interview in response to Ms. Winfrey's questioning suggest less than authentic remorse over such tactics and cheating due to doping.

To summarize, *TPOF* provides a deep dive into the communicative dynamics of leadership, which begin with sensemaking communications that resonate to form leadership attributions. Our examples give us an opportunity to problematize issues of race and diversity, in particular, but also social class and setting. From here, we move to broaden students' understanding of leadership as both individual and collective.

Wicked Problems and Collective Leadership

TPOF provides the foundation to understand how persons in authority frame problems to justify their preferred authority styles. We subsequently introduce

Grint (2005) who suggests a typology between managers and tame problems; leaders and wicked problems; and commander and crises. However, Grint does not introduce this typology to suggest a one-to-one correspondence, but the ways in which problem framing can be easily manipulated to align with power interests.

A *60 Minutes* profile of the American nuns who ran afoul of the Vatican in 2013 for their "feminist leanings" supplies an excellent example. It described the commission that Pope Benedict created to monitor and, potentially, censure the nuns' activities. The white, male monsignor who headed the commission framed the problem of the American nuns as a "crisis." Bob Simon, the CBS News correspondent, directly challenged such framing because it appeared trivial compared to the priest's sex abuse crisis plaguing the church at the time. What is not to be missed, however, is that this religious leader's framing of the American nuns' problem justifies the severest forms of censure, thus supporting Grint's (2005) argument. What should also not be missed are the articulate, measured, and cogent performances of the American nuns who emerge as leaders by virtue of their resistance. Gender and religiosity thus take center stage in this discussion of leadership.

The introduction of wicked problems provides the foundation for the second textbook of the course, *Share, Don't Take the Lead* (Pearce, Manz, & Sims, 2014), which details several different forms of collaborative leadership (e.g., distributed, shared, integrated, and rotated) in case study format. Student groups look for and present several televised examples of collaborative leadership, among them, episodes of *Grey's Anatomy* where the operating room environments, in particular, showcase distributed and shared leadership among medical professionals who frequently vary by gender, age, and ethnicity.

Lincoln, the Movie

The course ends with the 2012 movie, *Lincoln*, directed by Stephen Spielberg. The movie does a particularly good job of highlighting both the individual and collective leadership surrounding the passage of the 13th Amendment to abolish slavery. It problematizes issues of race, slavery, and civil rights as wicked problems demanding collaborative, often clumsy, solutions—whose failures, we point out, reverberate today. It showcases strong examples of framing by Lincoln, who manifests a heightened sensitivity to language through storytelling that, ironically, is not always welcomed. This film also reproduces the hero myth-making machinery of Hollywood, although there is also a strong emphasis on the collective, sometimes morally ambiguous, backstage maneuverings to get the bill passed that allows for many others to emerge as leaders. By showing the film in three class segments, we are able to assist with students' sensemaking for the many details of this film, which pulls course concepts together.

If we have been successful, including our use of television, we will have challenged the dominance of cognitive views of leadership by focusing on its relational, embodied, and collective aspects that is, a strongly *communicative* approach to leadership. We will have eschewed a romanticized view of leadership as individualist, heroic, white, and masculine in favor of more realistic and diverse portrayals. Finally, we will have attempted to present power as anything but a neutral resource that is, it is interest-laden, ideological, disciplining, and with both positive and negative aspects. However, there are more challenges for collateral learning beyond issues of gender, race, nationality, social class, the body, and a collective, relational view of leadership, as the next section reveals.

FURTHER LESSONS IN COLLATERAL LEARNING

Three forms of collateral learning around our television pedagogy (Dewey, 1963; Postman, 1985) pose special challenges with respect to the teaching of leadership communication. They include the valorization and degradation of leadership and the sacrifice of mundanity.

Valorization

Valorization paints leadership as a heroic and seemingly unattainable practice—even when leadership is cast as collective, not just individual. It is a topic of some debate in the leadership literature because certain theories are predisposed to hero anointing. For example, Yukl (1999) argued that charismatic and transformational leadership theories often valorize leaders, typically by casting their vision (and personal persuasive qualities) as the proximal cause of success, thus ignoring the multitude of factors that must also align for a vision to take effect (e.g., Steve Jobs' and Apple).

A typical example of valorizing individual leaders in our media examples is the movie *Sister Act*. As mentioned above, the clips portray a charismatic leader who takes an off-key, mediocre choir and turns them into a powerhouse chorus, only to be given an opportunity to perform for the Pope. The plot is more nuanced if shown in its entirety, but the (incredulous) outcome remains. While using a woman of color in the leadership role is a good tool for incorporating diversity into media examples, these clips also unintentionally accentuate extraordinary individual achievement with undifferentiated followers whose only role is to embody the leader's vision.

However, consider *Grey's Anatomy,* a drama centered on doctors at a teaching hospital who engage shared or distributed leadership during operations. In one example of high drama, the senior medical staff member appears to abdicate her teaching responsibilities as a junior colleague struggles during an operation of a patient whose life is on the line. Contra all outward appearances, the senior colleague summarily announces that the patient isn't going to die. Instead, she urges her junior colleague to rely on her instincts to make the correct decisions. Lo and behold, the junior colleague chooses wisely, and the patient survives. Students certainly see the shared leadership manifest in the clip, but it's hard not to miss how both doctors also bask in the heroic light in which they have been cast.

Consider also the *60 Minutes* profile, mentioned earlier, of a group of nuns who ran afoul of the Vatican for their so-called "feminist" ideas concerning the role of women in the traditionally patriarchal Catholic Church. This profile demonstrates how leadership emerges through acts of collaborative resistance, but also how problems get framed to suit one's preferred style of authority. The clip highlights two sisters, in particular, as leaders of separate branches of their movement, but it also criticizes the patriarchy and marginalizes the many other nuns with whom the two leaders collaborate. Despite the talk of collaboration by the sisters, *60 Minutes* portrays them as heroic, if unlikely, leaders by dint of the movement's success and the growing positive media coverage.

Degradation

Degradation as a form of collateral learning diminishes leadership and devalues authority, chiefly when the televised content uses satire to entertain and amuse. Such content can salvage an otherwise dull or abstract lecture, or it can powerfully portray the consequences of bad leadership behavior. In terms of collateral learning, however, it may be particularly harmful to Millennials who already harbor feelings of distrust toward society (Drake, 2014).

One well-loved media example in our course involves the *Saturday Night Live* clip of GM's Mary Barra and the Congressional hearing over the aforementioned safety recall that they handled so poorly. As we indicated above, Kate McKinnon's "Mary Barra" dodges questions, obfuscates, and outmaneuvers her way out of dealing with the safety issues. This comedic portrayal degrades leadership by portraying this female executive as untrustworthy, self-serving, and unilaterally failing to take responsibility for her company's actions. It completely elides the dilemma that Barra faced vis-à-vis conflicting goals between shareholders and stakeholders, which does not justify the abdication of responsibility, but better explains it. The clip also has the potential to accentuate Millennials' distrust of society, including (female) leaders of large corporations (Drake, 2014; Cillizza, 2015).

Another powerful example of leadership degradation via humor occurs in *The Office* episode, "Diversity Day." While the episode nicely demonstrates the key framing concepts of discourses, mental models, and core framing tasks—which can be very abstract concepts when first presented to students—it displays the same issues as the *SNL* skit. The office manager, Michael Scott, is an inept and clueless leader who takes his people on a wild ride of heavy-handed and insensitive diversity training that he personally designed. The episode is relatable to anyone who has had an ineffective and oblivious leader, but that is precisely what contributes to the degradation. Showing the highly amusing episode runs the risk of portraying all leaders as essentially inept and insensitive, especially toward diversity issues, thus reinforcing Millennials' general disillusionment with workplace leaders, and their lack of trust in others (Cillizza, 2015; Drake, 2014).

Sacrifice of Mundanity

Televised content that sacrifices mundanity marginalizes the ordinary, everyday aspects of a leader's job, thus creating the impression that the work of leadership is far more glamorous than it actually is. However, the mundanity of simple conversations, even just listening to direct reports, is central to the perceived competence and effectiveness of those in leadership positions (Alvesson & Sveningsson, 2003). Such content is, unfortunately, less stimulating to students. We know this because some complain that the movie, *Lincoln,* which features the mundane, lacks sufficient action in their view. It is as if singular portrayals of coaches of underdog teams who inspire come-from-behind victories (e.g., *Coach Carter, Hoosiers*) or *Terminator*-like action stars are the only leaders for which we should be aiming to get and hold their attention.

However, we do contribute to this state of affairs. Returning to the *Sister Act* clips with the Whoopi Goldberg character taking the choir to unforeseen heights, we do not show the necessary relationship building with choir members or indications of endless practice hours, which are just as essential to the choir's phenomenal success. The same sacrifice of mundanity occurs in Itay Talgam's TED talk regarding the conducting styles of the world's major orchestra conductors. While the clip elevates the physical embodiment of leadership style, it sacrifices portraying the mundane moments of rehearsals or other private meetings, which more likely contribute to their success as orchestra leaders. (It also valorizes conductors by showing only their public performances, in which they are the focus of attention, with undifferentiated orchestra members.)

Likewise, the clips contrasting CEOs Robert Murray, discussing the Crandall Canyon mine disaster, and Tony Hayward, discussing the BP oil spill in the Gulf of Mexico, are certainly moments of high drama. Both are in crisis mode to salvage the reputations of their companies amidst the catastrophic problems at hand. These are just a few of the many examples we could supply of sacrificing mundanity, not to mention the valorization and degradation of leadership.

Remaining Reflexive

While Postman (1985) warned of television's negative effects in education, he also provided hope for educators by suggesting that they remain reflexive. This has certainly helped us to address all of the forms of collateral learning that we have described in chapter, albeit with varying degrees of success. Our own reflexivity takes three forms. First, a Millennial always co-facilitates the course, as an undergraduate teaching assistant (TA), along with an experienced instructor. While the TA takes on the typical responsibilities (e.g., some grading, logistics, and so on), regular pre- and post-class meetings allow the professor and TA to discuss the pace of learning in the class and how Millennials are processing its contents.

Second, having a Millennial as a co-facilitator also affords us the opportunity to continually reflect on our own standpoints or positionalities. We are white and middle class, able to take full advantage of the opportunities of higher education. One of us is a professor and PhD who is a woman, and the other a master's student (formerly a TA) who is a man. Both of us are Catholic. One of us is a Baby Boomer and, as mentioned, one of us is a Millennial. Although we differ in a number of ways, we do not differ by race and must therefore be particularly sensitive to issues of white privilege and the ways in which leadership is often raced, not just gendered. We also do not differ by nationality, as we are both American, and thus must be sensitive to the ways in which leadership on the global stage may be profoundly different based on values quite foreign to the Westerners. Our students, of course, often differ by race, gender, age, and nationality.

Finally, when discussing our media examples, we strive to share our positionalities with the class to facilitate better classroom engagement, which Millennials say they desire (McGlynn, 2005). In fact, sharing positionalities may allow the student-facilitator relationship to become a place where discussions of collateral learning from media examples can more readily be challenged. While requiring students to share their positionalities back with instructors would be intrusive, in sharing our positions our hope is that students would eventually share challenges only they can see due to their respective standpoints.

With this foundation, consider two media examples that require a particularly high level of reflexivity, the aforementioned ABC special on the 40th anniversary of Dr. Martin Luther King's *I Have a Dream Speech* and the movie, *Lincoln*. Both media examples valorize individual leadership *and* showcase collective leadership. *Lincoln* clearly shows that the president could not accomplish passage of the 13th Amendment on his own. He requires help from congressional leaders and representatives, cabinet members, and even (morally dubious) outside liaisons (lobbyists before their time?). The ABC special features the other leaders of the civil rights movement, many of whom were interviewed for the documentary. Their presence signifies that Dr. King was an integral part of a movement and part of a network of leaders promoting equality. While each leader pays a steep price for their principles for which they stood making valorization, perhaps, inevitable, students must be continually reminded to focus on the *creative tension* between individual and collective leadership. That is, it is rarely a case of individual *or* collective leadership, but individual *and* collective leadership because they interpenetrate and build upon one another. Millennials' inclination is to focus on the former only, perhaps because the Hollywood myth-making machinery for heroes has done too good a job.

As we have mentioned previously, Millennials prefer action to the mundane. They must be encouraged to see how Dr. King also engaged in multiple acts of everyday leadership through many simple and private conversations with government leaders, Civil Rights leaders, and other supporters of the civil rights movement. Lincoln, of course, conversed with his advisors, listened to citizens, kept company with low-level staff until the wee hours of the night as they waited for news on the war, visited hospitals, and so on. We acknowledge that such content may inevitably bore some students, getting them to affix value to such scenes is crucial to shaping their own leadership styles and the value they place on taking the time and effort to hold such conversations.

Finally, the presentation of these two examples raises racial questions that are ongoing concerns for us. The movie *Lincoln* makes clear the pain and costs of a history of slavery, the effects of which African American students in the class may still feel today. How do we best remain sensitive to this, especially given our own positionalities? We often meet with African America students individually or in groups after class to gauge their reactions, comfort level, and concerns regarding this example. While we have been met with only positive feedback in the past, we must acknowledge that those who disagree might be choosing to remain silent. Regarding the documentary, although Dr. King's speech is widely regarded as the most important speech of the twentieth century, is it an example that has been "whitewashed" that is, one made more palatable to the majority of white students than other examples might be (e.g., Malcolm X)? We sometimes incorporate class assignments that give students the opportunity to select their own televised or movie portrayals of leadership, and it is noteworthy that the movie, *Malcolm X,* is a frequently chosen subject (for both black and white students).

No media example will ever be perfect, and we recognize that. However, we also recognize that reflexivity around our own pedagogical choices in televised content is vitally important to balance the learning desires of Millennial students with our teaching goals.

CONCLUSION

In this chapter, we have considered what it means to incorporate examples from television and other media into a Millennial-filled, 4000-level class on leadership communication. We have placed that class into a historical context with the existing literature on leadership and leadership communication. We examined what teaching Millennials requires, how we employ television examples, and what those examples may impart to student in terms of collateral learning. In addition to issues of gender, race, nationality, social class, the body, and a collective, relational view of leadership, we have found that our examples often valorize leadership, degrade it, or sacrifice the mundane aspects of leaders' job in lieu of its more glamorous aspects.

Only by remaining reflexive are we able to carefully navigate the various channels of collateral learning around leadership communication, although it is not always easy to do. However, at a time when the world needs leaders more than ever, understanding how we teach leadership to Millennials is vital. Hopefully, the thoughts presented here can begin the process of moving away from unchecked collateral learning toward shaping Millennial leaders who are better able to address the problems of tomorrow.

APPENDIX

Leadership Communication Video List

What is Leadership?

Several videos give students an opportunity to debate a definition of the concept.

1. SNL takes on Mary Barra of GM (4:08). This video raises questions of ethics and gender.
2. NBC. (April 5, 2014). *The GM ignition switch congressional hearings* [video file]. Retrieved from: http://www.nbc.com/saturday-night-live/video/gm-hearings-cold-open/2770788

3. Cincinnati Zoo Director, Thayne Maynard, discusses the shooting of Harambe, the gorilla.
4. WLWT Channel 5. (June 11, 2016). *Zoo director Thayne Maynard talks about gorilla exhibit's reopening* [video file]. Retrieved from: http://www.wlwt.com/news/zoo-director-thane-maynard-talks-about-gorilla-exhibits-reopening/39937852
5. From the Big Short, we have "Meet Michael Burry" (1:17). Must a leader be a good communicator?
6. Paramount Pictures. (December 7, 2015). *The big short—"meet Michael Burry" featurette (2015)—Paramount Pictures* [video file]. Retrieved from: https://www.youtube.com/watch?v=wP4ESIjfpLk
7. El Chapo (2:41). Must leaders be positive role models?
8. Rolling Stone. (January 9, 2016). *Watch two minutes of El Chapo's exclusive interview, just before his recapture* [video file]. Retrieved from: http://www.rollingstone.com/culture/videos/watch-two-minutes-of-el-chapos-exclusive-interview-just-before-his-recapture-20160109
9. First Followers—The Dancing Guy (2:57). Examines leadership that eschews individualism.
10. Sivers, D. (February 11, 2010). *First follower: Leadership lessons from dancing guy* [video file]. Retrieved from: http://www.youtube.com/watch?v=fW8ammMCVAJQ
11. Everyday leadership—Drew Dudley, TED Toronto (6:14). Leadership is for everyone.
12. Ted-ed. (August 15, 2013). *Everyday leadership – Drew Dudley* [video file]. Retrieved from: https://www.youtube.com/watch?v=uAy6EawKKME

Ten Leadership Theories in 5 Minutes

1. A quick overview of the major psychological and social psychological theories of leadership, this video provides foundation to contrast what a more communicative view of leadership looks like.
2. Morgan, S. (February 25, 2014). *Ten leadership theories in five minutes* [video file]. Retrieved from: https://www.youtube.com/watch?v=xB-YhBbtfXE

Leadership Style Videos:

These clips provide a good demonstration of autocratic, transformational, and charismatic leadership. The TED talk, however, reflects the ways in which the body manifests style.

1. Autocratic Leadership Style: George Patton trailer (4:38)
2. *Patton theatrical movie trailer (1970)* [video file]. (June 4, 2011). Retrieved from: http://www.youtube.com/watch?v=g-0dTpzNzwo

3. Leadership Style—TED talk on orchestra leaders (20:44)
4. Talgam, I. (July 2009). *Like the great conductors* [video file]. Retrieved from: https://www.ted.com/talks/itay_talgam_lead_like_the_great_conductors?language=en
5. Transformational Leadership Style: Sister Act (2 videos)
6. *Sister Act—Sister Mary Clarence taking over the choir* [video file]. (October 30, 2008). Retrieved from: https://www.youtube.com/watch?v=37hkxf5RaXc
7. *Oh Maria—Sister Act—Whoopi Goldberg | HD | lyrics* [video file]. (October 24, 2007). Retrieved from: http://www.youtube.com/watch?v=rHASQg8fR0s
8. Dark Side of Charisma—Jim Jones (44:29)
9. Jones, J. (November 18, 1978). *The Jonestown death tape (FBI no. Q 042)* [audio file]. Retrieved from: http://archive.org/details/ptc1978-11-18.flac16

Leadership Listening Videos

1. Ed Tronick's Still Face Experiments: This describes the basic human need to be heard.
2. University of Massachusetts Boston. (November 30, 2009). *Still face experiment: Dr. Edward Tronick* [video file]. Retrieved from: https://www.youtube.com/watch?v=apzXGEbZht0
3. Sesame Street John-John and Grover count backward: This describes "scaffolding," a key leadership listening skill.
4. *Sesame Street—Grover and John John count backwards* [video file]. (July 14, 2007). Retrieved from: www.youtube.com/watch?v=keJeDo5e9Qw
5. Mateo Listening: How mental models for listening get built. This is comic and gets student's attention.
6. *3-year-old Mateo makes his case for cupcakes: "Linda, honey, just listen."* [video file]. (March 10, 2014). Retrieved from: https://www.youtube.com/watch?v=TP8RB7UZHKI

Leadership Framing Breakdown

1. Robert Murray's television interviews dealing with the Crandall Canyon Mine Accident demonstrate how not to respond to an audience and how framing is used unethically.
2. *Murray Energy Pres CEO Bob Murray re Crandall Canyon Mine Disaster* [video file]. (June 13, 2014). Retrieved from: https://www.youtube.com/watch?v=4ke-yT0--Os
3. *Kyra Phillips interviews Bob Murray on Utah Mining Disaster* [video file]. (August 22, 2007). Retrieved from: https://www.youtube.com/watch?v=7s29fxVIVTc

4. Tony Hayward BP CEO. Poor handling of the Gulf Oil crisis: "I'd like my life back."
5. *BP CEO Tony Hayward: 'I'd like my life back'* [video file]. (May 31, 2010). Retrieved from: https://www.youtube.com/watch?v=MTdKa9eWNFw

Leadership Framing Components: Discourses, Mental Models, and Core Framing tasks

1. An episode of *The Office*: "Diversity Day" is used to examine framing components.
2. Novak, B. J. (writer), & Kwapis, K (director). (2005). Diversity Day [television series episode]. In A. Hamilton (associate producer), & M. Schur (co-producer) *The Office*. NBC.

Leadership Framing Component: Priming

1. This is good for showing how malleable the mind can be when we prime it. We can prepare ourselves for framing/leadership situations.
2. *Money Priming* [video file]. (August 18, 2009). Retrieved from: https://www.youtube.com/watch?v=hzP0yLyDsRs

Leadership Framing Component: Language Choices

1. ABC News Special on the 40th Anniversary of Martin Luther King's *I have a dream* speech examines specific language choices in leadership communication. This video also shows the shared network of leadership and influencers inside the civil rights movement.
2. Robbins, R. (producer). (August 28, 2003). *Peter Jennings reporting "I have a dream"* [television broadcast]. New York: ABC News.

Leadership Framing Component: Ethics and Moral Positioning

1. Review of Lance Armstrong's Admission of Doping through television interviews.
2. New York Daily News. (September 26, 2010). *"Nightline" airs Floyd Landis interview* [video file]. Retrieved from: https://www.youtube.com/watch?v=NLtgu1WFJu8&feature=related
3. Lance Armstrong Speaks with Oprah (start at 35:00)
4. *Lance Armstrong on Oprah part 1* [video file]. (December 14, 2013). Retrieved from: https://www.youtube.com/watch?v=2jtDH-10m2s

Leadership Problem Framing around Wicked Problems

1. *60 Minutes* clip involving how American nuns are behaving as resistance leaders and how the Vatican tried to reign them in.

2. *Nuns on a bus 60 Minutes* [video file]. (April 26, 2013). Retrieved from: https://www.youtube.com/watch?v=PAjkplR96Cs

Shared Leadership

1. Episode of *Grey's Anatomy* involving shared leadership during a hospital operation.
2. *Grey's Anatomy 6x11 "blink": Christina's solo surgery [HD]* [video file]. (January 15, 2010). Retrieved from: https://www.youtube.com/watch?v=zxRQxPc6Nqg

Shared Leadership, Framing, Crisis Leadership, Wicked Problems

1. The movie *Lincoln* is used to pull together almost all of the course concepts at the end of the semester.
2. Spielberg, S. (producer and director), & Kennedy, K (producer). (2012). *Lincoln* [motion picture]. United States: DreamWorks Pictures & Twentieth Century Fox.

NOTES

1. The authors would like to thank Omotayo Banjo for reading an earlier version of this chapter.
2. However, Murray did attend college (Mouawad, 2016).

REFERENCES

Ashcraft, K. L., & Mumby, D. K. (2004). *Reworking gender: A feminist communicology of organization.* Thousand Oaks, CA: Sage.

Cillizza, C. (April 30, 2015). Millennials don't trust anyone. That's a big deal. *Washington Post.* Retrieved from: https://www.washingtonpost.com/

Collinson, D., & Hearn, J. (1996). *Men as managers, managers as men: Critical perspectives on men, masculinities and managements.* London, England: Sage.

Collinson, D., & Tourish, D. (2015). Teaching leadership critically: New directions for leadership pedagogy. *Academy of Management Learning & Education, 14*(4), 576–594.

Considine, D., Horton, J., & Moorman, G. (2009). Teaching and reading the millennial generation through media literacy. *Journal of Adolescent & Adult Literacy, 52*(6), 471–481.

Denis, J., Langley, A., & Sergi, V. (2012). Leadership in the plural. *The Academy of Management Annals, 6*(1), 211–283.

Dewey, J. (1998). *Experience and education: The 60th anniversary edition.* West Lafayette, IN: Kappa Delta Pi International Honor Society in Education.

Drake, B. (2014). 6 new findings about millennials. *Pew*. Retrieved from: http://www. pewresearch.org

Eagly, A. H. (2007). Female leadership advantage and disadvantage: Resolving the contradictions. *Psychology of Women Quarterly, 31*(1), 1–12.

Eagly, A. H., & Karau, S. J. (2002). Role congruity theory of prejudice toward female leaders. *Psychological Review, 109*(3), 573–598.

Eagly, A. H., Johannesen-Schmidt, M. C., & Engen, M. L. (2003). Transformational, transactional, and laissez-faire leadership styles: A meta-analysis comparing women and men. *Psychological Bulletin, 129*(4), 569–591.

Fairhurst, G. T. (2007). *Discursive leadership: In conversation with leadership psychology*. Thousand Oaks, CA: Sage.

Fairhurst, G. T. (2011). *The power of framing: Creating the language of leadership*. San Francisco, CA: Jossey-Bass.

Fairhurst, G. T., & Connaughton, S. (2014). Leadership: A communication perspective. *Leadership, 10*(1), 7–35.

Fairhurst, G. T., Green, S. G., & Courtright, J. A. (1995). Inertial forces and the implementation of a socio-technical systems intervention. *Organization Science, 6*(2), 168–185.

Grint, K. (2005). Problems, problems, problems: The social construction of "leadership." *Human Relations, 58*(11), 1467–1494.

Heilman, M. E. (2001). Description and prescription: How gender stereotypes prevent women's ascent up the organizational ladder. *Journal of Social Issues, 57*(4), 657–674.

Kanter, R. M. (1977). *Men and women of the corporation*. New York, NY: Basic Books.

Kerfoot, D., & Knights, D. (1996). 'The best is yet to come?': The quest for embodiment in managerial work. In D. Collinson & J. Hearn (Eds.), *Men as managers, managers as men*. London, England: Sage.

Lin, T., & Cheng, B. (2007). Sex role first, leader role second? Sex combination of supervisor and subordinate, length of work relationship, and paternalistic leadership. *Chinese Journal of Psychology, 49*(4), 433–450 (in Chinese).

McGlynn, A. P. (2005). Teaching millennials, our newest cultural cohort. *The Education Digest, 71*(4), 12.

Mouawad, J. (April 30, 2016). A crusader in the coal mine, taking on president Obama. *New York Times*. Retrieved from: http://www.nytimes.com

Murray, A. (2011). Mind the gap: Technology, millennial leadership and the cross-generational workforce. The *Australian Library Journal, 60*(1), 54–65.

Nkomo, S. M. (1988). Race and sex: The forgotten case of the black female manager. In S. Rose & L. Larwood (Eds.), *Women's careers: Pathways and pitfalls* (pp. 133–150). New York, NY: Praeger.

Nkomo, S. M. (1992). The emperor has no clothes: Rewriting "race in organizations." *Academy of Management Review, 17*(3), 487–513.

Parker, P. S. (2005). *Race, gender, and leadership: Re-envisioning organizational leadership from the perspective of African American women executives*. Mawah, NJ: Lawrence Erlbaum.

Pearce, C. L., Manz, C. C., & Sims, Jr., H. P. (2014). *Share, don't take the lead: Leadership lessons from 21 vanguard organizations.* Charlotte, NC: Information Age.

Postman, N. (1985). *Amusing ourselves to death: Public discourse in the age of show business.* London, England: Penguin Books.

Ragins, B. (1991). Gender effects in subordinate evaluations of leaders: Real or artifact? *Journal of Organizational Behavior, 12*(3), 259–268.

Sheep, M. L., Fairhurst, G. T., & Khazanchi, S. (2017). Knots in the discourse of innovation: Investigating multiple tensions in a reacquired spin-off. *Organization Studies, 38*(3–4), 463–488.

Sinclair, A. (1998). *Doing leadership differently: Gender, power and sexuality in a changing business culture.* Carlton, Australia: Melbourne University Press.

Sinclair, A. (2005). Body possibilities in leadership. *Leadership, 1*(4), 387–406.

Varallo, S. M. (2008). Motherwork in academe: Intensive caring for the millenial student. *Women's Studies in Communication, 31*(2), 151–157.

Yukl, G. (1999). An evaluation of conceptual weaknesses in transformational and charismatic leadership theories. *The Leadership Quarterly, 10*(2), 285–305.

Chapter 2

Thank God It's Thursday

The Power of Shondaland, Gender, and Leadership

Creshema R. Murray

In their study of attitudes toward female authority, Rudman and Kilianski (2000) found that both women and men exhibited prejudice in their implicit attitudes toward female leaders. Yet, each Thursday, millions of *Grey's Anatomy* fans, "Scandal's gladiators," and *How to Get Away with Murder* fans gather around the television to see Meredith Grey tackle medical dilemmas, Olivia Pope overcome trials that threaten to bring down political figures in the nation's capital, and Annalise Keating work her magic in the courtroom. The Thursday night ABC television lineup has now been coined, Thank God It's Thursday, for the prolific lineup of shows produced by Shonda Rhimes and her Shondaland production company. These shows, along with their executive producer Shonda Rhimes, provide a shift in attitudes for television viewers as it relates to seeing women in workplace leadership roles in front of and behind the television lens.

This shift mirrors my personal changing attitude as it relates to my television viewership. Growing up, I recall sitting in front of the television and admiring Claire Huxtable lead her family and her law practice on *The Cosby Show*. I fell in love with Aunt Vivian on *The Fresh Prince of Bel-Air* and went around asking all of my friends to call me Professor Murray because I wanted to be just like Professor Vivian Banks. On *Living Single*, Khadijah James gave me hopes of owning my own magazine, and Gina Waters and Pam James on *Martin* had me investigating all of the workplace opportunities available at a public relations firm. These black women and their workplace leadership roles on television shaped the way I viewed female leadership. I looked at each woman like a hero that could do it all. These characters were beautiful, witty, fun loving, stylish, intelligent, and extremely successful. They all possessed characteristics that most ten-year-old girls would aspire to attain. I faithfully sat in front of my television each week yearning to learn more about juggling relationships, family, and work; in an effortless manner, from each black female character.

Fast forward ten years to my junior year of college, the year was 2004, reality television was on the rise and my love for television was declining. Instead of seeing positive images of black women in leadership roles on television, I was faced with images of black women fighting over men, black women being sexually objectified, and in many instances black women not being present on my television screen (Gray, 2005). I was hurt and confused. I felt that television had betrayed me and I did not know where to turn. My exposure to television media caused an identity crisis, projecting a bias in how I viewed my gender, my race, and my body. The new messages and images depicted on television seemed to mirror inaccurate accounts of the society in which I lived. The effects of media exposure to audiences, regardless of culture, have a direct effect on the social perceptions, attitudes, beliefs, and actions of individuals that consume the messages put forth (Mastro & Tropp, 2004). I found myself continuously questioning my feelings that the contemporary television representation of African Americans was all a lie.

CULTURAL PORTRAYALS

Consumers often rely on the media to understand and define things that they have not seen for themselves (La Ferle & Lee, 2005). It is well known that African Americans have traditionally been cast in stories to make people laugh and not think about serious issues. Images of African Americans in the media have the potential to provide erroneous information about African Americans and further miseducate the masses about the significance of the black culture (Entman, 1994). Poindexter and Stroman (1981) listed four propositions that emerged during an empirical study of African Americans and television. Those four propositions are as follows: (a) portrayals, historically African Americans have been underrepresented in television portrayals; (b) television as a source of information, there has been a trend toward increased visibility of African Americans on television; (c) viewing behavior, African Americans are generally presented on television in minor roles and in low-status occupational roles; (d) and effects, stereotyping and negative connotations of African Americans continue to be presented in television programs. The significance of this information allows individuals to understand the impact and effects on viewer cultural perceptions as it relates to understanding what people view through the television lens.

The cultural politics of blackness in the media reveals that the prejudice in the media industry allows for continued biased beliefs and attitudes to surmount any notions of equality. Images of African Americans in the media are representations of irresponsible and uncontainable one-dimensional characters that neglect to reflect the true complexity of African Americans. Within this idea, it is evident to state that those images are profoundly represented in shows about families, black situational comedies, and entertainment programming. Gray (1995) suggests that there are three contemporary images of African Americans that are anchored in many traditional network practices such as (a) assimilation, (b) plurality, and (c) multiculturalism. These images that injure the race represent a long circulated vortex of negative descriptors that reassures an uneasy white audience that African Americans are ignorant and whites have supremacy (Abraham, 2003).

Oftentimes we see cultural representations of blacks in the media based on a historical system of categorization that supports an inefficient channel to cultural understanding (La Ferle & Lee, 2005). Skewed presentations of African Americans culture and experiences are merged into accounts of incongruent interior definitions of blackness that equates to stereotypes (Coleman, 1998). Gordon Berry (1980) in "Television and Afro-Americans: Past Legacy and Present Portrayals," uncovered six stereotypical myths regarding African American worth and legitimacy in society. They are as follows:

1. the black household headed by a single parent, most often the mother (e.g., *Thea* and *South Central*)
2. the domineering, overly aggressive black woman such as "Aunt Esther" from *Sanford and Son*
3. the use of black dialect (really, a caricature of black English resulting in black voice)
4. the black community as weak and destructive (e.g., the ghetto poor)
5. idolizing pimps, drug dealers, and other criminals, as prized figures by the black community (e.g., "Hustle Man" and "Jerome" of *Martin)*
6. the African American and subsequently the black community as a homogenous, monolithic group

The stereotypical myths presented by Berry (1980) were published almost forty years ago, yet the images are still profound stereotypes that the mass media use in present day representations of African Americans. These images were present during my young adult television viewership and oftentimes skewed my perceptions of black womanhood during my adolescent years.

THE SHIFT

One night after sitting around watching *Grey's Anatomy*, a new television show by the name of *Scandal* appeared on my television screen. The main

character, Olivia Pope, was an ivy-league graduate turned presidential campaign manager, turned White House press secretary, turned Washington,
D. C. political fixer (Aitkenhead, 2013). She was sensationally fierce, crafty
with words, and dripping with power. She was not like the other women that I
had seen on television and it seemed that all was right in the television world.
Even though Olivia Pope displayed numerous humanistic flaws, her character
remained the same, a leader in the political, social, and public relations world
(Maxwell, 2013). The character exuded multiples layers to explore, demonstrating traits of a transitional leader, showing tenets of a servant leader, and
proving that ethics and leadership should always go hand in hand.

Although social roles have changed dramatically for women in the workplace, they continue to be underrepresented in leadership roles (Rudman and
Kilianski, 2000). In the world of Olivia Pope, this statement could not be
farther than truth. Her organization, Pope & Associates is a public relations
firm dedicated to assisting political figures through communication crises.
People call on Pope & Associates to save the day. The more I analyzed
Olivia Pope, the more I needed to know about the purpose for her creation
in popular culture. I found myself wondering, why was Olivia Pope created?
I then began asking others, what messages does this character portray about
women? In small viewing groups I asked, how will black women be viewed
as a result of the actions of Olivia Pope on the screen? In my personal journal
I asked, is she like Claire, Aunt Vivian, or Khadijah? The more questions I
had about Olivia Pope and *Scandal*, the more I needed to know about the
people behind the lens of creating Olivia Pope. Each question and answer
led back to creator, writer, and executive producer Shonda Rhimes. Labeled
as one of the most prolific television producers of all time, Shonda Rhimes
is a pop-cultural force to be reckoned with. Rhimes, known for hit shows
Private Practice and *Grey's Anatomy*, has literally changed the way people
view television. Her characters are diverse, complicated, ruthless, and look
nothing like the traditional white male protagonists. Each show under her
leadership tackles complex social issues. A leader in every word, Rhimes
television shows explore topics such as homosexuality, abortion, interracial
relationships, infidelity, police brutality, rape, and HIV and AIDS. As a writer
and a producer, Rhimes controls multiple narratives about women and leadership. Each character is professionally accomplished, providing new realities
for viewers. Never before have television viewers experienced this cultural
phenomenon of care and diversity shown by Shonda Rhimes and her team.
As the woman in front of and behind the lens, Shonda Rhimes is a leader in
every aspect of the television industry. As owner of the production company
Shondaland, Rhimes provides a voice for female leadership that has been
missing in the media world. The stories told by a black female showrunner
debunk traditional workplace norms of what it means to be female and what

it means to lead. Shows produced by Shondaland provide a safe space for narratives for and about women of color; ushering in a cultural shift in the way that many Americans view leadership and the role of race and gender in the workplace. The power of Shondaland has paved the way for more women, black women in particular, to serve in leadership roles in front of and behind the lens. The impact of Shonda Rhimes on the ABC network can be felt throughout the television and production world as a gradual shift in visibility in female leadership stories has occurred. With this change, my love for television is no longer in a fragile state. The voice of powerful, strong, and ambitious female leaders are no longer memories from my childhood. I see myself in Olivia Pope, Annalise Keating, and Shonda Rhimes every week in front of and behind the lens.

REFERENCES

Abraham, L. (2003). Media stereotypes of African Americans. In P.M. Lester & S.D. Ross (Eds.), *Images that injure: Pictorial stereotypes in the media.* (pp. 87–92). Westport, CT: Praeger.

Aitkenhead, D. (June 28, 2013). Kerry Washington: Notes on a Scandal. Retrieved November 6, 2014.

Berry, G. (1980). Television and Afro-American: Past legacy and present portrayals. In S. Withy & R. Abeles (Eds.), *Television and social behavior: Beyond violence and children* (pp. 231–248). Hillsdale: Erlbaum.

Coleman, R. R. (1998). Blackface+Blackvoice=Black Situation Comedy. In G. R. Hodges (Ed.), *African American history and culture* (pp. 61–147). New York: Garland Publishing.

Entman, R. M. (1994). Representation and reality in the portrayal of blacks on network television news. *Journalism & Mass Communication Quarterly, 71,* 509–520.

Gray, H. S. (1995). *Watching race: Television and the struggle for "blackness."* Minneapolis, MN: University of Minnesota Press.

Gray, H. S. (2005). *Cultural moves: African Americans and the politics of representation.* Los Angeles, CL: University of California Press.

La Ferle, C., & Lee, W. (2005). Can English language media connect with ethnic audiences? Ethnic minorities' media use and representation perceptions. *Journal of Advertising Research, 45,* 140–153.

Mastro, D. E., & Tropp, L. R. (2004). The effects of interracial contact, attitudes, and stereotypical portrayals on evaluations of black television sitcom characters. *Communication Research, 45,* 140–153.

Maxwell, B. (February 7, 2013). "Olivia Pope and the Scandal of Representation." *TheFeministWire.com.* Retrieved November 6, 2014.

Poindexter, P. M., & Stroman, C. (1981). Blacks and Television: A review of the Research literature. *Journal of Broadcasting, 25,* 103–122.

Rudman, L., & Kilianski, S. (2000). Implicit and explicit attitudes toward female authority. *Personality and Social Psychology Bulletin, 26,* 1315–1328.

Chapter 3

Loyalty as Leadership

Learning and Performing Leadership in The Americans

Raymond Blanton

"You see my kind of loyalty was loyalty to one's country, not to its institutions or its office-holders. The country is the real thing, the substantial thing, the eternal thing; it is the thing to watch over, and care for, and be loyal to; institutions are extraneous, they are its mere clothing, and clothing can wear out, become ragged, cease to be comfortable, cease to protect the body from winter, disease, and death. To be loyal to rags, to shout for rags, to worship rags, to die for rags— that is a loyalty of unreason."

—Mark Twain, *A Connecticut Yankee in King Arthur's Court*

Americans watch more than five hours of television per day (Koblin, 2016). This is comparable to the time a child spends learning in the classroom. Television has the potential to shape not only how we understand ideas like leadership but also how we learn to perform leadership at home, in the classroom, and beyond. As a medium of learning, television has long centered its focus on two primary elements of life: home and work. Some television shows, like *Fuller House,* focus on the home with the workplace at the margins. Other shows, like *The Office,* concentrate on the workplace with the home at the peripheral. And still other shows, like *The Americans,* offer a unique blend and balance of home and work life. In this chapter, I explore several ways that leadership in the workplace is learned and performed in the television series *The Americans.*

The Americans is a period drama about a complex marriage between two deep-cover KGB (Komitet Gosudarstvennoy Bezopasnosti) spies posing as Americans in suburban Washington D.C. in the aftermath of Ronald Reagan being elected president. Broadly, the series confronts a broad range of issues related to nationalism, race, class, ethnicity, gender, sexuality, and the body in ways that complement the central aim of this book. Put differently, *The Americans* gives us opportunities to interrogate production, presentation, and power related to learning and performing leadership. As a scripted television series, *The Americans* animates numerous discourses related to leadership communication and style, loyalty, and the body. In recognition of the prominent role television plays in how we understand, shape and perform life, I argue that *The Americans* is ideally suited for confronting the varied ways leadership is learned and performed in the workplace. For instance, given the nuanced leadership roles that Philip (Matthew Rhys) and Elizabeth (Keri Russell) Jennings perform—loyal KGB operatives (nation) maintaining a pretend marriage (family) while using a travel agency (work) as cover, *The Americans* serves as a resourceful series for exploring the varied ways that leadership style and communication function in the workplace as a means of production, presentation and power.

Though there are many subjects of interest in *The Americans*, the focus of this chapter centers on the significance of loyalty in learning and performing leadership. Theoretically, I argue that leadership is learned and performed in this series through a "body of identifications," by way of "trivial repetition and dull daily reinforcement" (Burke, 1969b, p. 26). For instance, given the series' focus on various leadership styles, including authoritative (Russian), democratic (American), and laissez-faire (intelligence officers), and the versatile roles that intelligence officers must perform, *The Americans* enhances the breadth and depth by which the trivial repetitions and dull daily reinforcements of loyalty and leadership are learned and performed, figuratively in speech, tone, and attitude, but also by way of a literal body of identifications—a literal disciplining of the body.

First, I use the pilot episode as a case study to explore the underlying themes of loyalty in learning and performing leadership. Second, I demonstrate how the music featured in the series functions to reinforce important themes such as loyalty and allegiance, further enhancing the body of identifications. Third, and finally, I assess episode 5 from season 1 as a case study for exhibiting the specific ways loyalty disciplines the body. In essence, relying on Kenneth Burke's notion that a critic's conceptual and methodological work pivots on questions, I ask what is the significance of loyalty in the learning and performance of leadership in *The Americans*?

LEADERSHIP AND LOYALTY

According to Quintanilla and Wahl (2017), leadership is best understood not as a trait, a birthright, a job title, or even a matter of charisma, but as a dynamic relationship based on mutual influence and common purpose that seeks to affect real change (p. 217). In other words, for Quintanilla and Wahl (2017), excelling in communication is central to developing dynamic relationships and demonstrating effective leadership. Furthermore, Chip and Dan Heath's (2007) *Made to Stick* affirms the importance of leaders developing communication that stays with you while Jonah Berger's (2013) *Contagious* highlights how leaders should communicate in ways that spread. To lead means literally to show the way or to go before as a guide. Yet, in learning how to show the way, we must first learn what the way is. This implicates a process by which we acquire acumen and learn to act by observing and replicating the behaviors of others in specific situations. Learning how to lead, then, at some level, seems to be an exercise in becoming loyal to particular people, ideas, and ideals and to the values inherent in those particular periods and places.

Betty Jean Craige (1996) has noted, "When we examine the uses of the word freedom in the political rhetoric of the United States, among the various definitions and concepts, it is often relative to the notion of loyalty" (p. 36). More than a recent development, however, in his Introduction to Frederick Douglass' *My Bondage, My Freedom* (1855), James McCune Smith recognized the value of loyalty in Douglass:

> Diffident in his own abilities, reluctant at their dissuading, how beautiful is the loyalty with which he still clung to their principles in all things else [...] almost alone [...] even in the teeth of the opposition of those from whom he had reason to expect counsel and encouragement. (p. Xxiv)

Beyond politics, the *Navy SEAL* creed declares: "My loyalty to Country and Team is beyond reproach." For instance, former *Navy SEAL* Brent Gleeson (2012) describes loyalty as one of the core values of the *Navy SEAL* training program, emphasizing the importance of learning from day one the role of trust and loyalty in developing a team. In "from day one" we can identify, as children, how we learned loyalty to nation as we recited the Pledge of Allegiance (Craige, 1996, p. 104).

The origins of loyalty mean to maintain true or faithful allegiance. In essence, loyalty is central to nearly every facet of our relational, vocational, and public lives. Loyalty authenticates our living and working relationships. Loyalty is the central tenet of a marriage—both as a binding legal agreement and (for many) a spiritual covenant. Loyalty has become essential to enjoying leisurely benefits. Loyalty cards are standard public relations tactics for establishing, maintaining, and sustaining consumer relationships (Heath and Heath, 2010, p. 126). Airlines have made loyalty into a status symbol (Berger, 2013, p. 49). In other words, we learn and perform leadership through loyalty practices.

However, in order to better understand the full implications of loyalty as it pertains to learning and performing leadership, I situate loyalty in the context of Kenneth Burke's rhetorical framework. Specifically, I frame rhetoric not in terms of one particular address, "but as a general *body of identifications* that owe their convincingness much more to a trivial repetition and dull daily reinforcement than to exceptional rhetorical skill" (Burke, 1969b, p. 26). Relatedly, in describing cultivation theory in *Media Reception Studies* (2005), Janet Staiger has made the distinction that meaning is drawn from an "accumulation of media experiences that explains media influence" (p. 59). Staiger has noted: "Meaning-making is fundamental to social groups, and scholars' tasks are to find how everyday events function in constituting a society that is able to negotiate its differences to remain a unit" (p. 76). To this end, in foregrounding the everyday lives of two Russian spies posing as an American family with a travel agency, *The Americans,* through both a figurative and literal body of identifications, demonstrates how leadership is learned and performed as loyalty.

As a public intellectual, Kenneth Burke devoted much of his life and work to the relationship between our living and the arts. In his first book of criticism, *Counter-statement* (1957), for instance, Burke developed a theory of aesthetic form to examine the interrelation of art and life, noting that the artist must "master ways of exerting influence upon the minds and emotions of others" (p. 74). And still further, in *Attitudes Toward History* (1959), Burke defines history and "life in political communities" as concerned with "characteristic responses of people in their forming and reforming of congregations" (p. xi). In the Introduction to Burke's *Permanence and Change* (1984), Hugh Duncan has indicated the ultimate aim of art:

> If, in the suffering and horror of our time, we can develop a method for the analysis of what symbols do to us in our relations with each other, we may yet learn to lead a better life. Such is Burke's message to our time. (Xliii)

Furthermore, Burke has defined loyalty as a "summing up of many motivational strands" (Burke, 1969b, p. 110). Burke (1969b) further recognizes how these reinforcements function rhetorically in persuading us to perform leadership by emphasizing that we influence others insofar as we can engage with them by "speech, gesture, tonality, order, image, attitude, [and] idea, identifying" (p. 55) our ways with theirs. As it relates to *The Americans,* which relies on an array of motivational strands via dramatic dimensions of identification and division, Burke has noted that because we cannot "know for certain just where one ends and the other begins," this gives us an invitation to rhetoric (Burke, 1969b, p. 25). As a means of connecting our notion of loyalty to a body of identifications, Burke has recognized in *Philosophy of Literary Form*

(1973) that a leader's accomplishments are directly related to the backing of the people; and that for the backing of the people to be as strong as possible, they need to be treated well; and when they are, their gratitude will repay itself in the form of "increased loyalty" (p. 211). And when in violation, as indicated in *Attitudes Toward History* (1959), Burke has pointed to the "astounding exactitude" with which we tend to "allay our guilt by appropriate rituals and acts of loyalty to established social customs" (p. 128).

These theoretical lenses are quite transferable to matters of art and its relationship to life. In *Permanence and Change* (1984), for instance, Burke has noted:

> One cannot long discuss the question of meaning, as applied to the field of art, without coming upon the problem of piety. Santayana has somewhere defined piety as loyalty to the sources of our being. It would as well be present when the potter molds the clay to exactly that form which completely gratifies his sense of how it ought to be. (p. 71)

In sum, to summon the spirit of Burke's *Philosophy of Literary Form* (1973), art forms, and in this sense, *The Americans,* function as "equipments for living that size up situations in various ways in keeping with correspondingly various attitudes" (p. 304).

THE AMERICANS

In 2010, federal prosecutors arrested ten Russian agents living suburban lives as part of an espionage ring that sought to recruit Americans (Holson, 2013). According to Ellen Barry (2010), "illegals" are meticulously trained in the KGB's Directorate S, assume a fake biography, and live undercover for years with no diplomatic cover. Barry (2010) has noted, "In the lore of Soviet spy craft, few figures command as much respect as the 'illegals', steel-jawed agents with the intelligence of a chess grandmaster and the fortitude of a cosmonaut." *Americans* cocreator and writer Joe Weisberg has credited this event, in addition to his time with the Central Intelligence Agency (CIA), as the inspiration for the series, having noted that Phillip and Elizabeth Jennings are essentially the 1981 versions of the "illegals." Weisberg has also noted, "I wanted to do a show about a husband and a wife and their children who don't know and how it affects the kids" (Waxman, 2013). Series cocreator Joel Fields has affirmed this sentiment:

> *The Americans* is at its core a marriage story. International relations are just an allegory for the human relations. Sometimes, when you're struggling in your

marriage or with your kid, it feels like life or death. For Philip and Elizabeth, it often is. (Thomas, 2013)

Put differently, as a marriage story grounded in espionage, *The Americans* is foremost about the tensions inherent in dis/loyalty to nation, family, friends, and colleagues. Consider, for instance, Weisberg's description of his personal experiences at the CIA:

> It was painful. Fundamentally, lies were at the core of the relationships. I lied to all my friends and most of the people in my family. I lied every day. I told twenty lies a day and I got used to it. It was hard for about two weeks. Then it got easy. I watched it happen to all of us. (Holson, 2013)

We find further indication in Weisberg's novel, *An Ordinary Spy* (2008), as protagonist Mark Ruttenberg senses that a letter he has received may be an ops test about fidelity:

> He was supposed to be my friend. But he was also supposed to be a loyal Agency employee. As much as I liked him, and believed that he liked me, I just didn't know if he was someone who would or wouldn't do this, whether he would be loyal to me or to the Agency first. (p. 89)

As a former CIA officer, Weisberg brings an almost unrivaled realism to the series. This not only enhances the viewing experience, it also strengthens the potential for learning and performing leadership in ways that are also starkly real. June Thomas (2013) has noted: "There are certain similarities between the work of a CIA agent and a TV writer. They both deal with deception, misdirection, and recruitment—albeit of viewers rather than assets—and loyalty building." In essence, then, it is Phillip and Elizabeth Jennings—their artful deceptions, a pretend marriage, made-up back-stories, ever-changing identities, and quick-shifting loyalties that are at the series' core (Holson, 2013).

Pilot Episode: Case Study

A television pilot is essentially a pitch for a show to become a series. It is a model for future development. As such, it is enriched with backstory and prominent themes upon which the show often relies and builds upon. As I argue, the central theme in *The Americans* is loyalty. It is the explicit means by which we learn and perform leadership. For instance, the pilot episode begins with a ten-minute sequence that effusively emboldens the themes and tensions of loyalty that frame both the episode and the series (four seasons with five and six to come). Specifically, in a sequence that features Phillip and Elizabeth Jennings apprehending a traitorous ex-KGB captain, each must prove and perform their loyalty by choosing either to save an injured ally or fulfill their mission—friend or nation. Throughout the series, consistently, Elizabeth lists toward mission and nation, whereas Phillip favors family and friend. And it is this tension of dis/loyalty that makes *The Americans* an intriguing and informative platform from which to explore how we learn and perform leadership. Moreover, what makes the show stimulating is that our primary frame of reference lies with the KGB agents rather than FBI agent Stan Beeman—blurring the lines that separate our traditional sensibilities of good and bad (Leeds, 2013). As such, the series both humanizes the other (e.g., Russians) and universalizes the relevancy of learning and performing leadership in the workplace and home from various perspectives.

To be more specifics, throughout the pilot episode, Phillip demonstrates a progressive willingness to be disloyal. For example, after learning of the resettlement package their captive had received from the U.S. government, Phillip declares, "Maybe we could just defect ourselves. At least we'd be millionaires. We wouldn't have to worry about going to jail, leaving the kids all alone. A lot of our problems just go away." However, this merely sets the stage for one of the more prominent themes of this episode (and the series), that is, Phillip's struggle to reconcile the emotional toll of his double life. To this, Weisberg has noted, "Phillip, as a character, is always changing and going through these struggles [and this] affects the marriage and how it comes up against Elizabeth, who also changes, just more slowly than Phillip" (Egner, 2016).

Additionally, intensifying (intriguingly so) the theme of loyalty a bit further is the relationship between the Jennings and their new neighbors—FBI counter intelligence officer Stan Beeman and his family. Upon learning this, Phillip playfully quips, "I have to make sure I don't do any spying around here." Stan, teasing out the underlying tension of the series, responds, "Oh, you better not, especially for those Russians." And Phillip, "Oh yea, they're the worst, right? And Stan, "Oh, they certainly are Philip; they certainly are." Upon returning home after the discovery of their neighbors' identity, an underlying tension in Phillip's loyalties continues to unravel. In this telling sequence, building on the jest of his previous defection tease, Phillip poses his solution:

Maybe there's another way. Look, maybe this is an opportunity. Maybe this is the perfect time for us just to think about the life we've been living, but just, really living it. Just be us. What are you talking about? I'm saying we might be blown. I'm also saying we are Philip and Elizabeth Jennings. We have been for a very long time. So why don't we get ahead of this. And why don't we make the first move and offer ourselves to them. We could get a lot of money. We just get relocated, take the good life, and be happy. (Weisberg, 2013)

Persistently throughout the pilot, the tenuous loyalty of Phillip and the steady loyalty of Elizabeth are in stark contrast—revealing a tension in their marriage as well. Elizabeth's response, for example, is telling, "Are you joking? Is this a joke? You want to betray our country?" Phillip's response, "Well, after everything we've done I don't think it's such a betrayal." Most explicitly, when asked if Phillip cares about the Motherland, he remarked, "I do, but our family comes first." And here, again, just as it does in the opening ten-minute sequence, tensions related to loyalty emerge—teaching us by way of a body of identifications, dull daily reinforcements of speech, attitude and the like, how we are to perform as leaders. Interestingly, it is at the conclusion of this scene that we are first introduced to the distinct theme song of the show—something I will expand on in a subsequent section.

In concluding how loyalty plays out in the pilot, however, I turn to a sequence featuring Phillip and his son Henry, attending a middle school function honoring an American astronaut. The scene is infused with patriotic symbolism—hundreds of hand-held American flags waving as they sing the National Anthem—as the camera glides ever so closer upon the American flag. It is this sequence that inspires Phillip to finally defect and attempt to free their captive and make a deal with the Americans. But when Elizabeth walks in on the attempted coup, alluding to an important theme I will address more fully later in the chapter (body), Phillip learns of how the ex-KGB captain violated Elizabeth (raping her during her initial training) and immediately kills the captive captain, giving us a clear indication of where Phillip's loyalty lies, with Elizabeth, and perhaps nation.

Music

In the visual medium, and in *The Americans* more specifically, music is integral to animating narrative dimensions and meaning making. Composer Nathan Barr, for instance, told the *Hollywood Reporter* that he draws on various sounds to subtly reference the environments and themes for individual characters in order to emphasize the subtext in various scenes. To illustrate the influence of musical design, Barr noted:

> Philip's theme is sort of a deep, low cello part. Elizabeth has a hammer dulcimer theme and Noah Emmerich's Stan has a driving bass theme. Those instruments in addition to the actual notes being played I think help with the identity of those characters in whatever situations they find themselves. (Lewis, 2014)

Lewis (2014) further noted, "By highlighting the musical elements of specific characters' themes, Barr can play up how a particular person is affected by the events unfolding onscreen." As I contend, if learning and performing leadership as it is being enacted on the screen is also reinforced through the music, part of the body of identifications, the potential to strengthen the bonds of meaning, particularly as it relates to loyalty, becomes much stronger. In the pilot episode, for example, I offer four examples of songs that illustrate how the theme of loyalty in the narrative is reinforced through the music, further enhancing the body of identifications for learning loyalty. Of note, each of these songs is centrally concerned with relational in/fidelity and dis/loyalty.

First, Quarterflash's "Harden My Heart," released in September 1981 on the B-side of "Don't Be Lonely," opens the pilot episode. As the song plays above the din of bar chatter, we meet Elizabeth for the first time, seducing an employee from the Department of Justice. The song's emphasis upon the pain of betrayal is an early indication of the importance of allegiance and loyalty. Second, building upon the theme of betrayal in "Harden My Heart," Fleetwood Mac's "Tusk," released in September 1979 on the B-side of "Never Make Me Cry," though mostly instrumental (the lyrics are featured in the conclusion to both the song and the pilot episode), further substantiates the theme of dis/loyalty. Specifically, the lyrics are framed around a series of questions directly related to loyalty:

Why don't you ask him if he's going to stay? Why don't you ask him if he's going away? Why don't you tell me what's going on? Why don't you tell me who's on the phone? (Fleetwood Mac, 1979)

Both of these songs are concerned with in/fidelity and the consequences of dis/loyalty. The third song, Juice Newton's "Queen of Hearts," released in June 1981 on the B-side of "River of Love," which is featured during a mall sequence with Phillip and daughter Paige, again centers on the theme of loyalty. As the lyrics resound, "laying out another lie," we continue to find the theme of loyalty being reinforced throughout the episode. Fourth, and finally, Phil Collins' "In the Air Tonight," released in January 1981 on the B-side of "The Roof is Leaking," plays without dialogue as Elizabeth and Phillip dispose of the body of the traitorous KGB officer and concludes with a reconciliatory love scene. Specifically, the song is both lyrically and contextually about dis/loyalty both in the line, "Well if you told me you were drowning, I would not lend a hand" and "I know where you've been. It's all been a pack of lies." Collins, who wrote the song after his wife left him (with their children), noted, "I'm not quite sure what the song is about, but there's a lot of anger, a lot of despair and a lot of frustration" (Greene, 2016). It is a pain that is perhaps most viscerally felt after, "Well the hurt doesn't show but the pain still grows. It's no stranger to you and me," leading into the song's iconic drum sequence.

Uniquely, even the album titles upon which these songs are featured consistently allude to issues of dis/loyalty related to love and in/fidelity, "Don't Be Lonely," "Never Make Me Cry," "River of Love," and "The Roof is Leaking." In sum, as Hilary Lewis (2014) has noted, *"The Americans* is layered with various lies and truths. So it's only fitting that the music for the critically acclaimed series be equally complex." In sum, music in *The Americans* reinforces both figurative and literal dimensions of loyalty through a body of identifications in ways that enrich how we learn and perform loyalty as leadership.

THE BODY

In this section, I examine episode 5 from season 1 as a case study to demonstrate how *The Americans* enables us to interrogate production, presentation, and power through the body in an effort to substantiate Burke's body of identifications as the means by which we learn and perform leadership through loyalty. Specifically, in addition to my examination of a figurative body of identifications, as in speech, tone, attitude, here I explore the literal *body*. More specifically, after outlining generalities related to the body, I specifically examine how Nina, Phillip, and Elizabeth, respectively, use their bodies to perform loyalty as leadership. To this end, I find Deborah Hawhee's *Moving Bodies* (2009) helpful, particularly her playful take on Kenneth Burke's well-known notion of "equipment for living," that is, "Bodies as Equipment for Moving" (p. 9).

As I contend, perhaps the most fundamental and essential means of learning and performing leadership in *The Americans* comes by way of the body. As it relates to the series, drawing on his CIA training, Weisberg validates how often spies use their bodies to demonstrate their loyalty when he noted:

> One year, the KGB had so much luck recruiting secretaries of important foreign government officials that they declared an entire Secretaries Defensive. And some of the operations went so far that the officers married the targets—real weddings, not fake weddings! Even years later, after some of these agents were caught, the people they married were so in love that they never believed it and stayed true to them. (Waxman, 2013)

Interestingly, this idea forms the basis of my first example, Phillip, particularly in his alter ego character Clark, who marries FBI secretary Martha Hanson (Alison Wright). In essence, from beginning to end in episode 5, "Comint," the body and its dis/loyalty is in deep focus. Of note, the episode is directed by a woman, Holly Dale, and also features writing by women, including Melissa James Gibson and Sneha Koorse—contributing to a more robust representation of the tensions inherent to the issues of gender and sexuality related to the body that manifest in both this specific episode and the series overall. For instance, one of our first indications of this theme in the episode emerges when FBI agent Amador explains his romantic interest in Martha Hanson to colleague Stan Beeman. As Martha approaches, Amador offers a flattering comment about her shoes and calves to which she replies, "That's actually a sexist comment." Having witnessed the exchange, Amador's supervisor begrudgingly (indicated by an eye roll) defends Martha's rights and corrects Amador. However, we are left with a clear sense that her claims are frivolous, further strengthening the hunch that the standards of loyalty placed upon the body vary in degree between men and women.

In my first example, I examine Nina Krilova (Annet Mahendru) walking in a park with FBI agent Stan Beeman. In short, Nina has been blackmailed and recruited by Stan to acquire information from the Russians for the American government. Stan demands, "You need to find out what's going on. We don't have any leeway here. You're a beautiful, intelligent, intuitive, and beautiful woman. I have complete faith that you'll figure out a way to find out, all you can." Immediately after this plea, Stan asks Nina to trust him, in Russian. Nina replies, "But listen, that's not what you say when you want to say trust me. When you say it in that way, with those words. It's like trust me. It's like you don't have a choice" (Gibson, 2013). Heeding Stan's words, Nina begins using her body to figure out a way to find out what's going on by exchanging sexual favors for information, seducing Director Vasili Nikolaevich (Peter Von Berg). Interestingly, loyalty becomes a subject of interest. After their first sexual encounter, Vasili turns to her and asks, "Nina, do you know what loyalty is?" "Of course," she replies. "I recruited an agent here twenty-three years ago when I was visiting America on a student visa," he says. "But just now he's got the 'jitters'. I plan to reassure him that everything will be fine."

Again, loyalty becomes the framework around which the plot and narrative progression develops. And when Nina relays this information to Stan, he asks, "How did you get him to talk?" Nina responds, "I sucked his cock. Just like you told me to." Though Stan expresses immediate shock and dismay, indicating that he never said to do that, he essentially demands she continue using her body when he says, "Extradition is coming soon. But we're not there yet. In the mean time, we just have to keep working for the good of all concerned. We have to nail down when that meeting is happening, Nina." Her response is incisive, "We?"

In this second example, my aim is to continue emphasizing the importance of the physical body while also underlining the contrast between the male and female body. For instance, Philip's bodily performances of loyalty are generally confined to his relationship with Martha Hanson and physical activities with FBI agent Stan Beeman. After playing racquetball with Stan, for example, Phillip achingly declared: "My body is getting too old for racquetball." In the subsequent scenes, however, a stark contrast is seen (and felt) between Phillip's body and Elizabeth's, our third example. So after we learn of Phillip's aching body, Elizabeth returns from acquiring intelligence from an encryption specialist, one who favors sexually violent behavior—beating her with a belt. When Philip sees the marks on her back he is thrown into a rage. "What happened?" Elizabeth's response is telling, "It's nothing." Philip, visibly upset, "That's not nothing." And in this Elizabeth conveys a harsh reality that Phillip seems unaware of, "It happens sometimes, Philip." In a sense, Elizabeth responds to her plight in the stereotypical manner that a man might be expected to respond, with a sense of strength and duty, "I can handle it. It is my job."

Clearly, though all of these characters use their bodies to perform loyalty, it is evident that Elizabeth and Nina, women in general, face many more complex challenges and demands than their male counterparts. As such, there is a substantive difference in performing loyalty as leadership and its impact on the female body. This becomes most clear in the episode's conclusion in a scene featuring Elizabeth and her Russian handler Claudia (Margo Martindale): "Elizabeth, is everything okay? I've been in this business a long time. I won't say this job is twice as hard for women but it is something close to that." Again, knowing the demands of her loyalty on the body, Elizabeth declares, "I can handle it." Then the conversation, as if turning directly into the faces of the viewer, turns to equal rights for women:

> Have you been following the sad progress of this country's equal rights amendment? Honestly it makes me chuckle. These women here need to learn what you and I have known forever. You can't wait for the laws to give you your rights. You have to take them, claim them, every second of every day of every year. (Gibson, 2013)

CONCLUSION

In this chapter, I have accounted for several ways that leadership is learned and performed as loyalty through both a figurative and literal body of identifications. Specifically, I have argued that loyalty is central to leadership, and most especially in *The Americans*. For instance, toward the end of season one, Russian general Vijktor Zhukov (Olek Krupa) confirms the importance of loyalty when he indicates that Elizabeth was chosen because of her fear of surrender and loyalty. In the conclusion to the pilot episode, Elizabeth validates her selection when she declared to Phillip why she would not defect:

"Because I'm a KGB officer, don't you understand that? After all these years I would go to jail. I would die. I would lose everything before I would betray my country."

In accord with the themes of this book, *The Americans* has much to teach us as it relates to interrogating forms of production, presentation, and power in our learning and performing of loyalty as leadership. More than teaching us how leadership is performed simply *for* Americans, it offers us a more universal and fundamentally human story. As cocreator Joel Fields (Egner, 2016) has noted:

There is also a universal story being told in which the human becomes political: How we view our enemy. When we give ourselves over completely to a cause, however good it might be, there will be consequences. And to the extent that we blind ourselves to them or we dehumanize the other side, we will pay some price. It may be a price that is necessary for society, but we're kidding ourselves to think there isn't a price. And we're kidding ourselves if we think that there isn't a point of view on the other side that is also human. What we do with Phillip and Elizabeth is we show the consequences up close, and I think showing them up close gets you to examine them differently and wonder about it.

And wondering about it bolsters how television, and *The Americans* in particular, teaches us to explore issues related to leadership communication in the workplace and at home. Moreover, as the epigraph attests, Mark Twain's (1963) *A Connecticut Yankee in King Arthur's Court* reiterates the notion that loyalty to nation rather than its institutions or office-holders is real, substantial, and eternal.

For Twain, institutions are clothing that can be worn to the point that they cease to hold to their essential purpose and function. "To be loyal to rags, to shout for rags, to worship rags, to die for rags—that is a loyalty of unreason" (p. 84). And it is this "loyalty of unreason" that confronts our society at present. This is illustrated most distinctly toward the conclusion of the pilot episode, when Russian general Vijktor Zhukov outlines the difficulties of the Cold War for his time and ironically perhaps ours as well:

The American people have elected a madman as their president. He is extending their military forces on a massive scale. He is against nuclear arms control agreement. He makes no secret of his desire to destroy us. Our war is not so cold anymore. What happens behind enemy lines will determine the outcome of this struggle. (Weisberg, 2013)

Put differently, more than an intriguing series that enables us to think about how leadership is learned and performed, *The Americans* foregrounds the essential role that loyalty plays in our present cultural moment. As *Time* recently noted, "The president has been less concerned by competence than with loyalty" (Miller, 2017). As such, given the renewed Cold War tensions between Russia and the United States, *The Americans* is an invitation to explore the specific ways in which loyalty shapes how we learn and perform leadership.

REFERENCES

Barry, Ellen. (June 29, 2010). 'Illegals' spy ring famed in lore of Russian spying. *The New York Times*. Retrieved from http://www.nytimes.com/2010/06/30/world/europe/30sleepers.html

Berger, Jonah. (2013). *Contagious: Why Things Catch On*. New York: Simon & Schuster.

Burke, Kenneth. (1957). *Counter-Statement*. Chicago, IL: University of Chicago Press.

Burke, Kenneth. (1959). *Attitudes Toward History*. Lost Altos, CA: Hermes Publications.

Burke, Kenneth. (1969a). *A Grammar of Motives*. Berkeley, CA: University of California Press.

Burke, Kenneth. (1969b). *A Rhetoric of Motives*. Berkeley, CA: University of California Press.

Burke, Kenneth. (1973). *The Philosophy of Literary Form*. Berkley, CA: University of California Press.

Burke, Kenneth. (1984). *Permanence and Change: An Anatomy of Purpose*. Berkeley, CA: University of California Press.

Collins, Phil. (1981). In the Air Tonight. On *The Roof is Leaking* [CD]. Los Angeles, *Virgin-Atlantic* Records.

Costello, Mark. (December 30, 2007). The spy in the gray flannel suit. *The New York Times*. Retrieved from http://www.nytimes.com/2007/12/30/books/review/Costello-t.html

Craige, Betty Jean. (1996). *American Patriotism in a Global Society*. Albany, NY: State University of New York Press.

Douglass, Frederick. (1855). *My Bondage and My Freedom*. New York and Auburn: Miller, Orton & Mulligan.

Egner, Jeremy. (March 23, 2016). Joe Weisberg and joel fields discuss 'the americans,' Ronald reign and pastor tim. *The New York Times*. Retrieved from https://www.nytimes.com/2016/03/23/arts/television/the-americans-showrunner-season-4-interview.html?_r=0

Fleetwood, Mick. (1979). Tusk. [Recorded by Fleetwood Mac] On *Never make me cry* [CD]. Burbank, CA: *Warner Brothers* Records.

Fletcher, George P. (1993). *Loyalty: An Essay on the Morality of Relationships*. New York: Oxford University Press.

Gibson, Melissa J. (Writer) and Dale, H. (Director). (2013). *Comint* [Television series episode]. In Weisberg, J. (Executive Producer), *The Americans*. New York: FX.

Gleeson, Brent. (November 16, 2012). What great leaders have that good leaders don't: The difference between good and great leadership can be expressed in a singleword: loyalty. *Inc.* Retrieved from http://www.inc.com/brent-gleeson/what-great-leaders-have-that-good-leaders-dont.html

Greene, Andy. (February 29, 2016). Phil collins: My life in 15 songs. *Rolling Stone.* Retrieved from http://www.rollingstone.com/music/lists/phil-collins-my-life-in-15-songs-20160229

Hawhee, Debra. (2009). *Moving Bodies: Kenneth Burke at the Edges of Language.* Columbia, SC: University of South Carolina Press.

Heath, Chip and Heath, Dan. (2007). *Made to Stick: Why Some Ideas Survive and Others Die.* New York: Random House.

Heath, Chip and Heath, Dan. (2010). *Switch: How to Change Things When Change is Hard.* New York: Broadway Books.

Holson, Laura M. (March 29, 2013). The dark stuff, distilled. *The New York Times.* Retrieved from http://www.nytimes.com/2013/03/31/fashion/joseph-weisberg-uses-his-cia-time-in-the-americans.html?pagewanted=all&_r=1&

Koblin, John. (June 30, 2016). How much do we love tv? Let us Count the ways. *The New York Times.* Retrieved from https://www.nytimes.com/2016/07/01/business/media/nielsen-survey-media-viewing.html

Leeds, Sarene (October 5, 2013). 'The americans invade new york's paley center. *Rolling Stone.* Retrieved from http://www.rollingstone.com/movies/news/the-americans-invade-new-yorks-paley-center-20131005

Lewis, Hilary. (May 21, 2014). 'The americans' composer on incorporating '80s, Russian sounds into music for spy drama. *The Hollywood Reporter.* Retrieved from http://www.hollywoodreporter.com/live-feed/americans-composer-incorporating-80s-russian-706270

Miller, Zeke. (May 15, 2017). The quiet after the tweetstorm: President Trump goes silent. *Time.* Retrieved from http://time.com/4779092/donald-trump-tweet-storm-quiet/

Newton, Juice. (1981). Queen of Hearts. On *River of Love* [CD]. Los Angeles, CA: *Capitol* Records.

Quarterflash. (1981). Harden my heart. On *Don't Be Lonely* [CD]. New York: *Geffen* Records.

Quintanilla, Kelly and Wahl, Shawn. (2017). *Business and Professional Communication: Keys for Workplace Excellence,* Third Edition. Los Angeles, CA: Sage.

Staiger, Janet. (2005). *Media Reception Studies.* New York: New York University Press.

Thomas, June. (January 31, 2013). A conversation with the americans showrunners joe weisberg and joel fields: The only spy show on tv made by an actual spy. Retrieved from http://www.slate.com/articles/arts/interrogation/2013/01/the_americans_fx_spy_series_creators_joe_weisberg_and_joel_fields.html

Twain, Mark (1963). *A Connecticut Yankee in King Arthur's Court.* New York: The New American Library.

Waxman, Olivia B. (January 30, 2013) Q&A: The cia officer behind the new spy drama the americans. *Time*. Retrieved from http://entertainment.time.com/2013/01/30/qa-the-cia-officer-behind-the-new-spy-drama-the-americans/?iid=ent-main-lead

Weisberg, Joseph. (2008). *An Ordinary Spy: A novel*. New York: Bloomsbury.

Weisberg, J. (Writer), & O'Conner, G. (Director). (2013). *Pilot* [Television series episode]. In Weisberg, J. (Executive Producer), *The Americans*. New York: FX.

Wolf, Robert Paul. (1968). *The Poverty of Liberalism*. Boston, MA: Beacon Press.

Chapter 4

Politics, Race, Gender, and Leadership

An Analysis of Media Representation of Government Agency Training

Mia Long Anderson

In 2015, the CIA reported on the status of diversity within its ranks. The director's Diversity in Leadership Study revealed that diversity in senior leadership has decreased over the past 20 years (Central Intelligence Agency, 2015). At the time of the study, around 25 percent of the entire CIA workforce consisted of racial and minority officers, while racial and minority representation in the Senior Intelligence Service was closer to 11 percent. In fact, the study found that "agency leaders, managers, and supervisors do not prioritize diversity in leadership" (p. 2) and that "recruitment efforts to increase diversity of the workforce have not been a priority" (p. 3). Similarly, as of 2012, African Americans and Hispanics made up 4.7 percent and 7.1 percent of the FBI's special agents, respectively (Gerstein, 2015).

In stark contrast, ABC's *Quantico* centers on the training of a racially diverse group of government agents. The group, under the leadership of two African American CIA members, includes white, Muslim American, African American, Asian American, and Jewish trainees. In addition, in the season under study, two of the CIA trainees are actually undercover FBI agents serving under the leadership of an African American female senior FBI agent. The interaction among the trainees and between the agents and leadership allows for an in-depth study of media representations at the intersection of politics, race, gender, and leadership.

As Cranmer and Harris (2015) indicate in their analysis of *Remember the Titans*, "media has long been regarded as influential in shaping and altering individuals' perceptions of race and interracial interactions" (p. 153). In the same way, the media can also present images of how members of various races and genders embrace and "do" leadership. In line with Walker and Aritz's research (2015), the present study draws upon multiple definitions of leadership. One is that "leadership is exercised when ideas expressed in talk

47

or actions are recognized by others as capable of progressing tasks or prob-lems which are important to them" (Robinson, 2001, as cited in Walker & Aritz, 2015, p. 453). Secondly, leadership is viewed as "a process of influence and meaning management that advances a talk or goal, an attribution made by followers or observers, and a process, in which influence may shift and dis-tribute itself among several organizational members" (Walker & Aritz, 2015, p. 453). The current research also rests upon Goleman's (2000) six leadership styles as a basis for analysis.

This chapter offers a critical examination of the portrayal of leadership in the second season of the ABC television show *Quantico*. As with Cranmer and Harris' (2015) study, the project "deconstructs the communication and interracial interactions" of the government employees (p. 156). Specifically, the project analyzes the leadership styles of African American CIA and FBI leaders Owen Hall (CIA), Lydia Bates (CIA), and Miranda Shaw (FBI), from the viewpoint of social identity theory and self-categorization theory.

Quantico lends itself to such a study for a variety of reasons. First, the three leaders on the show are all African American. In addition, two of the leaders are female (Lydia and Miranda), and two of the leaders are family members (Owen and Lydia). Secondly, the leaders work for two different organizations, with Lydia and Owen appearing to serve different covert missions within the same organization. In this way, the show is prime for focus on social iden-tity theory and self-categorization theory, as the leaders (and recruits) align with others differently within various contexts, according to allegiances to a certain organization or mission, along lines of leadership, and in the area of gender. Thirdly, the three leaders serve in dissimilar capacities, with Miranda Shaw serving as deputy director of the FBI, and Lydia and Owen serving as CIA trainers. This becomes significant in the comparison of leadership styles exhibited during a time of crisis and a period of stability. Finally, findings from this study enhance the body of knowledge related to race and leadership, gender and leadership, politics and leadership, and media representation of leadership.

It is worth acknowledging that *Quantico* does not present the most accu-rate picture of these governmental agencies. Because it is a scripted show, it provides a director's vision of a writer's perception and notions of how leadership is enacted in a government agency. In addition, as previous stud-ies indicate, diversity is not a strong suit of either organization (CIA, 2015; Gerstein, 2015). However, the diversity reflected on the show may provide insight into how leaders "do" leadership in diverse situations (as Lydia and Owen with their recruits) versus less diverse situations (as Miranda serves as the prime African American senior official at the bureau). What follows is a review of relevant literature, followed by a critical analysis of each person's leadership style as indicated by their conversations and actions on the show, along with suggestions for future research.

THEORETICAL FRAMEWORK

Social Identity Theory

Turner et al. (1987) define a psychological group as "one that is psychologically significant for the members, to which they relate themselves subjectively for social comparison and the acquisition of norms and values" (p. 1). In social identity theory (Tafjel & Turner, 1979), Tafjel (1981) asserts that one's personal identity (how they see themselves as a unique individual) and their social identity (how they see themselves as a psychological group member) are of equal importance in the construction of their self-concept (Rivenburgh, 2000). The concept of social identity is defined as "that part of an individual's self-concept which derives from his knowledge of his membership of a social group (or groups) together with the value and emotional significance attached to that membership" (Tafjel, 1978, p. 63). The theory asserts that everyone strives to obtain a positive social identity (Simon & Brown, 2000). The positive valence of social identity is established by differentiating one's social categorization (ingroup) from the identities of those outside that group (outgroup).

Further, the desire for positive social identity can lead to the development of ideological belief structures among those viewing television programs (Mastro, 2003). Hence, for viewers, "the potential for televised images to influence intergroup comparison is highly conceivable" (p. 99). Sung (2013) also notes that "media representations play an important role in shaping the ways in which audiences understand and make sense of the social world" (p. 26). Though Mastro (2003) focuses on the impact of televised images as it relates to race and ethnicity, media portrayals may influence other aspects of one's assessment of various aspects of society, extending even to comparisons of leadership styles (e.g., minority versus nonminority leaders, female versus male leaders, younger versus older leaders). As such, constructed portrayals of leadership on television have the ability to affect viewer thoughts on leadership, regardless of any stereotypical images that may persist.

Intergroup differentiation and intragroup similarity are positively correlated. In other words, just as group members look for similarities to members of their ingroup, they also seek to define differences displayed by the outgroup. In turn, group members begin to assimilate into their group to increase these similarities and differences (Schneider, 2004). Such activity is illustrated in studies through the manipulation of ingroup and outgroup distinctions that affect the behavior of those who believe themselves to be a part of the ingroup (Jetten, Spears, & Manstead, 1996; Simon, Hastedt, & Aufderheide, 1997). The need to behave and make judgments similar to those of other ingroup members is also exhibited through empirical research (Jetten et al., 1996; Simon et al., 1997; Biernat et al., 1996).

Self-categorization Theory

Self-categorization theory (Turner et al., 1987), sometimes referred to as the social identity theory of the group, seeks to explain the assumptions that need to be made about psychological group formation in order to understand social categorization studies on intergroup behavior conducted by Tafjel. To do this, self-categorization theory develops the concept of social identity and the assumption of an "interpersonal-intergroup continuum" of social behavior (Turner et al., 1987, p. viii). It draws from the ideas of group psychology, individualism, and interactionism (Turner et al.) to produce a framework for group interaction and its impact on development of the self-concept presented in social identity theory (Tafjel & Turner, 1979).

Self-categorization theory (Turner et al., 1987) further develops social identity theory (Tafjel & Turner, 1979) by noting that self-conception occurs on multiple levels of inclusiveness (Hewstone, 2000). Turner et al. suggest that there are at least three levels of self-categorization that serve as important factors in the social self-concept. The superordinate level of the self as human being bases self-categorization on one's identity as a human being with similarities to other humans versus alternate life forms. The intermediate level of ingroup-outgroup categorizations is based on social similarities and differences. This intermediate level focuses on the membership in social groups such as classifying oneself as African American, male, or working class. The subordinate level of personal self-categorizations is based on differences between the person as a unique individual and other ingroup members (p. 45).

According to the theory, people self-categorize "depending on whether a social categorization into ingroup and outgroup can meaningfully be applied to the current social context" (Simon et al., 1997, p. 311). In one setting, it may be more advantageous for someone to group himself according to race whereas in another setting, benefit may be derived from categorizing himself based on educational experience or gender. People may also categorize themselves within a subset of a larger group in a nested pattern of sorts, choosing to identify with a smaller group to which positive attributes are ascribed, but dissociate from the broader, encompassing group to which negative attributes are attached (Biernat et al., 1996). The idea is that there is a tendency for one to categorize himself in the group that will provide association with a higher status (Chattopadhyay, George, & Lawrence, 2004).

People self-categorize based on the social categories accessible to them at the time either through those valued and frequently employed aspects of the self-concept, referred to as chronically accessible, or those made self-evident and salient in the present context, referred to as situationally accessible (Hogg & Reid, 2006). Hogg & Reid provide examples of gender and race as two social categorizations that are often both chronically and situationally accessible.

Discovering optimal fit within a social group is a process within itself. People evaluate accessible categories based on similarities and differences among people and how well the group prototype explains why people act the way they do (Hogg & Reid, 2006). After this evaluation using comparative fit and normative fit, people strive to categorize. The process of determining optimal fit through categorization continues until the group member self-categorizes within a group that displays similarities that relate to their personal characteristics (e.g., race, gender, status within organizational structure, etc.; Hogg & Reid, 2006).

LEADERSHIP STYLES

As Holmes et al. (2003) indicate, leadership can be largely viewed as "a performance in which an effective leader successfully integrates the achievement of transactional objectives with more relational aspects of workplace interaction" (p. 32). This idea of "doing leadership" developed over time, a far cry from the preceding thoughts of leadership as a byproduct of instinctive traits rather than learned ability. Indeed, early leadership research reflects the thought that the ability to lead is innate, and the task is to identify those who were born to lead (Bernard, 1926; Horner, 1997). In essence, a person's personality, along with their physical, mental and emotional characteristics, determined their success as a leader. As Horner (1997) asserts, this position failed to assess "the situational and environmental factors that play a role in a leader's level of effectiveness" (p. 270).

Subsequent research rested on the thought that great leaders are identified by what they do rather than who they are. In this sense, leadership skills can be taught and learned; leaders can be developed, placing leadership research within both a training and organizational framework (Horner, 1997). At the same time, research offered two ways in which leaders were oriented—people-driven and outcome-driven (Blake, Shepard & Mouton, 1964). Leaders could then be classified based on their more frequently practiced orientation, with consideration of the moderating factor of flexibility (Horner, 1997).

Other leadership research embarked upon the influence of context in shaping leader behavior, incorporating the situation and environment into leader evaluation. For example, Fielder (1967) viewed leadership effectiveness as the product of leadership style and a particular situation's suitability for leader influence (Horner, 1997). More recently, studies in leadership have focused on the intersection of leadership and organizational culture, enhancing the call for more leadership skills in a workplace environment in which culture sometimes changes. To that end, as Horner (1997) asserts, "leaders are also involved in managing the culture by establishing an explicit strategic direction, communicating that direction, and defining organizational vision and values" (p. 272).

Goleman (2000), citing research conducted by the consulting firm Hay/ McBer, highlights six leadership styles: coercive, authoritative, affiliative, democratic, pacesetting, and coaching. The coercive style requires submission, typically producing a negative outcome. However, the coercive style can be beneficial during a crisis or in an effort to rein in lax employees. The authoritative style brings people together in their work toward a particular vision, mission, or goal. The authoritative leader often exhibits ambition, initiative, and temperance. Instead of the "Do what I tell you" stance of the coercive style, leaders utilizing the authoritative style say, in essence, "Come with me" (p. 9). When exerting this leadership style, a leader will portray confidence and empathy (Goleman, 2000). As the most effective leadership style, the authoritative style results in increases in every area of an organization. Because people understand the vision of the authoritative leader, followers tend to be more devoted to the organization.

The affiliative style puts people first, working to build relationships and good communication. According to Goleman (2000), this style works best in an effort to "build team harmony, increase morale, improve communication, or repair broken trust" (p. 9). There are disadvantages to the affiliative style, though, as its focus on commendation does nothing to identify and curtail subpar performance. It also leaves people without clear direction. For these reasons, research suggests that the affiliative style be used in conjunction with another style, such as the authoritative style, to offset the lack of clarity and organizational standards (Goleman, 2000).

The democratic style provides followers with a voice, including them in idea and policy formation. Employees are also able to express their concerns, resulting in better employee morale. Because of their high involvement in organizational processes, employees also "tend to be very realistic about what can and cannot be accomplished" (p. 11). The democratic style works best in two instances: (1) when the leader is unclear about the direction of the organization and needs the help of others, and (2) when new ideas are needed to work toward a well-defined vision. When not executed properly, the democratic style can result in lengthy brainstorming meetings and a delay in decision-making. The style also will not work if employees are not well informed or knowledgeable.

While the democratic leader asks "What do you think?," the pacesetting leadership style demands "Do as I do, now" (Goleman, 2000, p. 10). The pacesetting leader, in all her ambition and initiative, sets a standard of excellence for the organization. Those who cannot meet that standard may feel swamped and may be replaced by more competent employees. Such a work environment breeds feelings of distrust, with low commitment, direction, or feedback. The democratic leadership style works well "to get quick results from a highly motivated and competent team," though it most often produces negative results (p. 10).

The coaching style focuses more on an employee's future rather than the present tasks of the organization. There is a drive to develop others, from a long-term perspective. Though the coaching style tends to be used the least, it often produces positive results (Goleman, 2000). To that end, Goleman asserts, "Leaders who ignore this style are passing up a powerful tool: its impact on climate and performance are markedly positive" (p. 12). The coaching style works best with employees who recognize their weaknesses and have a desire to change. When coached properly, employees feel the leader genuinely cares about them and their future. Employees may also be more open to try new things. The reverse holds true as well, with the coaching style being less effective in an environment where followers oppose change. One reason the coaching style is used infrequently is the amount of time leaders must spend teaching and developing employees.

No leadership style must be used alone. An effective leader may use one style or alternate between various styles. As Goleman (2000) states, "being able to switch among the authoritative, affiliative, democratic, and coaching styles as conditions dictate creates the best organizational climate and optimizes business performance" (p. 3). In fact, it is these four of the styles that consistently produce positive results.

LEADERSHIP AND RACE

There are numerous theories stemming from the study of leadership, many of which produce models whereby one may ascertain best practices for successful leadership (Fielder, 1967; Liden, Sparrowe, & Wayne, 1997; Scandura & Schriesheim, 1994; Stogdill, 1974; Bass & Stogdill, 1990; Pearce, Conger, & Locke, 2008; Antonakis, Avolio, & Sivasubramaniam, 2003; Jago, 1982). Within this research are bodies of work on leadership styles and leadership within the contexts of race (Bartol, Evans, & Stith, 1978; Logan, 2011; Chao, 2017; Shin, Heath, & Lee, 2011; Madlock, 2008) and gender (Eagly & Johnson, 1990; Eagly, Johannesen-Schmidt, & van Engen, 2003; Korabik, 1990).

In line with Hogg & Reid's (2006) use of race and gender as two chronically and situationally accessible social categorizations, Ospina and Foldy (2009) declare that exploring race-ethnicity provides context within leadership research. The researchers argue that "race-ethnicity is often central to how individuals and collectives define themselves, either explicitly or implicitly" (p. 876). In this way, a person's race will influence their actions and reactions in the workplace, whether in the role of leader or employee. Pauliené (2012) further exerts that gender and culture both impact workplace behaviors. At the intersection of race, leadership, and power, then, is an underlying examination of the balancing of societal inequities within the assumed authority of previously marginalized voices (Ospina & Foldy, 2009).

As Ospina and Foldy (2009) highlight, studies of race and leadership have focused largely on the effects of race on perceptions of leadership and the enactment of leadership, along with the social reality of race. Various scholars found that race can act as a constraint to nonwhite leaders, who may have their authority challenged or be evaluated on means other than merit (Bartol, Evans, & Stith, 1978; Ospina and Foldy, 2009; Knight, Hebl, Foster, & Mannix, 2003). In addition, African American leaders may be seen as less effective than their white counterparts, with informal ostracizing in terms of consideration for positions of leadership and reprimand for past mistakes (Sackett & DuBois, Vecchio & Bullis, 2001; Rosette, Leonardelli, & Phillips, 2008; Walker, Madera, & Hebl, 2013).

Ospina and Foldy (2009) assert "recent organizational trends that amplify functional demands to cultivate both connectedness *and* difference provide an important setting where the complex reality of race-ethnicity becomes part of the phenomenon of leadership" (p. 877). To that end, scholars have attempted to categorize leadership traits along racial and gender lines. For example, in their comparison of black and white leaders, Bartol, Evans, and Stith (1978) found leaders to perform similarly in some instances, though black supervisors of employees of various races tended to "initiate more leader behaviors" than evident when leading black employees (p. 296).

LEADERSHIP AND GENDER

In addition to race, gender has been the focus of numerous leadership studies (Eagly, Karau, & Makhijani, 1995; Eagly, Johannesen-Schmidt, & van Engen, 2003; Korabik, 1990; Trempe, Rigny, & Haccoun, 1985; Yoder, 2001). In their study of women and leadership, Walker and Aritz (2015) highlight the typical characteristics attributed to feminine and masculine leaders. For example, feminine leaders are indirect, person-oriented, and collaborative, often providing supportive feedback. Conversely, masculine leaders are more direct, confrontational, and competitive, focusing more on the task than the people (Eagly & Johnson, 1990; Walker and Artiz, 2015, p. 455).

For women in a male-dominated society, then, the challenge becomes, to not appear "too masculine or too feminine" (Biereman, 2016, p. 119). As Biereman asserts, the ideal leader is often presented as masculine, with women exhibiting feminine characteristics often placed in positions where they are overlooked or undermined. Further, women may face obstacles in recruitment, training, and promotion that their male counterparts do not encounter. In an effort to counteract this, female leaders may adopt more masculine leadership traits. When female leaders are also a racial minority, their acceptance as a leader may face additional criticism (Parker, 1996; Sutton & Terrell, 1997; Jean-Marie, Williams, & Sherman, 2009).

ANALYSIS

Resting upon the backdrop of social identity theory and self-categorization theory, the current research explores how three African American (and two female) government representatives "do" leadership. Manganello et al. (2008) asserted that seven episodes, randomly selected, are needed for character-based analysis of a weekly series. Though the previous study focused on content analysis of sex on television, the basis of the assertion was determined applicable to the current study. The researcher viewed all episodes of ABC's *Quantico* airing in Fall 2016 (September 25 through November 27), resulting in an analysis of the first eight episodes of the second season. The analysis focused on the leadership styles and social identities of Owen Hall, Lydia Bates, and Miranda Shaw.

Owen Hall's Leadership Style

Owen Hall has worked for the CIA for over 20 years, many of which have been spent as a trainer to CIA recruits. Owen often expresses resentment for being removed from the field. Throughout the show, he works to find out who blew his cover, which ultimately led to his reassignment as a trainer. Though this subplot is vital to Owen's identity, it does not take away from the standard of excellence he exhibits and expects at the CIA recruit training facility, the Farm.

Throughout Owen's interactions with the trainees, he uses three leadership styles. Owen often uses the authoritative style in which he explains the overall goal of an exercise, or of the training experience as a whole, but allows the trainees to establish their own paths to meeting the set goal. For example, there is an exercise in which recruits are trained on surveillance. After the training session, recruits are blindfolded, thrown into vans, and dropped off in the middle of the woods, with the instruction to get back to the Farm by dark. Though the goal is clear, the recruits are tasked with finding their own way.

There are times, though, when Owen utilizes the democratic style, giving trainees a voice in decisions. In one instance, the trainees are tasked with using information they are given to decide if there should be a drone strike. The team must work together to reach its own unanimous decision within a predetermined amount of time. Owen's addition of the time element to the democratic style actually offsets its disadvantages, in that employees (or in this case, trainees) do not have the opportunity to engage in lengthy meetings. In addition, with Owen remaining in the room with them during their discussion and giving clear initial instructions, the recruits do not feel leaderless (Goleman, 2000).

Owen also practices the pacesetting style of leadership by setting and demonstrating high performance standards (Goleman, 2000). This works particularly well in the instance of CIA training, as the recruits are "self-motivated and highly competent" (p. 3). When the recruits make it to the Farm, Lydia and Owen explain that there will be a daily ranking of the recruits. If any recruit is at the bottom of the board twice, they will be sent home. Owen demonstrates his own high performance standards during an exercise in advanced interrogation techniques. Owen tasks the students with getting him to expose the alias he used when he worked in the field using such techniques. Owen endures over 14 hours of various types of torture before the waterboarding of his daughter convinces him to reveal his codename.

Finally, Owen incorporates the coaching style into his repertoire, specifically in his dealings with CIA recruits (and undercover FBI agents) Ryan Booth and Alex Parrish. In separate one-on-one conversations, Owen commends both Booth and Parrish for their prior work with the FBI. In one instance, Owen tells Parrish that he is the one responsible for her selection as a recruit, stating he believes in her abilities to succeed. Further, Owen tells Booth that he sees similarities between the two of them, with the understanding that Owen considers himself one of the best.

In terms of race, Owen never positions himself in that light. In line with the tenets of social identity theory and self-categorization theory, he appears to identify more as a former field agent and a current trainer than as an African American male. In no instance does he highlight his race as having any influence on his leadership or early removal as a field agent. Though there are a few instances in which he has conversations with Alex addressing her flirtatious actions, he does not discuss matters of gender or portray gender as a major part of his identity. He doesn't treat the recruits differently based on their race or gender. In all situations, he appears to see his former role and identity as a field agent as the more salient identity, rather than identifiers of race or gender.

As it relates to Walker and Aritz's (2015) discussion of masculine and feminine leader characteristics, Owen primarily displays masculine characteristics with his competitive nature and his sense of autonomy. On multiple occasions, he manages to create situations that stump the recruits, and on one occasion, fluster a fellow CIA agent. Owen expresses autonomy often, seeing himself as a lone ranger, one who was ousted by the CIA, but believes he can still perform the duties of a field operative. Still, Owen possesses the feminine characteristic of collaboration when he works with his co-trainer Lydia and recruit Léon to achieve certain tasks and recruit exercises.

Lydia Bates' Leadership Style

Lydia Bates is a CIA agent who has traveled extensively conducting CIA fieldwork. She longs to return to the field, but her return is a bit prolonged until she achieves clearance mid-season, only to return to the Farm. Lydia is Owen's daughter and, though the two work together in training recruits, there appears to be resentment toward Owen for his absence (due to fieldwork) during her childhood. This resentment is illustrated in Lydia's harsh treatment of her father's desire to find out who blew his cover. At one time, she tells him that he made so many mistakes, the CIA was looking for a way to excuse him from duty.

Lydia chiefly expresses two leadership styles: pacesetting and coaching. However, by default as a trainer, she engages in the democratic style in her assignment of certain tasks to the recruits. Lydia demonstrates her pacesetting style by placing demand for high standards upon all recruits. To that end, she may single out certain recruits by engaging in conversations in which she scolds them for their efforts, or lack thereof. For example, there are multiple instances in which Lydia criticizes Alex for her poor performance, though in some situations we find that her rebuke was only to test Alex's stressors.

Despite her reprimands, Lydia also embraces the coaching leadership style. With recruit, Dayana Mampasi, Lydia takes extra time during a surveillance exercise to point out Dayana's weaknesses and counsels her on ways to be better. Similarly, and in light of a previous situation in which she ignores Alex's request to talk, Lydia takes the time one evening to encourage Alex in her work at the Farm. This may be particularly helpful to Alex, as Goleman (2000) indicates that coaching works best with those who recognize their weaknesses and desire to change.

Like Owen, Lydia does not dwell on race. However, there is a phone call with another agent in which undertones of gender appear. During that phone conversation, Lydia asks if she has not been placed back in the field because of an implied sexual exchange she had with that agent. Otherwise, Lydia too seems to identify more as a CIA operative than an African American or a female, rarely drawing on either identity.

Finally, Lydia displays both feminine and masculine leadership styles. In line with feminine leadership styles, she is collaborative with Alex (though it is later revealed as a ruse) and Owen. She also provides supportive feedback, in a few instances, to Dayana and Alex. Among masculine leadership styles, Lydia operates autonomously, at one point encouraging Alex to do the same.

In fact, she asks Alex, after revealing her prior deception, if she thinks "this is the Girl Scouts where we're all in it together." Like Owen, and perhaps because of their roles as trainers and the portrayed nature of government agencies, Lydia is more task-oriented than people-oriented.

Miranda Shaw's Leadership Style

Miranda Shaw is the deputy director of the FBI. However, she is also an undercover terrorist involved in a high-stakes terrorist situation. She must navigate between maintaining her cover and making sure a terrorist attack is successful. She is the direct supervisor to multiple FBI operatives, including CIA recruits Alex Parrish and Ryan Booth.

Miranda's leadership style differs from that of Lydia and Owen. This may be because Miranda is working in the midst of a crisis, and is, in fact, a terrorist who has helped orchestrate the crisis within which she (and the nation) is involved. Miranda appears to use the authoritative style with her subordinate Shelby, showing self-confidence and, at times, empathy (Goleman, 2000). In one situation, Miranda takes Shelby with her to meet with a recently pardoned convict who will be used in a hostage exchange. As Goleman indicates this style may be more effective with Shelby because she is not as experienced as Miranda.

There are instances with Alex and Ryan where Miranda also uses the democratic leadership style. In meetings with the two undercover agents, she allows Alex and Ryan to offer their opinions on who should be the focus of the undercover investigation, though Miranda ultimately assigns next steps.

Most often, though, Miranda interchanges between the coercive and pacesetting styles. Throughout the crisis, she argues her reasoning to other leaders and, among both leaders and subordinates, is often the one to dictate next steps. For example, at one point, there is discussion of how to address a hostage situation. In the face of opposition, Miranda rebuts a colleague's rationale and makes a direct order. One example of Miranda's use of pacesetting is when she attempts to abruptly remove Alex from the Farm because she feels she has failed her mission. Alex refuses to leave and asserts her independence and determination to continue as a recruit.

Miranda never overtly addresses her race or gender, though she is portrayed as one of few African Americans or African American females in such a position of authority at the FBI.

Miranda largely uses masculine leadership styles. In each instance, she is very direct, making tough decisions among colleagues and delivering orders to subordinates. Likewise, she is quite confrontational. In one episode, she is told that a four-star general has been called in to handle the terrorist threat. She is heard expressing her defiance to military inclusion. She later confronts the general with that fact, though the general excuses Miranda's complaint and continues with her duties. In meetings with her colleagues, Miranda also dominates speaking time, often incorporating a raised voice into conversation.

IMPLICATIONS

According to self-categorization theory, people self-categorize "depending on whether a social categorization into ingroup and outgroup can meaningfully be applied to a social context" (Simon et al., 1997, p. 311). Chattopadhyay et al. (2004) further assert that people tend to categorize in the group that will equate to a higher status. In the instance of *Quantico*, it becomes evident early in the second season that the height of status among CIA members is as an agent working in the field. To that end, race and gender are not salient identifiers and tend to have very little influence in choice or reception of leadership styles. The leaders identify and associate more with recruits in whom they see qualities that good field agents possess. This surpasses racial, ethnic, and gender classifications. Rather than race, the leaders at times focus on the trainees' cultural backgrounds. However, even these conversations focus on how the cultural background can positively impact the success of the trainee. Even among recruits, those who consider themselves top recruits seek to identify with other recruits, with a lesser focus on race, culture, or gender.

Quantico also displays the use of multiple leadership styles by Owen, Lydia, and Miranda. This supports the assertion that leadership style alternates according to context. Even within the two agencies, Miranda uses leadership styles indicative of the crisis the agency now faces, while Owen and Lydia adopt leadership styles for a variety of contexts, all supporting proper CIA training. Though none of the leaders uses the affiliative style, Owen and Lydia's use of positive leadership styles can create "the best organizational climate and optimizes business performance" (Goleman, 2000, p. 3). Conversely, Miranda's mostly negative styles of leadership may have contributed to one employee's distrust of her (Shelby) and another employee's independence from her (Alex).

The present study may deepen the conversation and need for research on the use of leadership styles within various contexts. It also illuminates other areas of study. For instance, scholars may want to study the intersection of family roles and leadership. In *Quantico*, Lydia and Owen seem to be able to keep their professional and personal lives clear. This may not always be the case. It would be interesting to see how co-leadership with family members impacted leadership style as well as social identity. Though some research exists on leadership and government (Trottier, Van Wart, & Wang, 2008), there is a need of further study on leadership styles used within federal government agencies. Such a study could also lend credence or rebuttal for the nature of leadership *Quantico* exhibits.

CONCLUSION

Quantico presents an interesting, albeit fiction, portrayal of leadership in the CIA and the FBI. Illuminating three African American leaders, the show is prime for studies in leadership and theories, such as social identity theory and self-categorization theory. Though prior research shows that African Americans hold few leadership roles in the CIA and FBI, statistically speaking, these leaders do not present their race or gender as the more salient identity. Rather, they esteem the identity of a field agent or, in one instance, a high-ranking official as the more important identifier. Whether this portrayal of little focus on race and gender as salient identities is accurate is questionable, as it is, in fact, the scripted assessment of a television writer. Still, the lesser role attached to race and gender may consequentially impact the context and reasons for which certain leadership styles are implemented.

REFERENCES

Antonakis, J., Avolio, B. J., & Sivasubramaniam, N. (2003). Context and leadership: An examination of the nine-factor full-range leadership theory using the Multifactor Leadership Questionnaire. *The Leadership Quarterly, 14*(3), 261–295.

Bartol, K. M., Evans, C. J., & Stith, M. T. (1978). Black versus white leaders: A comparative review of the literature. *Academy of Management Review, 3*, 293–304.

Bass, B. M., & Stogdill, R. M. (1990). *Bass & Stogdill's Handbook of Leadership: Theory, Research, and Managerial Applications.* New York, NY: Simon & Schuster.

Bernard, L. L. (1926). *An Introduction to Social Psychology.* New York: Holt.

Biereman, L. L. (2016). Women's leaadership: Troubling notions of the "ideal" (male) leader. *Advances in Developing Human Resources, 18*(2), 119–136.

Biernat, M., Vescio, T. K., & Green, M. L. (1996). Selective self-stereotyping. *Journal of Personality and Social Psychology, 71*, 1194–1209.

Blake, R. R., Shepard, H. A., & Mouton, J. S. (1964). *Managing Intergroup Conflict in Industry.* Houston, TX: Gulf Publishing Co.

Central Intelligence Agency. (2015). *Director's Diversity in Leadership Study.* Retrieved from https://www.cia.gov/library/reports/dls-report.pdf

Chao, C. (2017). The Chinese female leadership styles from the perspectives of trait and transformational theories. *China Media Research, 13*(1), 63–73.

Chattopadhyay, P., George, E., & Lawrence, S. A. (2004). Why does dissimilarity matter? Exploring self-categorization, self-enhancement, and uncertainty reduction. *Journal of Applied Psychology, 89*, 892–900.

Cranmer, G. A., & Harris, T. (2015). "White-Side, Strong-Side": A critical examination of race and leadership in *Remember the Titans*. *Howard Journal of Communications, 26,* 153–171.

Eagly, A. H., & Johnson, B. T. (1990). Gender and leadership style: A meta-analysis. *Psychological Bulletin, 108*(2), 233–256.

Eagly, A. H., Karau, S. J., & Makhijani, M. G. (1995). Gender and the effectiveness of leaders: A meta-analysis. *Psychological Bulletin, 117*(1), 125–145.

Eagly, A. H., Johannesen-Schmidt, M. C., & van Engen, M. L. (2003). Tranformational, transactional, and laissez-faire leadership styles: A meta-analysis comparing women and men. *Psychological Bulletin, 129*(4), 569–591.

Fielder, F. E. (1967). *A Theory of Leadership Effectiveness.* New York: McGraw-Hill.

Gerstein, J. (February 13, 2015). Amid race talk, FBI struggles to hire black agents. *Politico.* Retrieved from http://www.politico.com/story/2015/02/fbi-black-hiring-115185

Goleman, D. (2000). Leadership that gets results. *Harvard Business Review, 78*(2), 4–17.

Hewstone, M. (2000). Contact and categorization: Social psychological interventions to change intergroup relations. In C. Stangor (Ed.), *Stereotypes and Prejudices* (pp. 394–418). Philadelphia, PA: Psychology Press.

Hogg, M. A., & Reid, S. A. (2006). Social identity, self-categorization, and the communication of group norms. In *Communication Theory* (16th ed., pp. 7–30). International Communication Association.

Holmes, J., Schnurr, S., Chan, A., & Chiles, T. (2003). The discourse of leadership. *Te Reo, 46,* 31–46.

Horner, M. (1997). Leadership theory: Past, present and future. *Team Performance Management, 3*(4), 270–287.

Jago, A. G. (1982). Leadership: Perspectives in theory and research. *Management Science, 28*(3). 315–336.

Jean-Marie, G., Williams, V. A., & Sherman, S. L. (2009). Black women's leadership experiences: Examining the intersectionality of race and gender. *Advances in Developing Human Resources, 11*(5), 562–581.

Jetten, J., Spears, R., & Manstead, A. S. (1996). Intergroup norms and intergroup discrimination: Distinctive self-categorization and social identity effects. *Journal of Personality and Social Psychology, 71* (6), 1222–1233.

Knight, J. L., Hebl, M. R., Foster, J. B., & Mannix, L. M. (2003). Out of role? Out of luck: The influence of race and leadership status on performance appraisals. *The Journal of Leadership and Organizational Studies, 9*(3), 85–93.

Korabik, K. (1990). Androgyny and leadership style. *Journal of Business Ethics, 9*(4/5), 283–292.

Liden, R. C., Sparrowe, R. T., & Wayne, S. J. (1997). Leader-member exchange theory: The past and potential for the future. *Research in Personnel and Human Resources Management, 15,* 47–119.

Logan, N. (2011). The white leader prototype: A critical analysis of race in public relations. *Journal of Public Relations Research, 23*(4), 442–457.

Madlock, P. E. (2008). The link between leadership style, communicator competence, and employee satisfaction. *Journal of Business Communication, 45*(1), 61–78.

Manganello, J., Franzini, A., & Jordan, A. (2008). Sampling television programs for content analysis of sex on television: How many episodes are enough? *Journal of Sex Research, 45*(1), 9–16.

Mastro, D. (2003). A social identity approach to understanding the impact of television messages. *Communication Monographs, 70*(2), 98–113.

Ospina, S., & Foldy, E. (2009). A critical review of race and ethnicity in the leadership literature: Surfacing context, power and the collective dimensions of leadership. *The Leadership Quarterly, 20*, 876–896.

Parker, P. S. (1996). Gender, culture, and leadership: Toward a culturally distinct model of African-American women executives' leadership strategies." *The Leadership Quarterly, 7*(2), 189–214.

Pauliené, R. (2012). Transforming leadership styles and knowledge sharing in a multicultural context. *Business, Management and Education, 10*(1), 91–109.

Pearce, C. L., Conger, J. A., & Locke, E. A. (2008). *The Leadership Quarterly, 19*(5), 622–628.

Rivenburgh, N. K. (2000). Social identity theory and news portrayals of citizens involved in international affairs. *Media Psychology, 2*, 303–329.

Robinson, V. M. J. (2001). Embedding leadership in task performance. In K. Wong, & C. W. Evers (Eds.), *Leadership for Quality Schooling* (pp. 90–102). London, England: Routledge.

Rosette, A. S., Leonardelli, G. J., & Pillips, K. W. (2008). The white standard: Racial bias in leader categorization. *Journal of Applied Psychology, 93*(4), 758.

Sackett, P. R., & DuBois, C. L. (1991). Rater-ratee race effects on performance evaluations: Challenging meta-analytic conclusions. *Journal of Applied Psychology, 76*, 873–877.

Scandura, T., & Schriesheim, C. (1994). Leader-member exchange theory and supervisor career mentoring as complementary constructs in leadership research. *Academy of Management Journal, 37*(6), 1588–1602.

Schneider, D. J. (2004). *The Psychology of Stereotyping*. New York: The Guilford Press.

Shin, J., Heath, R. L., & Lee, J. (2011). A contingency explanation of public relations practitioner leadership styles: Situation and culture. *Journal of Public Relations Research, 23*(2), 167–190.

Simon, B., & Brown, R. (2000). Perceived intragroup homogeneity in minority-majority contexts. In C. Stangor (Ed.), *Stereotypes and Prejudices* (pp. 326–337). Philadelphia: Psychology Press.

Simon, B., Hastedt, C., & Aufderheide, B. (1997). When self-categorization makes sense: The role of meaningful social categorization in minority and majority members' self-perception. *Journal of Personality and Social Psychology, 73*, 310–320.

Stogdill, R. M. (1974). *Handbook of Leadership: A Survey of Theory and Research.* New York, NY: Free Press.

Sung, C. C. M. (2013). Language and gender in a US reality TV show: An analysis of leadership discourse in single-sex interactions. *Nordic Journal of English Studies, 12*(2), 25–51.

Sutton, E. M., & Terrell, M. C. (1997). Identifying and developing leadership opportunities for African American men. *New Directions for Student Services, 80*, 55–64.

Tafjel, H. (1978). *Differentiation between Social Groups*. London: Academic Press.

Tafjel, H. (1981). Social stereotypes and social groups. In J. C. Turner, & H. Giles (Eds.), *Intergroup Behaviour* (pp. 144–167). Oxford; Chicago: Blackwell; University of Chicago Press.

Tafjel, H., & Turner, J. C. (1979). An integrative theory of intergroup conflict. In W. G. Austin, & S. Worchel (Eds.), *The Social Psychology of Intergroup Relations* (pp. 33–47). Monterey, CA: Brooks/Cole.

Trempe, J., Rigny, A., & Haccoun, R. (1985). Subordinates satisfaction with male and female managers: Role of perceived supervisory influence. *Journal of Applied Psychology, 70*(1), 44–47.

Trottier, T., Van Wart, M., & Wang, X. H. (2008). Examining the nature and significance of leadership in government organizations. *Public Administration Review, 68*(2), 319–333.

Turner, J. C., Hogg, M. A., Oakes, P. J., Reicher, S. D., & Wetherell, M. (1987). *Rediscovering the Social Group: A Self-Categorization Theory*. Oxford, England: Basil Blackwell.

Vecchio, R., & Bullis, R. (2001). Moderators of the influence of supervisor-subordinate similarity on subordinate outcomes. *Journal of Applied Psychology, 86*, 884–896.

Walker, R. C., & Aritz, J. (2015). Women doing leadership: Leadership styles and organizational culture. *International Journal of Business Communication, 52*(4), 452–478.

Walker, S. S., Madera, J. M., & Hebl, M. R. (2013). Effects of leader race and leader mistake on patronizing behaviors. *Journal of Business Diversity, 13*(1/2), 52–64.

Yoder, J. (2001). Making leadership work more effectively for women. *Journal of Social Issues, 57*(4), 815–828.

Part II

PRESENTATION OF IDENTITY

Chapter 5

"Boy bye"

A Textual Analysis of Angela Rye and the Politics of Representation of Black Women in Cable Television News

Loren Saxton Coleman

Angela Rye, former executive director of the Congressional Black Caucus and White House staffer, and founder and current director of IMPACT, a political advocacy group, is a political commentator on Cable News Television Network, CNN. During CNN's 2016 Democratic National Convention coverage in July, Rye and her reaction to one of Donald Trump supporter's positions on Trump's charity work garnered significant attention on traditional and social media channels. Rye's reaction, now labeled as the "eye roll heard 'round the world," transformed into an Internet and social media sensation, inspiring hashtags, such as "#ryeroll," (Heil, 2016). In early August, Rye's reaction to former Trump campaign manager, Corey Lewandowski, went viral again, as she used Beyoncé's lyrics, "boy bye," to convey her disagreement and disapproval with Trump's request for the release of President Obama's acceptance letter and transcripts from Harvard University (Heil, 2016).

Rye, with years of leadership experience in politics and law and political advocacy and civic engagement, has been both praised and criticized for her choice of words and facial expressions during her recent segments on CNN. In this chapter, I argue that her candor and use of popular culture references call into question the standards of representation and participation for black women, more specifically, black females in leadership positions, in television cable news. More specifically, Rye's *unapologetic* verbal and nonverbal presence and the reaction to her presence on CNN sheds light on how television news structures both provide opportunities for the exercise of agency, and simultaneously reinforces discriminatory racialized and gendered structures. Rye's nonverbal expressions and use of popular culture references cut through political jargon, and she asserts herself as a knowledgeable and reputable political commentator. Yet, Rye, to some audience members, simultaneously reinforces the angry, black woman stereotype. This chapter will explore how the complexity in representations of Rye, as a black female leader, in television news media point to how structures of race and gender both limit and provide opportunity for black women to exercise agency via media.

Using cultural studies as a theoretical and methodological guide, I will explore a cultural text: #ryeroll. Cultural studies investigate how power is produced and legitimized in cultural texts, like a Twitter hashtag (Kellner, 2015). Similarly, cultural studies also examine how people can resist this power, and create oppositional or alternative readings of the text (Kellner, 2015). Therefore, this textual analysis will explore the production, consumption, representation, regulation and identity of the #ryeroll to critically examine the representation of Angela Rye via media as a leader in politics and civic engagement. More specifically, this textual analysis will: (1) highlight the constitutive role representation plays in the formation and transformation of culture; (2) explore how Rye exercises agency in her political contributions on CNN; and (3) interrogate how that exercise of agency is limited by and also, helps transform structures of race and gender in cable television news media.

POLITICAL COMMENTATORS, MEDIA, AND CULTURE

Walter Lippmann questioned the public's ability to actively and knowledgeably participate in public opinion (Bro, 2012). Similar to Plato's idea of the "philosopher's kings," Lippmann believed that "a class of expert, who in a responsible way, can help direct the course of society for and on behalf of the public," (Bro, 2012, p. 434). Lippmann's meritocracy proposal was consistent with his idea that the general public did not have the expertise, or really, the desire to understand media messages, specifically those relating to politics. For Lippmann, the expert class of people included researchers from universities, analysts from think tanks and political commentators (Bro, 2012).

According to Bro (2012), Lippmann believed political commentators were necessary in establishing a link between politicians and the public. Bennett (2012) stated that political commentators operate within news organizations to describe and discuss politics. Bro (2012) postulated that many political commentators are former journalists, or formerly trained journalists. Within news organizations, political commentators can offer their professional expertise, while also acting as publicity agents for their respective news organizations, thus contributing to their popularization (Bro, 2012). Political commentators have gained traction in media, often participating in conversations within news organizations about topics, such as sports, culture, technology, and economics (Bro, 2012). Here, the literature highlights the role of political "pundits" or commentators in the formation of public opinion via public discourse in media.

Depending on the topic of discussion, news organizations rely on various political commentators as expert sources. For example, scholars have assessed how black journalists framed conversations on race during the elections of President Barack Obama (see Campbell and Wiggins, 2015). This research is part of a larger body of scholarship that explores the challenges of diversity in print and broadcast newsrooms (e.g., see Campbell, 1995; Nishikawa et al., 2009; Squires, 2009). While this literature does not speak specifically to diversity of political pundits, it does contribute to the understanding of how black women are represented in news media. This literature also helps build context on the standards of journalism, and how these standards condition the exercise of black women's agency in broadcast news.

BLACK WOMEN ON TELEVISION

Significant research has been done on the representation of black women on television. Black feminist scholar Patricia Hill Collins (2000) identified controlling images, or stereotypes, of black women in media. According to Collins, the portrayal of mammies, matriarchs, welfare recipients, sapphire, and hot mommas, has played an active role in the oppression of black women in social and cultural life. These stereotypes normalize and legitimize racism, sexism, and classism (Collins, 1990). Black feminist cultural studies scholar bell hooks (2013) argued that media are the most pervasive vehicles of imperialist white supremacist capitalist patriarchy, for short—white supremacy. This term hooks (2013) uses helps explain how interlocking systems of race, class, gender, and economics marginalize black women, in particular. Like Collins, hooks (2013) explicated how media representations function to restrict and limit black women. While many scholars have examined controlling images in entertainment television, research has also shown that those stereotypes persist in broadcast news.

For example, Nishikawa et al. (2009) found that black journalists are conditioned by mainstream news standards. More specifically, black journalists are less likely to be advocates when reporting news. In contrast, Meyers and Gayle (2015) examined how black women specifically challenged mainstream news standards to resist hegemonic newsroom standards. Examples of specific acts of resistance Meyers and Gayle (2015) found in their interviews include the following: using African American sources as experts, not using stereotypical African Americans, using white images and voices to achieve balance on issues, such as welfare and crime, encouraging African American sources to improve their appearance before being videotaped, and informing coworkers about racial issues. Here, while Meyers and Gayle (2015) specifically focused on how black women journalists "encode resistance" in the newsroom, their work highlights how this resistance is conditioned by structures of race, gender, and class. Black female journalists' attempt to avoid selecting stereotypical African American sources or encouraging African American sources to improve their appearance perpetuates the idea of the necessity of a socially palatable or unitized representation of African American women.

Although the aforementioned research does not specifically discuss black female commentators, Meyers and Gayle's (2015) emphasis on resistance and the exercise of agency in the newsroom helps build context for the argument made in this chapter. As mentioned earlier, political commentators use media to help shape and frame the public's understanding of politics. While Bro (2012) noted that many political commentators are formerly trained journalists, some are not, like Angela Rye, who is a trained lawyer. hooks (2013) and Collins (1990) research on black women stereotypes perpetuated in media help explain how controlling images of race and gender still work to condition Rye's exercise of agency as a political commentator and analyst.

The goal of this chapter is to analyze Angela Rye, a black female political commentator in television news media. Using cultural studies as a theoretical and methodological guide, this chapter explores the way in which Rye's identity, as a leading voice on politics and civic engagement, is formed in media, and the production, consumption, and regulation of the representation of her identity via the hashtag, #ryeroll.

ON THEORY AND METHOD

The study of culture in cultural studies is the study of texts and practices of everyday life, (Storey, 1996). Therefore, culture is not static or narrowly defined. Storey (1996) stated, "It is political in a quite specific sense—as a terrain of conflict and contestation," (p. 2). This statement speaks to the fluidity and transformative nature of culture, and therefore, cultural texts. Through textual analysis, cultural studies research highlights the constitutive role of culture in the production of our social, political, and economic world.

Textual analyses examine the subjective forms of social and cultural life to explore how people are constituted as social and political individuals (Johnson, 1986/87). Individuals produce and consume texts, exercising some control over the processes of their social lives. In the production and consumption of texts, some subjective forms are prioritized over others. Some forms reproduce existing forms of racial or spatial oppression or domination, while others provide alternative representations and interpretations of social life.

Raymond Williams and Richard Johnson asserted that culture and cultural analyses are complex whole processes. Similarly, Johnson (1986/87) stated that the text is reconstituted to include various moments of representation and reproductive practices across different genres. After examining forms and processes of production across different kinds of evidence, analyses point to common experiences of social and cultural life.

Roushanzamir (2004) stated that texts are defined by the researcher, and critical textual analyses focus on evidence of social practice, not representations of cultural and social life. Kellner (2015) and du Gay (1997) noted that textual analyses research should not prioritize one social practice or cultural process, such as production, over another. The circuit of culture provides a methodological framework that explores the articulation of a cultural phenomenon, such as a hashtag.

Twitter is a microblogging site that allows users to send 140 maximum character messages. Users can engage with one another via retweeting (RT), or by mentioning (@) a specific user in a tweet. Hashtags are another form of interaction on Twitter (Florini, 2014). A hashtag, which is created using the "#," "followed by the phrase to indicate the topic of the tweet (#hashtag)," (Florini, 2014). Twitter users can contribute to specific conversations using a hashtag, such as #ryeroll.

Scholars, like Florini (2014) and Brock (2009) have studied Twitter and Black Twitter using cultural studies as a theoretical and methodological guide. While my chapter is not focused on Black Twitter, their research on Twitter helps contextualize my research in the following ways. Florini (2014) and Brock's (2009) research on the performance of racial identity on Twitter examined the articulation of race, thus highlighting the communication process as a discursive process of linked, but distinct moments. Hall (1980) highlighted these moments as production, circulation, distribution/consumption, and reproduction. Later Richard Johnson (1986/87) and Paul du Gay (1997) identified these discursive processes as the circuit of culture.

More specifically, the circuit of culture explores how a cultural artifact is, "represented, which social identities are associated with it, how it is produced and consumed, and what mechanisms regulate its distribution and use," (du Gay, 1997, p. 3). Each moment in the circuit is distinct and will be separated for purpose of analysis, but is not mutually exclusive in the production and negotiation of meaning. Richard Johnson stated that circuit of culture analysis investigates how, "everyone participates, however, unequally, in the cultural process of making meanings and fixing and shifting identities," (Johnson et al., 2004, p. 10). In other words, using a circuit of culture analysis of a Twitter hashtag, this chapter will investigate how cable television audiences and Twitter users helped create meaning of Angela Rye, as a black female political commentator, and leading voice in civic engagement and politics.

In this chapter, I employ the circuit of culture to conduct a textual analysis of the cultural artifact: #ryeroll. The timeline of analysis was determined by two media moments—Rye's eye roll during a CNN panel at the Democratic National Convention (DNC) on July 27, 2016 and the presidential election night on November 9, 2016. Moments of *production, consumption,* and *representation* were examined through a textual analysis of Rye's CNN video clips and transcripts of July 27, 2016 and August 2, 2016, the hashtag "#ryeroll" and emergent hashtag "#boybye," and accessible tweets using Advanced Twitter Search from Angela Rye's Twitter handle (@Angela_Rye) from July 27, 2016 to November 9, 2016. Moments of *representation* were further examined, along with *identity* and *regulation* via a textual analysis of media coverage of Rye's two CNN video clips that appear on Rye's Twitter handle and the hashtags, "#ryeroll" and "#boybye" from July 27, 2016 to November 9, 2016.

WHO IS ANGELA RYE?

Angela Rye, Esq. is the cofounder and director of IMPACT strategies, a political and civic engagement organization in Washington, D.C. She currently serves on the boards of several organizations, such as the Congressional Black Caucus Institute and Women in Entertainment Empowerment Network. Previously, Rye has also served as the executive director and general counsel to the Congressional Black Caucus for the 112th Congress. Rye is also a CNN commentator and NPR political analyst (About Angela, n.d.).

Producing and Consuming #ryeroll

On July 27, 2016, Rye appeared on a CNN Tonight panel at the Democratic National Convention in Philadelphia. She was featured on a panel alongside CNN anchor Don Lemon, political commentators Kayleigh McEnany, Maria Cardona, Peter Beinart, and CNN political director David Chalian. The panel was reviewing the speakers for the night, which included both President Bill Clinton and Secretary of State Hillary Clinton. In critiquing Bill Clinton's 42-minute speech about Secretary Clinton, Lemon asked McEnany to respond to President Clinton's claim that Secretary Clinton was "the best darn change-maker in America."

As a Trump supporter, McEnany responded with criticism of Secretary Clinton's management of Libya, Iraq, and Syria. Within the camera frame, Rye turns her head away from McEnany and rolls her eyes. When Lemon interjected by naming Secretary Clinton's work on school and adoptive parents, McEnany responded:

Well that's great. You know Donald Trump has done great things in his private time, too, for veterans, all across his foundation. He's done great things, too. We've all done great things in our lives and I commend her for helping children, that's a commendable thing.

During McEnany's response, the camera pans out to include Rye and Cardona. As McEnany stated "Donald Trump has done great things," Rye rolled her eyes and then turns to Cardona, who also widened her eyes. The camera shot did not include McEnany, even as she was speaking, which suggested that the visual focus should be on Rye and Cardona's reaction to McEnany.

Mainstream news standards recommend that reporters should speak objectively, void of opinion (Tuchman, 1978). Therefore, Rye's visual reaction was not consistent with recommendations for standard newsroom posture. On one hand, Rye's representation perpetuated the angry black woman stereotype, which is seen as ill-mannered and unable to control her emotion. However, Rye's eye roll and smirks during McEnany's response challenged mainstream news standards, and thus, also subverted this standard newsroom posture, calling for a reconceptualization of standards of professionalism on cable television for political commentators.

After CNN aired this panel on television, #ryeroll emerged on Twitter. It seems that the hashtag was used to both challenge and perpetuate existing norms as it relates to black women in media and mainstream news standards. For example, on July 27, 2016 @HassanDarkside retweeted:

@therachelpotter: This girls face on @CNN is everything. (emojis). #myTHOUGHTS exactly.

Here, this tweet seems to praise Rye for showing her raw emotional reaction to McEnany's comments. Similarly, on July 30, 2017 @ac_witdahoodie tweeted:

@angela_rye I just found out about the #ryeroll and I am so happy to see you are clapping back at the haters and dumbasses (emojis).

On Angela Rye's Twitter mentions on July 28, @clarknt67 tweeted:

@angela_rye broke all the rules of media training and we (emoji) her for it. #eyerollequeen

In all three tweets, Twitter users are participating in the production of #ryeroll, and simultaneously, in the consumption of #ryeroll. More specifically, these three examples speak to the celebratory nature of some of the tweets that used #ryeroll and/or mentioned @angela_rye. These tweets speak to the consumers' resistance to restrictive newsroom standards. This is one exemplar of a subversive regulation of #ryeroll, as the last example specifically mentions how Rye "broke all the rules of media training," thus exercising a form of agency in media. In other words, Twitter users' celebration of Rye's eye roll is an act of resistance against restrictions on newsroom standards, and the controlling images of black women on television. However, that agency was conditioned.

While some tweets praised Rye for her overt display of disapproval of McEnany's comments, other Twitter users condemned her. For example, @copter_dave tweeted on July 29:

> **@angela_rye as a veteran I'm embarrassed for you. Keep it classy and unbiased.**

Here, this tweet conveys support of mainstream news standards, which suggests that commentators should remain unbiased. Similarly, this tweet suggests that Rye's representation created meaning and an identity that lacked sophistication or professionalism during this segment, which reinforces the sapphire stereotype, who is seen as loud, boisterous, and overbearing (Reynolds-Dobbs et al., 2008). Just seven days later, another hashtag emerged on Twitter.

On August 2, 2016, Rye was featured on a CNN Tonight show with CNN anchor Don Lemon. The panel featured CNN commentators Bakari Sellers, Corey Lewandowski, and Republican political consultant John Brabender. The main point of discussion of this panel was in response to President Obama's criticism of the then Republican presidential nominee, Donald Trump. Brabender stated that President Obama created Donald Trump, and Lewandowski followed with a statement that Donald Trump was the exact opposite of President Obama. He stated, "Donald Trump is strong decisive, clear about what he wants to accomplish." Rye immediately disagreed, and the conversation continued about the appropriateness of President Obama questioning the qualifications of Donald Trump to serve as president. While Lewandowski communicated that President Obama should not personally attack the Republican nominee, Rye reminded him and the audience that Trump challenged President Obama's American citizenship and his acceptance and matriculation at Harvard University.

Then, the following exchange ensued between Rye and Lewandowski.

Lewandowski: So, did he ever release his transcripts of Harvard?
Rye: By the way, tell me about those tax returns. Corey, while you're at it.
Lewandowski: Well, you raised the issue. I'm just asking you. You raise the issue. Did he—did he ever release his transcripts or his admission to Harvard

University. You raised the issue so just yes or no. The answer is no.
Rye: Corey, in this moment, I'm going to Beyonce you. Boy, bye. You're so out
of line right now. Tell your candidate to release his tax returns.

Bakari Sellers laughed after Rye made her remarks and it appeared that
Lewandowski and Brabender did not have any visible facial reaction to Rye's
use of Beyoncé lyrics. In the video clip, Rye used lyrics from "Sorry," a
Beyoncé song from the recent album, *Lemonade,* to dismiss Lewandowski's
statements about President Obama's transcripts. Rye's use of Beyoncé's lyrics coupled with her dismissive hand gesture worked to convey discontent
and lack of relevance of Lewandowski's statements. In this moment, Rye's
use of this popular culture reference challenges mainstream newsroom norms
that suggest that political commentators primarily use knowledge from
political experience, and traditional political language (Bro, 2012). Here, Rye
regulated traditional newsroom standards, and prioritized black popular culture and its subversive nature. Once again, a conversation on Twitter started
via #boybye.

This hashtag's production also allowed for the consumption of the television moment, and created the space for users to challenge and perpetuate
existing representations of black women on television news. For example, @
chasethekat23 tweeted on August 3, 2016:

**@Angela_rye U were fire tonight! Poise, style, educated & not afraid to put
one in their place when needed. You're my new sheroe!!! #boybye**

Here, @chasethekat23 praised Rye for her class, level of intellect and courage to challenge Lewandowski, who is a white man. Similarly, @mohaginy
tweeted on August 3, 2016:

**When you're black, highly educated and give NF! Love this woman!
@angela_rye #Boybye**

@MatthewJHarris7 tweeted on August 18, 2016:

**@Angela_rye Everything you pop up on CNN I get my whole life! I adore
you. Smart, quick, and no nonsense. Thank you! #boybye**

Here, all three tweets specifically used the word "educated" or "smart" to
describe Rye, which refutes the stigma that emotion or bias lends itself to
inaccuracy and lack of intelligence in news media. It also challenges the
notion that black women in positions of leadership and influence are represented as primarily angry or sassy in media. In both tweets, users pointed

to Rye's level of education, not her emotion, before emphasizing her assertiveness. However, some tweets still perpetuated the angry or ghetto black woman stereotype. For example, @sheldonbeatly tweeted on August 22, 2016:

@Angela_rye I LOVE IT! Dropping knowledge with the right amount of "hood"! #boybye

Although this tweet was celebratory, the conveyed message that black women who display emotion, or operate outside traditional newsroom norms are representing themselves as "hood," is consistent with literature on more contemporary stereotypes in media, such as the "crazy black bitch," (CBB). Reynolds-Dobbs et al. (2008) stated that the CBB is often portrayed as angry, unprofessional, and argumentative.

Several Twitter users expressed discontent using the hashtag or in @angela_rye's mentions. For example, @kevinpsweeney tweeted on August 10, 2016:

This is how a CEO talks! Your so ghetto.

Here, this tweet specifically challenged Rye's leadership capacity and leadership style. The use of the word ghetto is consistent with black women represented on television as, sassy, or overly demanding black women (Squires, 2009). Similarly, @micankusi tweeted on August 30, 2016:

@CNNnewsroom @angela_rye laughing during your apology for laughing while the pastor spoke=classless. Everyone deserves respect.

While these last two tweets do not use the #boybye hashtag, they are indicative of a negative sentiment toward Rye and her representation on CNN. Both tweets point to a perceived lack of professionalism in Rye. In some ways, these tweets also further delegitimize Rye's position of authority as a political commentator and, perpetuate the production and consumption of the controlling unqualified, unprofessional, and sassy CBB stereotype.

After #boybye emerged on Twitter, research showed that #ryeroll continued to be a topic of conversation as Rye appeared on CNN throughout the 2016 presidential election coverage. On August 3, 2016 @IamNurseTrish tweeted:

THIS is who I raise my daughter to be—@angela_rye #ryeroll #angelarye.

On August 16, 2016 @TheSouthernGent tweeted:

@angela_rye nothing more beautiful than an educated and powerful black woman #cmonsomebody #ryeroll.

On October. 10, 2016, @Mexic_anaT tweeted:

@Angela_rye always so articulate and damn fierce! Not sure how you don't lose your mind. #ryeroll #tellem.

In the aforementioned tweets, it seemed that Rye was celebrated as a black female political commentator. In these three tweets, it appeared that Twitter users were impressed by her ability to assert herself as an expert and leader. This response to Rye is consistent with Cartier's (2014) call for literature to examine black women in future texts. Although her analysis was primarily of fictional black female characters, the concept of future text is applicable to Rye's analysis. In future texts, consumers can move away from feeling compelled to label representation as positive or negative, and instead appreciate the production and consumption of new and more complex identities of black women in media (Cartier, 2014). In these tweets, Rye, as a future text, was represented as credible and purposeful in her exercise of authority.

Representing and Regulating #ryeroll

Rye garnered media coverage from varying outlets after her eye roll at the DNC. To further investigate practices of representation, identity, and regulation, this section analyzes online media coverage. Articles were selected for analysis using the #ryeroll and #boybye feeds and @Angela_Rye mentions from July 27, 2016 to November 9, 2016. Tweets using the specific hashtag pointed to the articles selected for analysis, and mentions with article links that discussed either Rye's eye roll at the DNC or Rye's use of Beyoncé lyrics to shut down Corey Lewandowski were also selected for analysis. A total of eight articles were analyzed from the following news sources: the *Cut* of *New York Magazine*, the *Huffington Post*, the *Root*, the *Grio, Essence,* and the *Washington Post*.

On July 27, the *Cut* published a story online titled, "Chatting with Angela Rye About the Eye Roll Heard 'Round the World." The online magazine also tweeted it from its account @TheCut on July 27. In this article, writer Dayna Evans interviewed Rye about the "eye roll heard 'round the world." The article stated that Rye mentioned that her visual display of emotion is often calculated so that she does not appear as the "angry black woman." Although CNN is supportive of her contribution, this point is an exemplar of how pervasive and regulatory this controlling image of black women is in television media. Evans also noted that while many Twitter users praised Rye's eye roll, others thought her display of emotion was "childish."

Evans noted that Rye stated that she did not have a "poker face," like CNN political commentator Wolf Blitzer, who Rye stated was somewhat of a mentor. This points to two important factors. It is evident that Rye's identity is regulated or conditioned by the mainstream norm that news anchors should employ a "poker face," or unbiased, emotionless face. On a more critical level, Rye pointed to a white male as a standard of an effective "poker face," which supports hooks (2013) argument that white male patriarchy structures still regulate traditional newsrooms, and thus, conditioned Rye's exercise of agency.

On July 28, *Huffington Post* published the article, "This Woman Eye-Rolling At A Trump Supporter Is All of Us." The article was retweeted on July 28 by several Twitter users. For example, @writeplayrepeat retweeted the story's link with this original copy: **It shall henceforth be known as the #ryeroll @Angle_rye.**

The *Huffington Post* writer Alanna Vagianos labeled Rye's eye roll as "an eye-roll for the history books." The title and first couple paragraphs of this story pointed to how Rye's eye roll was representative of people that rejected Donald Trump's presidential campaign slogan, "Make American Great Again."

On August 3, the *Huffington Post* published an online article in its Black Voices section titled, "Angela Rye to Trump Supporter: 'I'm Going to Beyonce You. Boy, Bye.'" In this article, the *Huffington Post* writer Zeba Blay mentioned how Rye had become popular because of her "epic eye rolls" at the DNC, and the use of Beyoncé lyrics to dismiss Trump supporters. Blay called this moment "glorious," providing an example of the positive and lovable representation of Rye.

On August 4, the *Washington Post* published the online article, "Meet Angela Rye, who shut down a former Trump staffer with Beyonce grade shade." The article was retweeted by several users. For example, on August 4 @LynnReedSelhy retweeted the story's link with this original copy:

Love my sister Link @angela_rye Great @washingtonpost profile #ryeroll #boybye.

The article addressed both Rye's use of Beyoncé lyrics and her eye roll at the DNC. Like the *Huffington Post* article, the *Washington Post* article mentioned how Rye was aware that she was representative of people that rejected Donald Trump's personal attacks on President Obama, and those who were overall frustrated with the discriminatory rhetoric used during Trump's presidential campaign. The *Washington Post* article also noted that Twitter users both praised and criticized Rye's use of Beyoncé lyrics. Rye, who was interviewed for the article, stated that the praise and criticism was ideologically aligned. More specifically, Trump supporters labeled her "ghetto and unprofessional," while those who opposed Trump told Rye that she spoke for them and she spoke the way they would speak to their friends.

Trump supporters' labeling of Rye's representation as "ghetto and unprofessional," is consistent with the Collins' (1990) conversations on controlling images of black women in media, specifically sapphire. It also provides evidence of how mainstream newsroom standards regulate political commentators. In contrast, people who opposed Trump indicated that Rye was not only representative of their opposition, but also that Rye was relatable and accessible to them. Here, the formation of collective identity with Rye is consistent with scholarship that points to an increase in audience engagement with news when people feel empowered about a specific issue (Bennett, 2012).

As Rye continued to appear on CNN panels, article links continued to circulate on Twitter about her. For example, *Essence* magazine published an online article titled, "7 of CNN Commentator Angela Rye's Most Lit Moments." This article was retweeted several times on Twitter. For example, @architataylor retweeted the article link with this original copy:

Proud to call @angela_rye my former boss lady! #ryeroll #tellemwhatsup.

The first two moments detailed in the article were Rye's use of Beyoncé's lyrics and then, her eye roll at the DNC. *Essence*, a black-owned publication that celebrates black culture, praised Rye's display of emotion while disseminating facts about issues relevant to the black community, like police brutality.

The *Root* published a similar online article on October 4 titled, "The Politics and Faces of Angela Rye." Unlike previously mentioned articles, the *Root* writer Yesha Callahan described Rye's professional experiences to help establish credibility and legitimacy as a political commentator, first. It was noted that Rye was the founder and director of IMPACT strategies in the second full paragraph of the article. Therefore, it seemed that the *Root* prioritized Rye's expertise in political advocacy and civic engagement. Callahan did not mention Rye's facial expression until the sixth paragraph in the body of the article.

The *Huffington Post* published an online article in its Black Voices section on October 31 titled, "CNN Commentator Angela Rye's Bes Moments Will Brighten Your Day." One Twitter user, @serenity_pat,among others, retweeted the article with this original copy:

THIS is why we love @angela_rye.

The *Huffington Post* writer Rachel Gebreyes article's organization is consistent with the aforementioned the *Root* article. Rye was immediately identified as a leader and expert in politics, as Gebreyes identified Rye as a former director of the Congressional Black Caucus in the first sentence of the second paragraph. Again, Rye's expertise and qualifications were immediately identified to substantiate her position as a political commentator.

Similarly, an article published on the *Grio* on November 1 identified Rye as the "Black community's unofficial defender." According to the article, Rye was represented as the black community's unofficial defender because of her willingness and capability to address stigmas about the black community, often perpetuated by the Republican Party. The article overwhelmingly praised Rye as it iterated how Black Twitter often celebrated after Rye would challenge and sometimes even dismiss stereotypical rhetoric from Trump supporters. The *Grio* writer Niki McGloster wrote in her article titled, "It Was Love at First Eye-roll with Angela Rye":

> Not only has Rye's off-the-cuff digs and cultural volleying made her an unforgettable part of the election coverage, but also her audaciousness in the face of folks who'd rather a Black woman remain silent on matters that affect her community. Rye doesn't cower or falter. She's articulate and, from where I'm sitting, pretty damn on point ... And because she does it so brilliantly, it nearly shatters the Angry Black Woman trope.

Here, McGloster's statements explicitly highlighted how Rye's representation is conditioned by crippling stereotypes. However, as McGloster noted, Rye's candor and intellect help to dismantle that stereotype. Similarly, this article pointed to why representation is important, and more importantly, how it is constitutive of cultural life. She wrote:

> her dedication to fight against the ridiculous notion that all black folks are poor and uneducated (needing to be saved by the Great White Trump) and her ability to bridge a gap between government illiterate Millennials and need-to-know politics. She easily makes you want to sit through a few round of CNN and join the conversation. Hell, most importantly, it makes you want to vote.

Here, McGloster emphasized that Rye's representation is important for several reasons. First, it helps challenges the stigma that black people are uneducated. Second, CNN consumers, specifically those who are in the millennial generation, can collectively identify with Rye's prioritization of political awareness and civic engagement through her use of popular culture references. Third, Rye's purposeful efforts to challenge misconceptions about the black community and courage to take on Trump supporters motivates people to action, specifically to vote.

Online media coverage overwhelmingly praised Rye for her eye roll and "Beyoncé grade-shade." However, it's important to note that six out of the eight articles were published in either strictly online publications, or sections of online publications that largely focus on issues pertinent to the black community. However, even among those articles, there were some distinct differences, such as the *Root*, the *Grio* and *Huffington Post* writers' explicit prioritization of Rye's leadership experience and qualifications.

DISCUSSION

Rye's leadership experience in IMPACT strategies and the Congressional Black Caucus coupled with her extensive background in law qualify her as an expert and leader in politics and public affairs. This chapter's goals were to explore the representation of Angela Rye via cultural analysis of #ryeroll, a hashtag that emerged just after Rye's eye roll at the DNC in Philadelphia. Guided by the circuit of culture, my textual analysis examined Twitter hashtags and mentions, and online media coverage to investigate the articulation of Angela Rye as a leading voice politics and civic engagement, in moments of production, consumption, representation, regulation, and identity.

Rye's popularity on Twitter and in media coverage could point to a growing acceptance and appreciation of black women serving in leadership positions in media, such as a political commentator. In the production and consumption practices of #ryeroll, some Twitter users were impressed with Rye's honesty and courage. These practices may represent a shift in expectations for black woman on television media, in the political context. It may represent a movement away from traditional journalism policies, which are rooted in objectivity, fairness and accuracy (Tuchman, 1978).

Through the analysis of #ryeroll, this chapter also sheds light on how Rye's representation was regulated by dominant and stereotypical structures of race and gender. Although analyzed media coverage and most tweets seemed to praise Rye, there were some Twitter users that overtly disapproved with Rye's representation on CNN. For example, @GOPBlackduck tweeted on August 4:

This is the kind of black person CNN wants on its air?
Neck twisting, finger pointing Angela Rye. Sad stereotype.

This tweet is just one example of how Twitter users regulated Rye's representation using the "ghetto" black woman stereotype. Rye's representation was also regulated by the black superwoman stereotype, as conveyed in the *Grio* article. The black superwoman stereotype refers to a black woman manages difficult and unpopular work without fears or weaknesses of other women (Reynolds-Dobbs et al., 2008). As such, Rye, as a black woman leader on an international platform who willingly challenges dominant stereotypes of black communities, and consistently draws attention to issues pertinent to the black community, was represented as the "unofficial Black defender."

However, this analysis also provided evidence that Rye self-identified as a champion for the safety and sanctity of black lives. For example, on October 5, @max_ellis tweeted:

> **U r seriously just mean to people . . . like relax, this is America,**
> **People think differently than u do . . . ur such an angry person.**

@angela_rye replied:

> **It's hard as hell to be nice and happy about racism when my folks**
> **Are dying. You feel me?**

Here, Rye exercised agency when she challenged the sapphire stereotype as she conveyed that anger and frustration are appropriate emotions to display when advocating for the safety and sanctity of black lives.

This textual analysis also shows that although Rye's representation was regulated by dominant and crippling structures of race and gender, her representation also subverted these structures, as it contributed to the production of collective identity among Twitter users, both producers and consumers of #ryeroll. Hall stated, "Black popular culture has enabled the surfacing, inside the mixed and contradictory modes even of some mainstream popular culture, of elements of discourse that is different, other forms of life, other traditions of representation" (Hall, 1996, p. 470). In other words, Rye's use of popular culture language, like Beyoncé lyrics, and social media platform, Twitter, to engage with audiences helps create meaning that contributes to a more complex and often, contradictory, understanding and appreciation for black women as legitimate leading voices on cable television news, and legitimate leaders in civic engagement and political advocacy.

This research contributes to ongoing research on the representation and representation of black women on television, in a variety of contexts. It specifically calls for analyses to consider how black women in leadership positions can simultaneously challenge and perpetuate dominant structures of race and gender via practices of resistance. This research can develop practical models of diversity and inclusion in the workplace, and think critically about how these models can both challenge and perpetuate narrow understandings of black women as leaders.

REFERENCES

About Angela. Retrieved from http://angelarye.com/about-angela/

Bennett, L. (2012). *News: Politics of Illusion*. Glenview, IL: Pearson.

Blay, Z. (August 3, 2016). Angela Rye to Trump supporter: 'I'm going to Beyonce you. Boy, bye.' *Huffington Post*. Retrieved from http://www.huffingtonpost. com/entry/angela-rye-to-trump-supporter-im-going-to-beyoncé-you-boy-bye_ us_57a20149e4b08a8e8b602f1f

Bro, P. (2012). License to comment: The popularization of a political commentator. *Journalism Studies, 13*(3), 433–446.

Brock, A. (2009). "Who do you think you are?!": Race, representation and cultural rhetorics in online spaces. *Project on Rhetoric Inquiry, 6*, 15–35.

Callahan, Y. (October 4, 2016). The politics and faces of Angela Rye. *The Root*. Retrieved from http://www.theroot.com/the-politics-and-faces-of-angela-rye-1790857074

Campbell, C. (1995). *Race, myth and the news*. Thousand Oaks: Sage Publications.

Campbell, K. and Wiggins, E. L. (2014) Walking a tightrope: Obama's duality as framed by selected African American columnists. *Journalism Practice, 9*(2), 184–199.

Cartier, N. (2014). Black women on screen as future texts: A new look at black pop culture representations. *Cinema Journal, 53*(4), 150–157.

Collins, P. H. (1990). *Black Feminist Thought: Knowledge, Consciousness, and The Politics of Empowerment*. Boston: Unwin Hyman.

Du Gay, P., Hall, S., Janes, L., Mackay, H. and Negua, K. (1997). *Doing Cultural Studies: The Story of the Sony Walkman*. London: Sage.

Evans, D. (July 27, 2016). Chatting with Angela Rye about the eye roll heard 'round the world. *The Cut*. Retrieved from http://nymag.com/thecut/2016/07/angela-rye-cnn-tonight-eye-roll.html

Florini, S. (2014). Tweets, tweeps and signifyin': Communication and cultural performance on "black Twitter." *Television & New Media, 15*(3), 223–237.

Gebreyes, R. (October 31, 2016). CNN commentator Angela Rye's best moments will brighten your day. *Huffington Post*. Retrieved from http://www.huffingtonpost.com/entry/angela-rye-cnn_us_58174e51e4b0990edc32253d

Hall, S. (1980). Encoding/decoding. In S. Hall, D. Hobson, A. Lowe and P. Willis (Eds.) *Culture, Media, Language* (p. 51–61). London: Hutchinson.

Hall, S. (1996). What is this 'black' black in popular culture? In D. Morley and K-H. Chen (Eds.) *Stuart Hall: Critical Dialogues in Cultural Studies* (p. 465–475). New York: Routledge.

Heil, E. (August 3, 2016). Meet Angela Rye, who shut down a former Trump staffer with Beyonce-grade shade. *The Washington Post*. Retrieved from https://www. washingtonpost.com/news/reliable-source/wp/2016/08/03/meet-angela-rye-who-shut-down-a-former-trump-spokesman-with-beyonce-grade-shade/?utm_term=. eba7a93c2c23

Hooks, B. (2013). *Writing Beyond Race: Living Theory and Practice*. New York: Routledge.

Johnson, R. (1986/87) What is cultural studies anyway? *Social Text, 16*, 38–80.

Johnson, R., Chambers, D., Raghuram, P. and Tincknell, E. (2004). Cultural studies and the study of culture: Disciplines and dialogues. In *The Practice of Cultural Studies* (p. 1–25). London: Sage.

Kellner, D. (2015). Cultural studies, multiculturalism and media culture. In G. Dines and J. Humex (Eds.) *Gender, Race, and Class in Media: A Text Reader* (p. 9–20). Thousand Oaks: Sage Publications.

Lewis, T. (August 10, 2016). 7 of CNN commentator Angela Rye's most lit moments. *Essence*. Retrieved from http://www.essence.com/2016/08/10/angela-rye-cnn-election-2016-clinton-trump

McGloster, N. (November 1, 2016). It was love at first eye-roll with Angela Rye. *The Grio*. Retrieved from http://thegrio.com/2016/11/01/angela-rye-is-our-black-hero/

Meyers, M. and Gayle, L. (2015). African American women in the newsroom: Encoding resistance. *Howard Journal of Communications, 26*, 292–312.

Nishikawa, K. A., Towner, T. L., Clawson, R. A. and Waltenburg, E. N. (2009). Interviewing the interviewers: Journalistic norms and racial diversity in the newsroom. *The Howard Journal of Communication, 20*, 242–259.

Reynolds-Dobbs, W., Thomas, K. M. and Harrison, M. (2008). From mammy to superwoman: Images that hinder black women's career development. *Journal of Career Development, 35*(2), 129–150.

Roushanzamir, E. (2004). Chimera veil of "Iranian Women" and processes of U.S. textual commodification: How U.S. print media represent Iran. *Journal of Communication Inquiry, 28*(1), 9–28.

Squires, C. (2009). *African Americans and the Media*. Cambridge: Polity Press.

Storey, J. (1996). *Cultural Studies and the Study of Popular Culture*. Athens, GA: University of Georgia Press.

Tuchman, G. (1978). *Making News*. New York: Free Press.

Vagianos, A. (July 28, 2016). This woman eye-rollng at a Trump supporter is all of us. *Huffington Post*. Retrieved from http://www.huffingtonpost.com/entry/this-woman-eye-rolling-at-a-trump-supporter-is-all-of-us_us_579a0a09e4b01180b531e272

Chapter 6

Pinned Down by Profit

Managing the Branded Body in Total Divas

Kristen L. Cole and Alexis Pulos

In this chapter, we explore the representation of leadership, management, and control in the E! reality television series *Total Divas*. *Total Divas* follows the personal and professional lives of the WWE Divas, the female wrestling division of the World Wrestling Entertainment Inc. (WWE). The primary business endeavor of the WWE is professional wrestling but since its incorporation in the early 1980s, they have also expanded into other forms of entertainment, including film, music, video games, product sales, and, most recently, reality television. The WWE's most recent partnership with E! to produce the reality television show *Total Divas* has been a relative success. *Total Divas* first aired on July 28, 2013 and as of January 2017 it is in its sixth season. During the first six episodes of its sixth season, the show drew an average of 600,000 viewers and ranked consistently in the Top 50 Original Cable Telecasts (Metcalf, 2017). In addition to highlighting the everyday lives of some of the WWE's most recognizable female Superstars, the show offers a peek into the organizational culture of the WWE, including negotiations of power and control as they relate to employee goals and responsibilities, and the corporation's institutional visions.

Utilizing critical discourse analysis and pulling from Barker's (1999) theoretical model of organizational control, we reveal how interaction between management and members of the WWE Divas division reflects a new form of organizational control, which we refer to here as *neoliberal control*. We argue that this form of control is constructed and reaffirmed through the discourses presented by the WWE and embodied by the Divas. This reiterative process of constituting and reaffirming control results in a strong company brand but at the cost of depoliticizing the bodies that constitute that brand. In other words, the organizational control of bodies—and, in this case, female bodies—becomes justifiable. Neoliberal control therefore leads to a black boxing of labor and identity, where bodies are viewed entirely in terms of their brand value.

Since *Total Divas* is relatively young in comparison to its professional wrestling counterpart, there is limited scholarship that specifically addresses the reality show. Studies that do analyze *Total Divas* (e.g., Dunn, 2015) are concerned primarily with gendered representations rather than representations of organizational dynamics. However, there is a significant body of scholarship on the WWE's organizational practices in general, which provides a starting point for our present analysis of *Total Divas*.

THE BUSINESS OF WRESTLING

The popularity of professional wrestling ebbs and flows, but during times of peak ratings and viewership the WWE has garnered "more than 500 million regular viewers" (Deeter-Schmelz & Sojka, 2004, p. 133). Analyzing the marketing strategies employed by WWE, Bajaj, and Banerjee (2016) reveal that WWE is successful as a "marketing spectacle" because of its ability to maintain a cosmopolitan image (p. 80). The success of this diversified image occurs through WWE's alignment of their audience's personalities with their brand's personality, which they achieve by ensuring that their performers "maintain their characters outside the arena" (p. 75). By branding employees as performers across multiple media platforms (television, film, websites, video games, etc.), the WWE is able to appeal to and market their organization to a broader audience.

WWE Superstars are so commodified that it is difficult, and sometimes impossible, for them to be seen as separate from the company. For example, in 2010, former WWE CEO Linda McMahon ran for political office but she was unsuccessful because constituents could not distinguish between her WWE storyline and the legitimacy of her campaign (Walker, 2012). In fact, the WWE brand and their product-based storylines are so thoroughly cultivated for their fans that, according to Deeter-Schmelz & Sojka (2004), the "WWE is more representative of a subculture of product consumption than an entertainment venue" (p. 134). The WWE's commitment to narrative and character commodification is arguably a consequence of their evolution from sport to sports entertainment (McLean, 2000). As Barrett and Levin (2015) note, after 1989, when the WWE publicly acknowledged that the outcomes of their wrestling matches were predetermined, they were able to focus less on actual wrestling and more on character development and storylines, which "became as essential to the [WWE] product as the wrestling matches themselves" (p. 470). Shifting focus to characters and storylines offered greater branding opportunities, which meant more screen time for the women of WWE.

WWE and fans refer to wrestling entertainment in the 1990s as the Attitude Era. This era boasted more adult-oriented storylines and character development, which included cross-gender interpersonal drama that carried overt and outward physical violence against the women in WWE (Barrett & Levin, 2015). The WWE's next progression, from the Attitude Era into the PG or family-oriented era, saw an end to physical violence against women but an increase in physical and sexual intimidation. Barrett and Levin (2015) suggest that these acts are subtler and that "men's aggression toward women has not been eradicated but, rather, channeled through more socially accepted psychological avenues" (p. 484), which is more difficult for viewers to recognize as violent or abusive.

Covering up the explicitness of sexism in WWE gave way to the newest era, sometimes referred to as the Divas Revolution. On April 4, 2016, WWE announced that although "the term 'divas' fit [the] female characters back in the day when the product was not as child-friendly," the term no longer reflects the women's division (Wagner, 2016, para. 5). Instead, "from this point forward," all WWE performers "male and female—will be known as 'Superstars'" (Wagner, 2016, para. 7). Alongside this name change, the WWE also established a Women's Championship and announced their commitment to give female talent more screen time in future matches and storylines. Although these representational changes reflect a positive, progressive direction for women in the WWE, the issue of branding as it relates to labor (and, in this case, gendered labor) remains a concern, which is what we turn our attention to next.

Wrestling as Immaterial Labor

What the above literature points to is that the WWE's evolution from sport to sports entertainment and adult to family entertainment has resulted in a shift from overt to covert practices of representation. This shift not only obscures sexism and gender discrimination but also the many facets of wrestling as work. Chow and Laine (2014) point out that wrestling is and always has been about physical labor, particularly "the performance of the labouring body" (p. 44). However, as a form of entertainment, this labor is complex because it is largely immaterial. What this means is that "the wrestler generates value for the promoter through ticket sales and other corporate promotions, through merchandising and selling of the wrestler's image," therefore "the labour that the wrestler is paid for is representational labour, that is, the presentation of a storyline" (Chow & Laine, pp. 44–45). In fact, because wrestlers are contracted employees, their working conditions "place enormous demands on their bodies without adequate remuneration, insurance, or job security" (Chow, 2014, p. 80). Chow (2014) refers to the labor economy of wrestling as "precarious," meaning that it is "flexible and temporary employment" that does not afford "job security, pensions, stable working hours or contract, and maternity pay" (Chow, 2014, pp. 80–81).

Employment precarity is not unique to the labor of wrestling but is a central component of service and passion industries. Chow (2014) suggests, "under neoliberal economic policy, precarity has become an increasingly universal condition," which affects "service-sector workers, temporary migrant workers, and salaried workers in the creative industries and other forms of 'immaterial labor' (those forms of labor that produce information, affects, and attitudes, as opposed to material commodities)" (Chow, 2014, p. 81). The distinction between shift or service workers and wrestlers is that wrestling is "passion work" (Smith, 2008, p. 159). Meaning, like many forms of performance (acting, modeling, professional sports, etc.), "workers are driven by their passion for artistic and creative practice and will therefore endure difficult and unpredictable working conditions" (Chow, 2014, p. 81). Wrestlers are motivated by their passion to not only sell themselves but also their bodies. As Chow (2014) states, "in the economy of wrestling, bodies are reproduced and endlessly circulated as commodities." In these working contexts, the body is disciplined not only for "what it can *do*" but also "what it looks *like*" (p. 81).

Having spent time as an amateur entertainment wrestler, Chow (2014) claims that "the wrestler/worker prefigures and models the way in which precarious and unstable work forces workers in all industries to adopt certain disciplinary procedures in order to survive in a freelance world" (Chow, 2014, p. 81). These disciplinary procedures not only include working on bodies to adhere to strict physical standards but also constructing narratives and values about the business of wrestling that are "difficult to commodify" (Chow, 2014, p. 82). For example, many wrestlers will attempt to reframe exploitation by focusing on the "affects, affinities, and relationships" facilitated by the work (Chow, 2014, p. 82). These alternative conceptions of the industry reflect a unique process of control. To help understand this process, which is central to our analysis of *Total Divas*, we turn next to a discussion of the different levels, or eras, of organizational control.

THEORIES OF ORGANIZATIONAL CONTROL

Organizational control is a central component of organizational theory that has shaped management practices for decades. Following the basic assumptions of Bernard (1968) and social contract theory, Barker (1999) asserts that a defining element of any organization is the need for individuals to "surrender some autonomy in organizational participation," to an extent, for the collective will of the organization (p. 35). To reach goals, the organization requires buy-in on the employee's end, with the understanding that this agreement will be mutually beneficial. In sum, organizational members submit to the constraints of the organization in order to accomplish the larger, mutually beneficial, goals of the organization. However, because organizations exercise their ability to achieve goals through the management of members' abilities and capacities, control is bound to systems of power that are not easily established or managed, which is a central dilemma of organizational society (Tompkins and Cheney, 1985).

Over the past five centuries, organizations have gone through four broad paradigm shifts to create a system of control that effectively balances their needs with those of their employees (Edwards, 1981). First is *simple control*, where capitalists openly exercise their power through direct, authoritarian, and "personal control of work and workers by the company's owner or hired bosses, best seen in the nineteenth-century factories and in small family-owned companies today" (Barker, 1999, p. 36). Through this regime of control, bosses set work rates, hire and fire members, and wield institutional power for their own interests over those of the worker or organization. This detached form of labor relations, alongside abuses of power, leads to labor unrest, making simple control inefficient for growing organizations (Tompkins and Cheney, 1985, p. 182).

Due to rising inequality, labor tensions, and tyrannical forms of exploitation, organizations turned to a more technical form of supervision. According to Edwards (1981), technical control embeds mechanisms of management "in the physical technology of the firm, designed into the very machines and other physical apparatuses of the workplace" (p. 161). Parallel to the technological advancements of the industrial revolution, the control of the blue-collar worker was transferred to the technology of the plant, which set the pace and direction of labor processes. While this technical flow of continual production was seen in the meatpacking and textile industries, it was epitomized at Ford's Highland Park plant where the role of the foreman, who traditionally directed and inspected work, was eliminated in favor of the assembly line process (Edwards, 1981, p. 168). However, like simple control, technical control can suffer from worker strikes that could shut down the entire production process.

Motivated to create less obtrusive means of control, large corporations implemented new forms of white-collar control through bureaucratic systems. Rather than resting power within single individuals or machines of production, bureaucratic control is "embedded in the social organization of the enterprise, in the contrived social relations of production at the point of production" (Edwards, 1981, p. 161). Work activities are governed by and through the rules of law that are passed down by the organization and its members, thereby giving control over to a hierarchical system that sets the legal-rules of reward and punishment. However, where the nineteenth-century mill owner overtly controlled workers and the textile factory offset management to technology, bureaucracy controls workers "by shaping their knowledge about the 'right' ways to act and interact in the organization" (Barker, 1999, p. 37). For example, when a worker seeks supervisor approval for a customer transaction, because that is what they are required to do, the control of the employee is hidden in the natural rules of that system. As bureaucratic organizations create and follow rule-based guidelines for how to act, the activities that enable organizational interaction come to constrain those same activities, thus transforming bureaucratic control into a "subtle but powerful form of domination" (Barker, 1999, p. 37). This powerfully oppressive bureaucracy is what Weber (1958) calls an *iron cage*, where bureaucracy consumes all other forms of control, ultimately making the system an immovable object of control.

In reaction to the changing dynamics of a postindustrial workforce, Tompkins and Cheney (1985) extended Edward's three control strategies by creating *concertive control*. In concertive control, "the necessary social rules that constitute meaning and sanction modes of social conduct become manifest through the collaborative interactions of the organization's members" (Barker, 1999, p. 39). For example, in developing technology sectors like Google or Microsoft, self-managing design teams absorb the responsibilities of the supervisor and are now able to set their own work schedule, coordinate with other groups, and order the material they need to complete their specific job functions. In this system, control emerges from the value-based interactions of the members who reward and punish effective and ineffective members, thereby creating their own self-generated means of discipline and control rather than relying on bureaucratic systems (Kanter, 1989; Ogilvy, 1990; Eccles & Nohria, 1992; Parker, 1992).

While concertive control offers more flexibility, the rise of neoliberalism challenges this team structure by moving the focus of control onto the body of an individual employee, a process we are calling *neoliberal control*. Neoliberalism, as Harvey (2005) states, "proposes that human well-being can best be advanced by liberating individual entrepreneurial freedoms and skills within an institutional framework characterized by strong private property rights, free markets, and free trade," which seeks to bring all human action into the domain of the free-market (p. 2). In this new system, labor becomes more flexible, decentralized, and outsourced, leading to a division of production that emphasizes differentiation through marketing and the "targeting of consumers according to lifestyle" (Phipps, 2014, p. 9). Unlike previous organizational systems of control, which focused on the central tasks of their members, neoliberal systems focus on the flexible opportunities for the individual and their ability to target the needs of the organization's consumers. For example, within new passion industries like the WWE, organizational members—removed from the matrix of production as a producer of this good or that (Giddens, 1991; Bauman, 1992)—are required to manage their "feelings, body language and expression in accordance with their employer's requirements, in order to produce the desired emotional states in customers" and successfully sell their body/performance as a product (Hochschild, 1983, pp. 9–10). By advancing and relocating the entrepreneurial and regulatory freedoms of a neoliberal market onto the social realm of the employee body, members learn to control and discipline themselves in relation to market demands on their body rather than through a concertive system.

In a neoliberal context, "the body is not only a site through which capital circulates as labor power, but it is also a cite through which capital circulates as commodities" (Guthman, 2009, p. 192). The construction of the body as both a source of labor and as a commodity leads to two conditions of power that can be seen at micro and macro levels: governmentality and responsibilization. Governmentality refers to the principles and rationales by which individuals become self-governing. Bodies are marked, perceived, and read through norms and averages that become principles and rationales for appropriate and inappropriate practices of embodiment. Choice, then, represents a right, which is the key to neoliberal subject formation; by exercising our choice, we are exercising our freedoms. However, with choice comes responsibility, which is what the concept of responsibilization addresses. Through a model of personal responsibility, the individual is expected to exercise choice and become responsible for his or her risks. Thus, neoliberalism produces a hypervigilance about self-control and self-discipline.

How does this translate into contemporary organizational culture and leadership? This question guides our analysis of *Total Divas*. Specifically, although *Total Divas* is advertised as a behind the scenes look into the WWE organization that exposes viewers to the intricate managerial and leadership styles of the entertainment industry, what we also witness is a careful crafting of a narrative of personal choice and responsibility in relation to brand and body management.

LEADERSHIP AND CONTROL IN *TOTAL DIVAS*

In *Total Divas*, members of the WWE women's division are consistently represented as negotiating their struggles with embodiments of identity but always with respect to what it means, personally, to be a WWE Diva. In doing so, the WWE Diva body is constructed as a site of character and brand management rather than a site of economic, social, and political meaning.

Although this might seem like a unique context of employee/employer inter-action, this representation points to a larger system of neoliberal leadership and management that attempts to locate organizational agency and branding in the individual, thus separating employers from the modes and processes of production that construct and control everyday identity and embodiment.

Neoliberal Discursive Formations

Our analysis of *Total Divas* is conducted based on the steps of critical discourse analysis (CDA) presented by Fairclough (2003), which calls for textual analysis, discussion of the text's discursive practices, and contex-tualization of broader social practices. As Milani (2008) states, "the aim of Critical Discourse Analysis (CDA) is to unmask how texts embody and (re) produce what one would call 'grand narratives of domination'—that is, broad ideological frameworks" (Milani, 2008, p. 33). In general, CDA focuses on the role of discourse in the "production and reproduction of power abuse or domination" (van Dijk, 2001, p. 96). Therefore, in utilizing CDA to analyze *Total Divas* we aim to make covert processes of power and control overt and explicate their social and cultural implications.

To uncover processes of power and control as they relate to management and leadership in the organizational context of *Total Divas*, we narrow our focus to highlight and interpret the discursive formations that manifest in conversations between management and employees. Discursive formations are the "resources or materials out of which identities are crafted" (Alvesson, Ashcraft, & Thomas, 2008, p. 18). More specifically, discursive formations are "official and informal representations that construct particular versions of self, work and organization" (p. 19). Barker (1999) expands this definition of discursive formations, as they relate to organizations, by claiming they are "sets of power relationships, knowledge about those relationships, and rules for the right way of behaving in terms of the power and knowledge" (p. 46). Therefore, discursive formations are "sets of possibilities," which "we use to create a workable shared meaning in the organization" (p. 46). In our analy-sis, we pay close attention to the kinds of conversations that highlight con-structions of identity as they relate to self (Divas) and organization (WWE), how these constructions facilitate or constrain power, and what these findings suggest for organizational relationships and meaning.

With respect to the neoliberal conditions of passion work such as wres-tling, we also consider Springer's (2010) definition of discursive formations, which he pulls from Foucault (2002) to claim that they "can be defined as a group of statements that belong to a single system of formulation" (p. 931). For example, Springer (2010) suggests the formulation of a "neoliberal dis-course," which "systematically constructs subjects and the world of which they speak" (p. 931). We utilize the tenets of neoliberal control set forth in the previous section to articulate the discursive formations that manifest in *Total Divas*, which construct and reflect these neoliberal subjects and their organizational life worlds. Although we surveyed all six seasons (83 episodes) to conduct our analysis, in the following sections we highlight several in-depth analytic examples that represent our larger findings. As mentioned previously, we look here specifically at interactions between Mark Carrano, the WWE Divas division manager, and his employees, the WWE Divas.

Neoliberal Control Inside and Outside the Squared Circle

The process of neoliberal control manifests, symbolically and materially, in the ways the Divas attempt to reframe the exploitation of their bodies and the precarity of their labor, which is seen throughout the *Total Divas* series in conversations between management and the employees. In nearly all of these interactions, the Divas encounter regulatory norms that are justified as brand management, which they internalized and performed for the sake of personal identity and responsibility. In other words, by focusing on personal goals and relationships, the source of institutional control and its implications are rendered invisible. The following analytic examples reflect these discursive formations of neoliberal control in the context of character development, narrative progression, and brand loyalty.

Character Development

The first way that neoliberal control takes form discursively in *Total Divas* is through personal adherence to developing distinct character identities, both in and outside the ring and on and off screen. For example, in season 3, episode 18, titled "Model Behavior," WWE Diva Paige approaches the manager of the Diva's division, Mark Carrano, about wanting to get a large tattoo on her chest. Mark's immediate reaction is to ask one of the male wrestlers in the room, Jerry Lawer, what he thinks. To which Jerry responds, "I'm not a big fan of tattoos on girls." From the start, this interaction constructs and reflects the mechanisms of self-regulation that are foundational to neoliberal control: the articulation of norms about the body, in this case dominant expectations about femininity in relation to appropriate or inappropriate body modifications. After hearing Jerry's reaction (even though Jerry has no formal managerial or leadership role in WWE), Mark tells Paige: "You have set yourself up as a brand so most likely we're going to say no to it but we'll try to get it approved." Here, Mark articulates Paige's responsibility for character evolution and brand management through a rhetoric of personal choice. He suggests that her past and present embodiments of character are what have created the brand, not the WWE's principles and rationales, thus removing the organization from the context of responsibility. In other words, it is her body so it is her brand—at least in terms of how it is practiced and regulated, since she has no legal or financial ownership over the brand.

Paige's personal responsibility for brand control is reaffirmed when Mark comes back to her with the company's decision regarding her tattoo request. He says, "you've built this brand up as you are now and now you want to change it completely, overnight. It's not going to happen." Paige responds, in a camera confessional, by saying "I'm sick of people telling me what I can and can't do with my own body. If I want to dress a certain way, if I want to change my hair color, I should be able to. This is mine. It doesn't belong to anyone. It just pisses me off. I'm not a child. Let me do what I want." Although it is clear that Paige is expressing ongoing frustrations with being under the watchful eye of the company, and likely even the scrutiny of patriarchy, in both of these expressions the principles and rationales for character development and evolution that are established and enforced by WWE remain unchallenged. In fact, at the end of the episode Paige goes to the tattoo parlor with the intention of defying the institution but decides not to go through with it because she does not want to compromise her professional dreams. She declares that it is her choice to be in the WWE and she has worked her whole life to fulfill the promises of this choice, therefore the consequences of getting a tattoo outweigh the restrictions of bodily autonomy. Paige's discourses construct and reflect a neoliberal subjectivity. She must be responsible and control her self-image appropriately, because it is her choice and her freedom to fulfill her personal goals. The WWE is positioned as a voice of reason, a sounding board, reminding the performers of their roles as good citizens of the company without being directly responsible for that commitment and its consequences.

Narrative Progression

In addition to character development, another way neoliberal control manifests discursively is through the illusion of voluntary and active participation in narrative progression. For example, in season 4, episode 1, titled "Diva Divide," WWE Diva Natalya wants to switch up her character's look because she wants to tell a more interesting story. Specifically, Natalya is interested in creating a dominatrix costume to make her character more assertive and powerful. When she approaches Mark Carrano about this idea, he immediately recoils and reminds her that WWE is a family show. In the end, Natalya compromises by toning down her costume, essentially adding some ruffles and eliminating suggestive props. In an interview with E! online about the episode Natalya says:

We don't have control over a lot of things, but when we get time to wrestle and the chance to tell stories. Even if we only have two minutes on Raw, it needs to help tell a story. Whether it's through social media, Total Divas, Raw, Smack-Down, NXT or whatever, there is still the story. … We have this beautiful division of girls being allowed to tell a story and taking the ball and running with it. Not just anyone can tell that story. (Clark, 2015, para. 1)

In other words, although the Divas have little control over their bodily accouterments, their responsibility is to tell a story that viewers will recognize and identify with. Therefore, self-regulation is a choice to be part of something bigger, and even something empowering. However, that larger entity is not the company, it is the story, which obscures the control of the organization and instead locates power in the individual who chooses to participate, or not participate, in moving the story forward.

Later on in the series, Natalya is faced with an unwelcomed narrative change for her character, which puts her face-to-face with the precarity of her employment. In season 6, episode 7, titled "A Win-Wine Situation," WWE decides to shift Natalya's character from good to evil. Upon finding out about this decision, Natalya confesses to fellow Diva, Summer Rae, "I really hope I can take this role and run with it. I'm nervous because I've been a good guy for so long." To which Summer Rae replies, "If you mess up then you won't have a job." Immediately, the responsibility for this change in creative direction is placed on Natalya, not WWE. Throughout the episode, it is made clear that Natalya embraces the weight of this responsibility. As she reflects on her various performances as a newly minted villain, she constantly worries about how the audience is reacting, stating "now they're not cheering me and now they're not booing me, they're just kind of confused. That's not good." She even acknowledges the consequences of not connecting with the audience, saying, "I'm frustrated and I feel like if this fails I can't go back to being a good guy. I'll probably get fired."

Later on in the episode, Natalya is so worried about making her new storyline successful that she decides to approach Mark Carrano about an idea she has to enhance her evil-turn narrative. Natalya suggests to him that she could team up with one of WWE's most hated characters, Eva Marie, in order to boost her villainous image. She claims, "If I could scoop some of her heat it's money." To which Carrano responds, "For you. What does it do for anything else?" Natalya, somewhat stunned by his blunt reaction, begins to articulate her response but is cut off by Mark who inevitably tells her "She's a newcomer. You're a veteran. Act like one. You don't gotta ride her coat tails. Be your own star." Mark walks away and Natalya is left with a baffled and defeated look on her face. However, she recommits herself to the new narrative and by the end of the episode she receives resounding boos from the

WWE audience. Natalya then confesses to the E! cameras that her fear of getting fired was essentially an overreaction. She states, "I think if I've learned anything from this situation it's that it just takes time. It takes time for the audience to transition. And patience is a virtue." Consistent with her previous sentiments, Natalya sees WWE not as a controlling entity and instead sees herself a vehicle for narrative progression. This reframing separates the worker (Natalya) from the conditions of commodification and labor by suggesting that the scenario is one predicated on personal choice and responsibility in relation to a narrative and its audience, not a company.

Brand Loyalty

Even in situations entirely outside the ring and entirely separate from WWE, such as external endorsements, the Divas are subject to forms of organizational control. Neoliberal control, specifically, manifests discursively in these contexts through embodied and internalized brand loyalty. For example, in the season 3 finale, episode 20, titled "The New Divas Champion," WWE Diva Eva Marie pursues an opportunity to develop her own line of hair extensions in partnership with a reputable hair extension company. During a photo shoot to promote her new line, she receives a call from Mark Carrano telling her: "So, legal gave me a heads up about some Instagram photos posted at a photo shoot. What photo shoot was it?" Eva Marie responds tentatively by telling him she is just adding some extra content to her website, to which he replies, "Who ran the website and who did all the approval for the photos? Is that you?" After Eva Marie tells him that her husband, Johnathan (who she affectionately refers to as her "husbanager") is responsible for making decisions regarding the content on her website, Carrano states:

> So, OK let's just think about this. And I'm going to be brief and frank with you so you do not get in trouble, okay? In the future you need to run everything through WWE legal and me. Because if you have your husbanager, or whatever you call him, doing approvals, we've got some major problems.

Eva Marie returns to the photo shoot and tells her husband, Johnathan, that she thinks it is best if they temporarily shut down the photo shoot in order to get WWE's approval first. Johnathan gets angry about the request and tells her "You're launching your own hair line with one of the biggest hair extension companies in the world. We're not going to shut that down because Mark Carrano called you up." She tentatively responds by telling him "That puts me in a really big bind because WWE is my breadwinner" Johnathan cuts her off before she can finish her sentence to remind her "WWE is one quarter of our income. WWE is one thing but this is planning a future." In a confession to the E! cameras Eva Marie says, "The last thing I want to do is upset WWE because that has helped create this brand. But with Johnathan I think he just sees it business, business, business and he doesn't understand that WWE really is my main focus."

This scenario reflects the level of legal control that WWE has over its employees, both on and off screen and in situations external to the company. As discussed previously, one of the ways WWE has managed to become such a successful company is by carefully regulating these character images, which go beyond the squared circle. However, the discourse that is constructed here reflects a much more insidious process of control. Even after Johnathan reminds Eva Marie that the legal repercussions she might face with WWE would not yield significant financial consequences, she still cites the importance of keeping ties with the company for the sake of her own brand. In other words, she reframes the company brand as a personal brand. In this case, brand loyalty is not developed by the company for the consumer but is located in the laboring body (Eva Marie). Therefore, it is her personal choice and responsibility to either maintain or violate the integrity of that (her) brand, for which the consequences are entirely her own.

NEOLIBERAL CONTROL AS SYMBOLIC VIOLENCE

Contrary to what these discourses might attempt to communicate, the consequences of neoliberal control are not self-contained. Springer (2010) suggests that analyses such as the one provided here are important because "we must look to discursive formations and subjectivations to understand the uptake of neoliberal ideas as a new political economic 'rationality'" (p. 933). Specifically, analyzing neoliberal discursive formations "affords an understanding of neoliberalism that recognizes a simultaneously top-down and bottom-up (re)reproduction through continually (re)articulated citational chains refracted both from the discourse of the subject, and from subject to discourse" (p. 931). As we can see in all of the analytic examples provided here, in a neoliberal-context control and power are not only enacted by management but they are also reaffirmed through the acceptance and justification of this power and control by the employees, thus rendering top-down processes natural and invisible.

Another implication of identifying these discursive formations is that they shine light on "how capitalism's structural inequalities are increasingly misrecognized as the emergent rationality of neoliberalism" (Springer, 2010, p. 933). Springer suggests that this misrecognition "represents not only the foundation of neoliberal 'commonsense,' but also, and not incidentally, the very essence of symbolic violence" (Springer, 2010, p. 933). In other words, processes of control that are continuously internalized, embodied, and justified become common sense. They are converted into rules of conduct that go unnoticed, which means that their power, consequences, and even their violence also go unnoticed. In the context of *Total Divas*, one of the most glaringly alarming consequences of this process of neoliberal control is that discursive emphasis on personal goals, choices, and responsibilities leads to a black boxing of sexism. Management can control the bodies of female employees—anything from how they perform femininity to silencing or minimizing their concerns over job security to squelching their upward financial mobility—while touting it as their personal sacrifice for the sake of participating in their passion and not because of systems and practices of gender discrimination.

Although we recognize that *Total Divas* seems like a unique organizational context, passion work is an increasingly popular venture. Between rhetorics encouraging people to pursue their passions and information-based economic marketplaces that force people to sell themselves alongside their labor (and to do it for low wages without contractual guarantees), the prevalence of neoliberal control and the reaches of its consequences are on the rise. Without being aware of how these discursive formations manifest and perpetuate through management and leadership practices, in real world and representational reality, we face the possibility of an organizational future where the separation between brands and bodies is indistinguishable.

REFERENCES

Alvesson, M., Ashcraft, K. L., & Thomas, R. (2008). Identity matters: Reflections on the construction of identity scholarship in organization studies. *Organization, 15*(1), 5–28.

Baja, V., & Banerjee, S. (2016). The spectacle of excess: A marketing-cum-financial analysis of WWE Inc. *The IUP Journal of Brand Management, 13*(3), 75–83.

Barker, J. R. (1999). *The Discipline of Teamwork: Participation and Concertive Control*. Thousand Oaks, CA: Sage.

Barnard, C. (1968). *The Functions of the Executive*. Cambridge, MA: Harvard University Press. (Original work published 1938).

Barrett, B. J., & Levin, D. S. (2015). "You can't touch me, you can't touch me": Intergender violence and aggression in the PG era of World Wrestling Entertainment (WWE) programming. *Feminism & Psychology, 25*(4), 469–488.

Bauman, Z. (1992). *Intimations of Postmodernity*. London: Routledge.

Chow, B. D. V. (2014). Work and shoot: Professional wrestling and embodied politics. *TDR: The Drama Review, 58*(2), 72–86.

Chow, B., & Laine, E. (2014). Audience affirmation and the labour of professional wrestling. *Performance Research, 19*(2), 44–53.

Clark, R. (July 6, 2015). WWE Diva Natalya discusses why the NXT women's division is succeeding, more. *EWrestlingNews*. Retrieved from http://www.ewrestlingnews. com/news/wwe-diva-natalya-discusses-why-the-nxt-women-s-division-is-succeeding-more

Deeter-Schmelz, D. R., & Sojka, J. Z. (2004). Wrestling with American values: An exploratory investigation of World Wrestling Entertainment™ as a product-based subculture. *Journal of Consumer Behaviour, 4*(2), 132–143.

Dunn, C. (2015). 'Sexy, smart and powerful': Examining gender and reality in the WWE Diva's division. *Networking Knowledge, 8*(3), 1–18.

Eccles, R. G., & Nohira, N. (1992). *Beyond the Hype: Rediscovering the Essence of Management*. Cambridge, MA: Harvard Business School Press.

Edwards, R. (1981). The social relations of production at the point of production. In M. Zey-Ferrell & M. Aiken (Eds.), *Complex Organizations: Critical Perspectives* (pp. 109–125). Glenview, IL: Scott, Foresman & Company.

Fairclough, N. (2003). *Analysing Discourse: Textual Analysis for Social Research*. New York: Routledge.

Foucault, M. (2002). *The Archeology of Knowledge* (2nd ed.). London: Routledge.

Giddens, A. (1991). Structuration theory: Past, present and future. In C. G. A. Bryant & D. Jary (Eds.), *Giddens' Theory of Structuration: A Critical Appreciation* (pp. 201–221). London: Routledge.

Guthman, J. (2009). Neoliberalism and the constitution of contemporary bodies. In E. D. Rothblum, S. Solovay & M. Wann (Eds.), *The Fat Studies Reader* (pp. 187–196). New York, NYU Press.

Harvey, D. (2005). *A Brief History of Neoliberalism*. New York: Oxford University Press.

Hochschild, A. (1983). *The Managed Heart: Commercialization of Human Feelings*. Berkeley, CA: University of California Press.

Kanter, R. M. (1989). *When Giants Learn to Dance*. New York: Simon & Schuster.

McLean, B. (October 16, 2000). Inside the world's weirdest family business. *Fortune Magazine*. Retrieved from http://archive.fortune.com/magazines/fortune/fortune_archive/2000/10/16/289655/index.htm

Metcalf, M. (January 25, 2017). ShowBuzzDaily's top 150 Wednesday cable originals & network finals. *ShowBuzzDaily: Entertainment Predictions, News & Reviews*. Retrieved from http://www.showbuzzdaily.com/articles/showbuzzdailys-top-150-wednesday-cable-originals-network-finals-1-25-2017.html.

Milani, T. M. (2008). Language testing and citizenship: A language ideological debate in Sweden. *Language in Society, 37*(1), 27–59.

Ogilvy, J. (1990). This postmodern business. *Marketing and Research Today, 18*(1), 4–20.

Parker, M. (1992). Post-modern organizations or postmodern organization theory? *Organization Studies, 13*(1), 1–17.

Phipps, A. (2014). *The Politics of the Body: Gender in a Neoliberal and Neoconservative age*. Cambridge, MA: Polity Press.

Smith, A. T. (2008). Passion work: The joint production of emotional labor in professional wrestling. *Social Psychology Quarterly, 71*(2), 157–176.

Springer, S. (2010). Neoliberal discursive formations: On the contours of subjectiva-tion, good governance, and symbolic violence in posttransitional Cambodia. *Environment and Planning D: Society and Space, 28*(5), 931–950.

Tompkins, P. K., & Cheney, G. (1985). Communication and unobtrusive control in contemporary organizations. In R. D. McPhee & P. K. Tompkins (Eds.), *Organizational Communication: Traditional Themes and New Directions* (pp. 179–210). Beverly Hills, CA: Sage.

Van Dijk, T. A. (2001). Multidisciplinary CDA: A plea for diversity. In R. Wodak & M. Meyer (Eds.), *Methods of Critical Discourse Analysis* (pp. 95–120). London: Sage Publications.

Wagner, L. (2016). From 'Divas' to 'Superstars': WWE embraces women's sports revolution. *NPR.* Retrieved from http://www.npr.org/sections/thetwo-way/2016/04/04/472989931/from-divas-to-superstars-wwe-embraces-womens-sports-revolution

Walker, J. (2012). A candidate commodified: Linda McMahon as a WWE product in the 2010 senate campaign. *Journal of Contemporary Rhetoric, 2*(1), 11–18.

Weber, M. (1958). *The Protestant Ethic and the Spirit of Capitalism.* New York: Charles Scribner's Sons.

Chapter 7

You Need to Be Younger to Succeed

Representations of Generational Distinctions and Gender in TV Land's Younger

Maxine Gesualdi

Younger, a sitcom on TV Land network, focuses on Liza, a 40-year-old, recently divorced mom who needs to find a job after leaving the workforce 15 years ago to raise her daughter. Because of her employment gap and age, Liza faces age bias and cannot find someone who will hire her. Having a "young" look, Liza is mistaken for a 26-year-old during a night out. Liza uses this misunderstanding to pose as a 26-year-old at her next job interview and gets hired at a publishing house. The show follows Liza as she navigates her new job and younger persona.

The viewer sees representations of gender and intergenerational struggles that often occur in the workplace as Liza encounters organizational life that is much different from when she left almost two decades ago. Liza's interactions with Kelsey, a millennial up-and-comer first-level manager, and Diana, a stubborn, 43-year-old, "old school" executive leader, demonstrate how leadership is conceptualized, constructed, and reinforced related to age and gender.

Through the main characters and other leaders within the fictional workplace setting in the show, viewers see that age bias and generational stereotypes can affect leadership enactment. The show also provides insight into how leadership is communicated and enacted beyond formal titles and hierarchical ordering. Through a close reading textual analysis of the interactions of Liza, Kelsey, and Diana in *Younger*, the chapter illustrates how leadership is created through interactions. In addition, the chapter uncovers norms about age of women in leadership as promoted through the characters' interactions.

TELEVISION'S ROLE IN SOCIETY

As we consume television, we are being socialized to a worldview managed by media producers and influenced by consumer tastes and expectations. Because television has become a "centralized system of storytelling" (Morgan, Shanahan, & Signorielli, 2009) that attracts viewers across demographic categories and geographic boundaries, messages sent through television have the power to create shared meaning in society. Television, then, can promote ideals and norms through the characters' actions and storyline arcs. Examining portrayals of people on television uncovers the ways we are socialized to view the world.

Because television reflects society, many social norms are supported through fictional portrayals of daily life. This promotion via television of *the way things ought to be* can be undermined by alternative interpretations and readings of the portrayals (Hall, 1980). However, most people are not media critics, and internalize the dominant messages in media portrayals (Morgan, Shanahan, & Signorielli, 2009). Media portrayals, therefore, can uphold dominant views of people in society related to social position, race, and gender.

Beyond social norms, television can illustrate how social institutions are expected to operate. Media representations shape our idea of work and organizations throughout our lives. For example, the children's television show *Sesame Street* features the interworking of Hooper's store, a central setting for the show. From Hooper's Store to Cheers to Dunder Mifflin, organizations often serve as a setting for human interaction on television because viewers can relate to lives spent as members of organizations. As Hassard and Holliday (1998) assert, "popular culture offers more dramatic, more intense and more dynamic representations of organizations than management texts" (p. 1). Therefore, analyzing television shows can uncover the various ways leadership is depicted and how these depictions can shape viewers' understanding of leadership. This chapter analyzes the emergence and operation of leadership within the organizational setting of *Younger* and uncovers the messages audiences receive about leadership, age and gender via the characters' words and actions.

THE STUDY OF LEADERSHIP

The study of leadership has many offshoots and varieties, making a single, concrete conceptualization of leadership impossible. However, the variety of leadership concepts in academic research and popular press is indicative of the complexity of leadership situations and the multifaceted nature of leaders. Modern theory on leadership focused on rational characterizations of what make a good leader. This rational approach first identified intrinsic traits (Judge, Heller, & Mount, 2002; Stogdill, 1948) of good leaders. The rational approach then expanded to identify behavioral styles that were more important than traits in determining success (Blake and Mouton, 1978).

Although these rational approaches have guided the study of leadership for many decades, other scholars have taken the study of leadership in less rational directions. For example, discursive leadership (Fairhurst, 2007) is the study of leadership that examines the "social, linguistic and cultural aspects of leadership" by "focusing on organizational discourse, both as language use in social interaction and the view of Discourse made popular by Michel Foucault" (p .viii). In other words, discursive leadership has two levels of analysis. First, it examines the dialogue between organizational members to uncover how members enact leadership qualities and react to the leadership of others. In addition, discursive leadership can also focus on the Foucauldian idea of discourse (Arribas-Ayllon & Walkerdine, 2011; Foucault, 1980), which is concerned with how the history of the concept of leadership is brought to bear on any current leader-follower situation in order to uphold dominant power structures in society. Focusing on leadership in this way creates a new understanding of leadership as a construction based on communication and interaction between organizational members, rather than a trait or behavior of an individual or a position in a hierarchy. This chapter follows in Fairhurst's (2007) recommendations of analyzing small-d discourse and focuses on communication between the characters to illustrate how each main character enacts leadership qualities and exerts her agency in the organization. The guiding idea of the analysis of *Younger* is that leadership status can be created and enacted through communication.

WOMEN, AGE, GENERATIONS, AND LEADERSHIP

Scholars of organizations examine variables such as gender and age and how these variables affect leadership. The study of age and leadership often focuses on chronological age (Oshagbemi, 2003; Walter & Scheibe, 2013) or generational age groups (Arsenault, 2004; Deal, Altman, & Rogelberg, 2010). Age has been characterized as a factor that affects leadership style, with older managers being more collaborative than younger managers (Oshagbemi, 2003). Age has also been characterized as emotional maturity, which is not equal to chronological age (Walter & Scheibe, 2013). Beyond these views of age as a demographic trait, age is often considered in relation to membership in specific generations such as Baby Boomers, Generation X, and Millennials (Arsenault, 2004; Deal, Altman, & Rogelberg, 2010). Generational membership has been linked to preferred leadership styles (Arsenault, 2004), such as Baby Boomers enacting a collegial and participatory style. In addition, generational differences show varied attitudes toward the idea of leadership (Salahuddin, 2010). For example, Generation X members prefer leaders who provide room for autonomy and individual development (Yu & Miller, 2005).

Few scholars look at the intersection of age and gender in organizational leadership. Although research concludes that mid-career women face obstacles (Cheung & Halpern, 2000), age itself has not been studied in relation to gender and leadership. The few studies that attempt to measure this intersection often study both traits individually as predictors of other factors such as transactional or transformational leadership style (Barbuto, Fritz, Matkin, & Marx, 2007). In one study that examined age and gender, there was no significant effect of age and gender on leadership style effectiveness (Barbuto, Fritz, Matkin, & Marx, 2007). Because most of the leadership studies prior to 1980 were conducted by males about males (Klenke, 1996), it is not surprising how little we understand about women and age and leadership. Because we do know that women face barriers to career success due to maternal status and gender norms of caregiving (Cheung & Halpern, 2000), it is safe to assume that cultural stereotypes of women at various ages also affect how women are seen in leadership roles, even if the academic research has not followed this path of inquiry.

MEDIA PORTRAYALS

Because *Younger*'s main character is a woman who is hiding her age, the analysis will also focus on how age and gender are depicted using a critical analysis of the interactions. Research about women in leadership tends to compare women's experiences to men's experiences (Klenke, 1996). This research essentializes feminine and masculine leadership qualities to characterize how women lead, which often follow stereotypes about women being better at relationships and men being better at competition. In popular press, women are often "treated as a scarcity, or are labeled as ineffective because cultural stereotypes hold that they lack important leadership attributes, or that they are heralded as possessing keys to effective leadership" (Klenke, 1996, p. 133). In other words, business and popular press characterize women leaders in various ways that treat them as anomalies in contrast to men who are expected to be natural leaders.

Media portrayals of women have been studied extensively since the first movies and television shows were produced. Research shows that women, especially older women, are underrepresented or portrayed within stereotypical roles (Collins, 2011; Daalmans, Kleemans, & Sadza, 2017; Gill, 2007; Ross, 2004; Tuchman, 1979). When women are shown to be working outside the home, they are depicted often as having unknown occupational status or in subordinate roles (Glascock, 2001; Lauzen & Dozier, 2005).

In addition to gender, media depictions of age are biased. Younger people are favored in television, with older people practically invisible (Eschholz, Bufkin, & Long, 2002; Lauzen & Dozier, 2005). In addition, women characters are often featured as younger than their male counterparts (Eschholz, Bufkin, & Long, 2002; Lauzen & Dozier, 2005). When organizational leadership is depicted on the screen, older men, not women, are most often depicted as leaders (Lauzen & Dozier, 2005). The show *Younger* features women of various ages in different types of leadership roles, with one character faking her age to appear younger. Therefore, the show provides a unique depiction of female leaders. Analyzing the show can help uncover how multigenerational women in leadership positions are portrayed and how the characters enact leadership through communication.

In summary, this chapter analyzes a television show that features issues of gender and age in the workplace in order to demonstrate how the characters enact leadership. Though the focus on discourse and communication encounters between the characters, it also will uncover the ways in which the characters uphold or challenge norms related to women and age in leadership positions. The results of this analysis add to our understanding of media portrayals of leadership as well as provides insight into how leaders establish their position through discourse.

DESCRIPTION OF *YOUNGER*

Younger debuted on TV Land in 2015 (Collins, 2015) and is scheduled for a fourth season in 2017. The main character of the show is Liza Miller, a 40-year-old, recently divorced mom who needs to find a job after staying home to raise her daughter for almost two decades. The series begins when Liza is navigating a divorce from her cheating, gambling-addicted husband. Liza's daughter is studying abroad in India for her senior year in high school. Liza lives in a New Jersey suburb of New York City but is selling her house because of the divorce. She moves in with her friend Maggie who lives in Brooklyn. Maggie is an artist and a lesbian who lives a bohemian life. Liza's goal when she moves to Brooklyn is to find a job. She had a successful career in publishing before she had her daughter. After she had her daughter, she stayed home while her husband supported the family. Therefore, Liza has a 15-year gap on her resume, which is scaring away employers. Liza interviews with much younger women and is finding that her age and time away from work outside the home is an obstacle to find a job.

After a particularly discouraging day on the job market, Maggie takes Liza to a local bar to drown her sorrows. At the bar, Maggie leaves Liza for a moment. In that moment, Josh, a 26-year-old tattoo artist hits on Liza. Liza begins to tell Josh that she is too old for him, and he answers by saying that she could not be much older than 26. This misunderstanding gives Maggie an idea, and she makes-over Liza to have her appear younger before her next job interview. Liza agrees that going into interviews as her current age is not getting her anywhere, so she decides in desperation to lie about her age in her next interview.

Liza's next interview was with Diana Trout at Empirical Press publishing. During the interview, Liza claims to be 26. Diana, who is 43, grills Liza regarding stereotypes of Millennials, including asking Liza what makes her special. Clearly exasperated by the young applicants for the position, Diana asks this question as a trap to find out how spoiled Liza is, consistent with Diana's own stereotypes of Millennials. When Liza answers, "I'm a grown up. I don't think I'm special," Diana realizes that Liza is different than previous applicants and hires Liza as her assistant.

After receiving the offer from Diana, Liza heads into the ladies' room to call Maggie. While in there, Liza meets Kelsey Peters, a 20-something-year-old editor in the company. Kelsey shares with Liza that she will have a tough time with Diana because Diana wants to destroy the younger women out of jealousy. Kelsey tells Liza that she moved up the ladder quickly and gives Liza encouragement that she can do the same.

The rest of the series focuses on how Liza creates relationships with Diana and other coworkers and the young man who mistook her for 26. The storylines focus on how Liza faces a new type of organization that is 24/7 online. The series also follows Liza's budding romance with Josh. Throughout the series, Liza must navigate her fake age and fight the urge to tell those at work and at home about her deception.

OVERVIEW OF ANALYSIS

To analyze *Younger*, I chose to examine all three seasons of the show. Within the 36 episodes, I isolated interactions and dialogue between Liza, Diana, and Kelsey that illustrate their leadership within the organization. I also critically analyzed how the interactions promote or challenge dominant norms of age and gender in leadership.

To analyze the interactions for leadership construction through discourse, I conducted a critical discourse analysis of the characters' interactions. In critical discourse analysis, the researcher is concerned with the "social meanings within langue and discursive strategies" (Hesse-Biber & Leavy, 2011,

p. 238). This type of discourse analysis goes beyond the spoken word by linking the dialogue to deeper meanings in our past and in our current social structures. Through this type of analysis, the ways in which the characters display expected or unexpected behaviors will be revealed.

For each major character, the analysis below outlines how discourse with the other characters establishes leadership within the organization. For each character, I provide an overview of her leadership communication as well as examples from show scripts. The information in parentheses is my addition to the dialogue for the example scenes.

Liza and Leadership

Liza has the least power in the organization because she is an assistant. However, because she had a successful career in publishing prior to having her daughter, she has experience beyond what is expected. Therefore, she has to make sure she is not too overbearing to ensure that it does not seem like she is overstepping her bounds. She also has to manage Diana's rage as well as Kelsey's sometimes unprofessional behavior. For example, in season 1, episode 4, Kelsey has too much to drink and is late for a meeting with her new author. Diana confronts Liza who has been working with Kelsey on the project:

Diana: (halting, angry) Liza. Why is Anton Bjornberg sitting by himself in our conference room?
Liza: (calm but hesitant) Uh, he's here for his first meeting with Kelsey.
Diana: (annoyed) Well, that explains why he's sitting in our conference room, but not the "by himself" part.
Liza: (calm and collected) Kelsey has been slightly delayed.
Diana: (more annoyed) How delayed?
Liza: (calm) That is undetermined at this time.
Diana: (more annoyed) What are you, the White House press secretary? If you don't tell me, I can't fix it.
Liza: (empathetic and lying) She was worked up about today and nervous about the deal, so I gave her some Ambien. There is a slight possibility she may still be asleep.
Diana: (alarmed) Oh, dear God (enters conference room … cheerfully) Anton. Diana Trout, head of marketing.
Anton: Hello.
Diana: Hi. This is my associate, Liza something. Kelsey's been slightly detained. Uh, let's chat a bit about marketing.

In this exchange, Liza keeps a cool head while Diana is annoyed. In addition, Liza covers for Kelsey because she knows the project is very important to Kelsey's career. Therefore, Liza demonstrates an understanding and cool leadership style as she tries to diffuse the situation and maintain professionalism for a colleague who was acting unprofessionally.

Because Kelsey sees Liza as a peer and socializes with Liza outside of work, Liza is able to advise Kelsey about work matters. This advice goes beyond boundaries of friendship into organizational leadership and mentoring. Following Kelsey's late arrival to the meeting with the new author in season 1, episode 4, Kelsey is mad because Liza did not stop Kelsey from celebrating the night before. In the interaction, Liza deflects Kelsey's blame and becomes a mentor to Kelsey by giving her some career advice:

Liza: (firmly) You know, you can rant and deflect blame all you want, or you can own this, take responsibility for it, and go fix it.
Kelsey: (defeated but inspired) You're right.

Diana and Leadership

Diana's leadership style is exemplified in her discourse with others in the organization. Through the use of a halting speaking style with extreme enunciation, Diana establishes her legitimate power in the organization. She uses a formal tone with everyone she meets and demands respect through her tone. Diana often begins and ends the dialogue with others and tends to punctuate her interactions with orders.

For example, Liza begins her first day on the job by bringing Diana coffee. Without even making eye contact, Diana barks orders at Liza.

Diana: (earnestly) I need you to set up a Twitter account for Jane Austen and start writing her tweets.
Liza: (puzzled) Jane Austen? Dead Jane Austen?
Diana: Yes, we're releasing Pride and Prejudice as an ebook. (dismissive) We need to make some noise in the twitterverse.
Liza: You want me to tweet?
Diana: (exasperated) As Jane. Are you deaf? Is that how you got into Dartmouth?
Liza: (sheepishly) No, of course not. (turns to leave)
Diana: (as Liza's leaving) Put it on Facebook and Match.com. And Christian-Mingle. (drinks coffee ... frowns ... yells out the door at Liza) Not hot enough!

Even though Diana uses her interactions to establish her power over the other characters, she also uses softer tones and allows more time for others to talk when the person she's interacting with is saying something agreeable to her. This softening establishes Diana as more of a collaborator than a dictator. For example, Liza works a side job as a cocktail waitress during a company event in season 1, episode 7. Diana finds out that Liza worked the event and asks her why. Liza says it is because she has to make a student loan payment of $1,800 (which is actually for Liza's daughter). Diana, seeing that Liza is working hard, leaves a check for Liza at her desk:

Liza: (enters Diana's office ... grateful) Diana, this is so generous of you, but I couldn't possibly take this.
Diana: (without looking up from computer screen ... cold) Consider it an early Christmas bonus.
Liza: (grateful) You have no idea how much this means to me. I don't know how to thank you.
Diana: (cold ... still looking at screen but grins for a split second) Well, you can start by bringing me that catalog copy I asked for.
Liza: (hurrying away) Of course.

Throughout the series, Diana comes to rely on Liza more for ideas and support. Diana's transformation into a softer leader does not go far, however. She continues to use her halting style to establish her power when needed. She commands her employees and keeps her distance through her formal conversational style and tone.

Kelsey and Leadership

Through her cheerful nature and positive outlook, Kelsey establishes herself as leader who is focused on growth of the organization and of the staff. She eschews Diana's style for a more visionary leadership that includes encouraging others to think about possibilities. For example, Kelsey signs a big author who is being sought after by many different publishing houses in season 1, episode 6. She gets the author to sign with Empirical. She announces the acquisition in a staff meeting:

Kelsey: (in cheerful voice) I am very happy to announce that Empirical is now officially the publishing house for the English translation of Anton Bjornberg's Kaleidoscope of Life. (with loud enthusiasm) We signed the Swede! (applause from group) Now, we're on a tight launch for the fall, which will be not a small challenge, because the preliminary translation might as well be in Swedish. But I start working with Anton first thing in the morning, and I'm confident that we can meet that deadline. So I will need marketing and cover artwork by the end of this week. Great. That's all from me.
Liza: (meeting adjourned, standing beside conference room table) Damn, girl. If I didn't know you, I'd be impressed.
Kelsey: I definitely want you on my marketing team. I'm gonna take you under my wing.

Diana: (approaching) Kelsey, congratulations. I don't know how you did it, (disdainful pause) but you did. (quickly) I'm here if you need me. (barking as she leaves the room) Liza!

Because she is driven, Kelsey can sometimes be caught up in her individual contributions, which allows Liza to step in and lead for Kelsey. For example, in season 1, episode 11, Liza sees an opportunity to help Kelsey with a major editing project for a new author's first book and offers to lead the project:

Liza: (dropping in Kelsey's office) You need anything?
Kelsey: (frustrated) Yeah, a book doctor for Megan Vernoff. Half of my regulars are busy competing for the Kardashian rewrite.
Liza: Where do you even find a book doctor, anyway?
Kelsey: Most of them are stay-at-home moms with Ivy League degrees. I mean, some of them had really promising careers. They just gave up to have kids, and now they're so far off track, they'd do anything. They don't even care about the credit. (under her breath) Another reason why we can never stop working.
Liza: (sheepishly) You know, I've done some creative writing. And I edited the Dartmouth Literary Journal. Maybe I could give the Vernoff book a try.
Kelsey: (relieved) Seriously? You want to write about the sex life of a woman in her 40s?
Liza: (ironically) I'm sure I can suppress my gag reflex if I'm getting paid enough. (pauses) That came out wrong. But I could use the money.
Kelsey: (relieved) Well, that's a good reason. See what you can do with chapter one.

DISCUSSION

Younger illustrates that organizational members establish their leadership through interaction with others. Liza's nurturing style establishes her as a collaborator who wants to put the organization's success ahead of her own success. With Diana, Liza waits her turn to speak and respects Diana's legitimate authority in the organization. However, Liza uses breaks in dialogue to insert her ideas and add value to the organization when she sees an opportunity. With Kelsey, her colleague who becomes more like a peer, Liza establishes a coaching leadership style. Because Liza has life experience that Kelsey does not have, Liza uses encouraging words and active listening skills to help Kelsey cope with obstacles and challenges in the organization.

Diana's formal and classical management style comes across in her halting tone and formal enunciation. She establishes her desire to collaborate through a softening of body language and by allowing others more speaking time. The use of cold, distant communication style and formal language establish her leadership within the organization. Diana matches her style in discussions with others to her legitimate power in the organization.

Kelsey's driven and positive style allows her to lead successful publishing efforts for the company. By focusing on her own career path, Kelsey establishes herself as an important contributor to company success and a good partner with Liza. However, because Kelsey is rising through the ranks, she also makes mistakes that could derail her success. Through her mentoring interactions with Liza, Kelsey is able to correct her path and maintain her leadership status within the organization.

Social norms and discourse regarding age and gender create an intersectional construct for women in organizations. Age is seen as a liability at every stage of a woman's career, as evidenced in academic research, popular press, and media depictions. Liza, Kelsey, and Diana largely operate within the norms of these. Liza's character is able to subvert the dominant discourse regarding women in leadership because she has the benefit of experience but also the exuberance of youth that catches the eye of the senior management. Therefore she is able to create a space for self-fulfillment and success without worrying about the confines that accompany an older woman in the workforce.

Although parental status is not at the center of this analysis, it is worth noting that none of these women have children as understood by their coworkers. Liza has a grown daughter, but because she is lying about her age and status, no one on the job knows she has this daughter. Therefore, not only can Liza operate unencumbered with age stereotypes of an older woman, she also does not need to deal with "working mother" stereotypes. This allows Liza again to be unfettered within the confines of the organization and can be seen as a type-A contributor in a sea of stereotypical slacker Millennials.

In all, *Younger* portrays leadership possibilities for women by empowering them to chart their own paths. The show reflects constraints in society for older women as evidenced by Diana's constant attempts to assert her legitimacy. By framing the show through Liza's vantage point, the show helps viewers question norms but not enough to depict a way to destroy them. Subterfuge is the only path as exemplified through Liza's lying about her age. And, in the series, the ruse is a path to succeed.

IMPLICATIONS

This chapter adds to leadership studies by focusing on media depictions of women leaders of various ages and how those characters use communication to establish leadership. Because this analysis focuses on the words and tones used by the characters, it goes beyond attributing leadership powers based on the characters positions in the hierarchy to addressing how they navigate their leadership through interaction. In addition, the chapter adds to the literature on media depictions of women and age. The analysis provides another data point in how media depictions uphold stereotypes, such as Diana being dismissive of the younger women. It also shows how viewers can subvert these norms, with Liza being able to establish a strong position in the show by straddling her two identities. The series shows that women can be powerful leaders at any age.

The chapter also provides a roadmap to use *Younger* as a teaching tool. Interactions of the characters from the series could be used in a classroom setting to demonstrate how leadership is more than a title. As demonstrated through Liza, Diana, and Kelsey, leadership is enacted through communication with others in the organization. Because Liza does not have formal power in the organization but is relied on by Diana and Kelsey to lead through innovation, the show demonstrates that leadership in organizations is not based on traits or behaviors but on the give and take between organizational members. Analysis of *Younger* in an organizational communication or management classroom can illustrate the various ways leadership is conceptualized.

Avid viewers of *Younger* may focus on the campy aspects of Liza's new sex life or Diana's obsession with handbags or Kelsey's cheating fiancée. However, a deeper analysis of the show offers examples of leadership styles as enacted by Liza, Diana, and Kelsey and how they communicate to establish their leadership in the organization. By focusing on three women of different ages in leadership roles, *Younger* provides insight into how women in leadership navigate expectations and create their own paths.

REFERENCES

Arribas-Ayllon, M., & Walkerdine, V. (2008). Foucauldian discourse analysis. *The Sage Handbook of Qualitative Research in Psychology*, 91–108. doi: 10.4135/9781848607927

Barbuto Jr, J. E., Fritz, S. M., Matkin, G. S., & Marx, D. B. (2007). Effects of gender, education, and age upon leaders' use of influence tactics and full range leadership behaviors. *Sex Roles, 56*, 71–83. doi:10.1007/s11199-006-9152-

Bazzini, D. G., McIntosh, W. D., Smith, S. M., Cook, S., & Harris, C. (1997). The aging woman in popular film: Underrepresented, unattractive, unfriendly, and unintelligent. *Sex Roles, 36*(7–8), 531–543. doi:10.1007/BF02766689

Berger, P. L., & Luckmann, T. (1966). *The Social Construction of Reality: A Treatise on the Sociology of Knowledge*. New York: Garden City.

Blake, R. R., & Mouton, J. S. (1978). *The New Managerial Grid*. Houston, TX: Gulf.

Cheung, F. M., & Halpern, D. F. (2010). Women at the top: Powerful leaders define success as work + family in a culture of gender. *American Psychologist, 65*(3), 182–193. doi:10.1037/a0017309

Collins, R. L. (2011). Content analysis of gender roles in media: Where are we now and where should we go? *Sex Roles, 64*(3–4), 290–298. doi:10.1007/s11199-010-9929-5

Daalmans, S., Kleemans, M., & Sadza, A. (2017). Gender representation on gender-targeted television channels: A comparison of female-and male-targeted tv channels in the Netherlands. *Sex Roles, 77*, 1–13. doi: 10.1007/s11199-016-0727-6

Eschholz, S., Bufkin, J., & Long, J. (2002). Symbolic reality bites: Women and racial/ethnic minorities in modern film. *Sociological Spectrum, 22*(3), 299–334. doi: 10.1080/02732170290062658

Fairhurst, G.T. (2007). *Discursive Leadership: In Conversation with Leadership Psychology*. Thousand Oaks, CA: Sage.

Fairhurst, G. T. (2008). Discursive leadership: A communication alternative to leadership psychology. *Management Communication Quarterly, 21*, 510–521. doi:10.1177/0893318907313714

Fairhurst, G. T., & Grant, D. (2010). The social construction of leadership: A sailing guide. *Management Communication Quarterly, 24*, 171–210. doi:10.1177/0893318909359697

Foucault, M. (1980). *Power/Knowledge: Selected Interviews and Other Writings, 1972–1977*. New York: Pantheon.

Garcia-Retamero, R., & López-Zafra, E. (2006). Prejudice against women in male-congenial environments: Perceptions of gender role congruity in leadership. *Sex Roles, 55*, 51–61. doi:10.1007/s11199-006-9068-1

Gill, R. (2007). *Gender and the Media*. Malden, MA: Polity Press.

Glascock, J. (2001). Gender roles on prime-time network television: Demographics and behaviors. *Journal of Broadcasting and Electronic Media, 45*, 656–669.

Hall, S. (1980). Encoding/decoding. In S. Hall, D. Hobson, A. Lowe, & P. Willis (Eds.), *Culture, Media, Language: Working Papers in Cultural Studies, 1972–1979* (pp. 128–13fl). London: Hutchinson.

Judge, T. A., Heller, D., & Mount, M. K. (2002). Five-factor model of personality and job satisfaction: A meta-analysis. *Journal of Applied Psychology, 87*, 530–541. doi: 10.1037/0021-9010.87.3.530

Klenke, K. (1996). *Women and Leadership: A Contextual Perspective*. New York: Springer Publishing Company.

Lauzen, M. M., & Dozier, D. M. (2005). Maintaining the double standard: Portrayals of age and gender in popular films. *Sex Roles, 52*(7–8), 437–446. doi: 10.1007/s11199-005-3710-1

Littleton, C. (July 15, 2015). TV Land thinks younger, shifts focus from Baby Boomers to Gen X. *Variety*. Retrieved from http://variety.com/2015/tv/news/tv-land-younger-jim-gaffigan-impastor-generation-x-1201541043/

Ross, K. (2004). Women framed: the gendered turn in mediated politics. In K. Ross, & C. Byerly (Eds.), *Women and Media* (pp. 60–80). Malden, MA: Blackwell Publishing Ltd.

Salahuddin, M. M. (2010). Generational differences impact on leadership style and organizational success. *Journal of Diversity Management, 5*(2), 1–6.

Signorielli, N., & Bacue, A. (1999). Recognition and respect: A content analysis of prime-time television characters across three decades. *Sex Roles, 40*(7–8), 527–544. doi: 10.1023/A:1018883912900

Stogdill, R. M. (1948). Personal factors associated with leadership: A survey of the literature. *Journal of Psychology, 25*, 35–71. doi: 10.1080/00223980.1948.9917362

Tuchman, G. (1979). Women's depictions by the mass media. *Signs, 4*(3), 528–542. doi:10.1086/493636

Walter, F., & Scheibe, S. (2013). A literature review and emotion-based model of age and leadership: New directions for the trait approach. *The Leadership Quarterly, 24*(6), 882–901.

Yu, H. C., & Miller, P. (2005). Leadership style: The X Generation and Baby Boomers compared in different cultural contexts. *Leadership & Organization Development Journal, 26*(1), 35–50.

Chapter 8

Transformational Leadership in Teams

BBC's New Tricks

Sharmila Pixy Ferris

INTRODUCTION

This chapter considers leadership in teams, focusing on transformational leadership in a popular police procedural TV show. BBC One's long-running *New Tricks* follows the daily working of the Unsolved Crime and Open Case Squad, a fictional cold case unit of the Metropolitan Police in London, England. The show compellingly demonstrates the role of gender and age diversity in transformational leadership.

THEORETICAL FOUNDATION

The transformational theory of leadership, first articulated by James McGregor Burns (Burns, 1978), has become increasingly popular over the decades (Ghasabeh, Soosa, & Reaiche, 2015). Transformational leaders establish a common vision, using rhetorical skills, and work with their group to execute the vision. A transformational leader, according to seminal research by Bass (1990, 1999), is characterized by charisma and the following components (defined briefly here, and discussed in further detail in the analysis section):

• Idealized influence: serving as role models for their followers.
• Inspirational motivation: motivating and inspiring, by providing meaning and challenge to their followers' work.
• Intellectual stimulation: stimulating followers' efforts to be innovative and creative.
• Individualized Consideration: paying special attention to each individual follower's needs for achievement and growth by acting as a coach or mentor.

Over the decades, transformational leadership theory has grown in popularity until it has become a staple in leadership studies and practice. In the three decades since its articulation, transformational leadership theory was found by Judge and Piccolo (2004) in a meta-analysis to have high validity, and has been applied in a wide range of contexts.

One important context in which transformational leadership theory has been applied is teams. Teams are integral to the twentieth- and twenty-first-century workplace (Jackson, Joshi & Zedeck, 2011). For students, understanding the various factors affecting successful teams is important for individual career success. As Burke, Stagl, Klein, Goodwin, Salas, and Halpin (2006) note, there's a need to better understand the relationship between leader behaviors and team performance outcomes. Transformational leadership theory offers a means to further this understanding, and from early in the research, transformational leadership has been applied to teams (Bass, 1990, 1999; Bass & Riggio, 2006). However, the early research on transformational leadership in teams (Bass, 1990; Burns, 1978) did not consider some factors of real importance today, including gender of the leader or age diversity in the team.

A consideration of age diversity in teams is increasingly important, given the aging of the workforce in the developed world (Küper, Rivkin, & Schmidt, 2017). Teams with objective age diversity can be less effective, but when team members' perceptions and diversity beliefs are positive, the impact on the team can be positive (Ellwart, Bündgens, & Rack, 2013). Students who better understand age as a factor in team functioning can be more successful when they work in teams, with reduced age stereotypes and less conflict.

A consideration of gender in leadership is also important, given the significance of gender in today's workplace. Although women's presence in the work force has substantially increased from the twentieth century into the twenty-first, women's leadership presence is still limited and women continue to be underrepresented at the higher levels of organizations. For example, today only 5 percent of Fortune 500 companies have women CEOs and women significantly lag behind men in senior management (Pew, 2014). Thus it is not surprising that the research on women and leadership is correspondingly limited (Paustian-Underdahl, Walker, & Woehr, 2014).

This chapter can add to the literature on leadership. Specifically, this chapter will build on the theory of transformational leadership to demonstrate how a woman leader can positively impact the performance of an age-diverse team through idealized influence, inspirational motivation, intellectual stimulation, and individualized consideration. These complex concepts can more easily be understood by students when illustrated by Detective Superintendent Sandra Pullman (in the BBC show *New Tricks)* as she works with her team of three older male detectives, a young police constable, and a middle-aged supervisor, using leadership skills to improve the team's performance.

METHODOLOGY: TELEVISION AS A LENS FOR STUDYING LEADERSHIP AND TEAMS

Television can be a lens for studying society through its reflection of cultural behaviors and norms. Since television programming often mirrors current societal trends and attitudes, analysis of popular TV shows can prove beneficial for understanding communication. Media representations often result from dominant racial, gender, and class ideologies (Hill Collins, 2000; hooks, 1992), so television can prove particularly useful in studying societal issues, including gender and age in the workplace. As Anderson and Ferris (2016) demonstrate, women have been grossly underrepresented as characters on television, in less screen time and lower lead roles; and when represented, women are often stereotyped and objectified. Gender stereotyping has been found to persist even in the rare TV shows, about women in stereotypically masculine professions such as the police force. Cox (2012) found that the TLC's *Police Women of Broward County* reinforced stereotyped gender roles, and showed language, clothing, and subject matter that objectify the female police officers depicted on the show. Today, TV shows that portray a strong female leader are increasing, but still rare enough to be notable (e.g., *Commander in Chief, State of Affairs* in the United States, *Borgen* in Denmark).

BBC One's *New Tricks* offers a compelling vehicle portraying a woman leader, demonstrating the role of gender in transformational leadership. The show is a British police procedural comedy-drama about a fictional cold case unit of the Metropolitan Police, known as the Unsolved Crime and Open Case Squad (UCOS), whose mission is to reinvestigate unsolved crimes. The characters in the show reflect many of the dynamics of the police workplace, with three senior male detectives (returning to the workplace after retirement) supervised by a younger, successful and career-driven woman. The show's title emphasizes *New Tricks* the team's age diversity, as repeated in its theme song, "You can't teach an old dog a brand new trick."

New Tricks began in 2003, proved very popular and ran for a rare twelve seasons on BBC One. While the cast of the show largely changed in 2013, the gender and relational composition of the team (a younger woman leader, three experienced, older male team members) was maintained, with gender and relationship dynamics forming a constant subtext to the plots as the team investigates old crimes. *New Tricks* thus offers an excellent teaching example of gendered leadership in a male-dominated workplace.

This chapter is limited to a consideration of the first season of *New* Tricks (Series 1) for several reasons. First, the debut season of the show establishes the characters who remain for ten of the twelve additional seasons. Second, the first season provides an opportunity to explore the establishment of leadership and relational dynamics as the characters meet, interact, get to know each other, and establish friendships and bonds. (See Appendix A for a character guide and Appendix B for an episode guide of series 1 of *New Tricks*. Please note that "seasons" are referred to as "series" in Great Britain, and the terms are used interchangeably here)

TRANSFORMATIONAL TEAM LEADERSHIP IN *NEW TRICKS*

From its pilot episode through its first season, *New Tricks* provides an enjoy-ably entertaining illustration of issues of gendered transformational leader-ship and age diversity in teams. The show revolves around the working of an unusual cold case team in the (London) Metropolitan Police Force. After a public relations disaster (a botched kidnapping rescue, during which she killed the kidnapper's dog), Detective Superintendent Sandra Pullman is punished by being sidelined into leadership of a new unit, Unsolved Crime and Open Case Squad (UCOS).

Age-diverse team. Due to a shortage of qualified personnel, Sandra is told to recruit from among retired detectives. She seeks out her former mentor, retired Detective Superintendent Jack Halford, and on his advice advertises for the new team. Sadly, a dismaying number of well-qualified retirees are either dead or incapacitated, and after many interviews Sandra finds only two candidates who meet her requirements, Brian Lane and Gerry Standing.

The three older members of the UCOS team, Jack, Brian, and Gerry, have "vast experience" (as their supervisor DAC Bevan makes clear at a press con-ference in Episode 4). But with experience, each of them brings the emotional baggage connected to their retirements. Jack Halford, of the highest rank, is a detective chief superintendent, thus outranking Sandra who used to work for him. Jack is haunted by the death of his wife Mary, who was a victim of an unsolved hit and run. He talks to his dead wife often, and believes she can help him solve his cases. Jack understands the bureaucracy of the Met-ropolitan Police but has little patience for its internal politics. Brian Lane is a retired detective inspector, forced into retirement by accusations during his alcoholic past of allowing a drug dealer to die on his watch. Brian is obsessed with what he perceives as a conspiracy to force him out of the Met. He is brilliant, but has an obsessive-compulsive personality, and when focused on a goal, will ignore the rules. Gerry Standing, the lowest ranking member of the team preretirement, is a retired detective sergeant, whose old-fashioned policing style is not politically correct. While not corrupt, Gerry was forced out of the Met by accusations of corruption, and nurses an ongoing grudge against DAC Bevan. Gerry always gets the job done well but often bends the rules to do so. The last member of the team is a young constable Izzy Clark (known to the team as Clarkie), who is assigned to them as administrative and IT support. Clarkie's life experiences as a young black man, and his knowledge of modern policing, place him a world apart from the three senior men on the team, aligning him more closely with Sandra in terms of knowledge and skills, if not experience or rank.

This age-diverse team of men is led by Sandra Pullman, a beautiful and dynamic woman. Successful and driven, Sandra is young to have reached the elevated rank of detective superintendent. Her age and relative lack of experience when compared to Jack, Brian, and Jerry could have led to problems, but this team illustrates the positive impact of team members' perceptions and diversity beliefs (Ellwart, Bündgens & Rack, 2013). Sandra values her senior detectives' experience and individual skills (Brian's memory, Gerry's interpersonal skills, and Jack's wisdom and guidance) and relies on Clarkie's research and administrative skills. The young constable respects the older men's experience and quietly assists them in their areas of weakness, such as technology. Jointly, their positive perceptions lead to a strong and successful team who solve every cold case they undertake.

Although the UCOS team consists of members whose skills and experience complement each other well, Deputy Assistant Commissioner Bevan (Sandra's boss) feels that they have problems due to personality issues and due to the reasons for their forced retirements from the police force. Sandra stands by her hires and refuses to back down when DAC Bevan criticizes both Gerry and Brian. Sandra insists that her team will get the job done. In this Sandra's leadership skills are evident; as a transformational leader she demonstrates *direct visioning behaviors* such as confidence in achievement of her goals (Bass, 1990).

Sandra Pullman's transformational leadership characteristics. Throughout Series 1, Sandra Pullman's transformational leadership is clearly evident, displayed from the very outset as she formed her new team. She actively *listens* (Bass, 1990) to Jack, who recommends that she hire Brian and Gerry for their skills. Sandra is *open* (Bass, 1990) to Jack's advice, despite her personal qualms is willing to give her team members a chance to prove themselves.

As Bass' ongoing research has made clear, a transformational leader has *charisma*, serves as a role models for followers (*idealized influence*), motivates and inspires them (*inspirational motivation*), stimulates followers' efforts to be innovative and creative (*intellectual stimulation*) and pays special attention to each individual follower's needs for achievement and growth (*individualized consideration*) (1990, 1999; Bass & Riggio, 2006).

Sandra's *charisma* is evident from the outset: she is dynamic and persuasive detective, fast-tracked through the system to achieve the status of Superintendent. She gets what she wants from her bureaucratic, obstructive boss, and maverick team by sheer force of will, and her charm is so strong that the men she investigates often find her irresistible even while they are under investigation. Although Bevan, her boss, has sidelined her rise through the ranks of the Metropolitan Police, by the end of series 1 he recognizes her remarkable success as leader of UCOS, congratulating her on her leadership and success rate, and offering her a promotion.

Sandra's personal life is messy and often lonely, but as Sandra tells her therapist, all her life she's been driven to be the best. She recognizes that "every inch up the pole comes at a personal price" (as her boyfriend notes in Episode 6) and has been willing to pay that price. As a leader she provides *idealized influence*, serving as a role model of success for Jack, Gerry, Brian, and Clarkie, and working alongside them to succeed. By first rehiring Jack, Brian, and Gerry, and then showing on an ongoing basis that she believes in their abilities, Sandra offers *inspirational motivation*, bringing meaning to their lives. Sandra excels at providing her team with *intellectual stimulation*, allowing them creativity and innovation, even when it leads Gerry and Brian to step outside of established police procedure, which is tied to Sandra's *individualized consideration* of each of her team members (more on both of these issues below).

Idealized influence. As a leader, Sandra serves as a role model of success for Jack, Gerry, Brian, and Clarkie. The three older men had their careers cut short by circumstances outside their control: Jack by the untimely death of his wife; Gerry accused of corruption and forced to resign; Brian, when an alcoholic, forced to retire due to the death of a drug dealer in his custody. Although Sandra is much younger than the three of them, she is in a career position they respect. Sandra's drive, ambition, and belief in their abilities inspire Jack, Brian, and Gerry to success. They begin to irreverently call her "bird in charge" behind her back (in several episodes beginning with their second case), and by their sixth case call her that to her face, also affectionately calling her a "forceful confident woman" (Episode 5). Sandra inspires her team by working alongside them, rather than directing from above. She is not unaware of Jack, Brian, and Gerry's problems and quirks, but utilizes these factors to promote the team's success.

Izzy Clark (known to the team as Clarkie) is on the other end of the spectrum, at the start of his career and at the bottom of the Metropolitan Police's career ladder. To him, Sandra provides a standard to which he can aspire. Clarkie is aware of the disadvantages of his race in the Metropolitan Police, as he clearly states to Brian in episode 5. Sandra, as a fellow minority, albeit one who has been fast-tracked to a position of power, becomes a role model to Clarkie. By valuing his administrative and IT skills, Sandra shows Clark he is an important member of the team and inspires him to aim higher.

Sandra's idealized influence is furthered through considerable and ongoing task motivation. When the team is stymied by a seventeen-year-old cold trail in their second case, the unsolved murder of a policewoman, Sandra focuses the team on their task by telling them she was at college with the murdered woman and would not give up on finding the murderer. She uses their dislike of Special Branch to keep the team motivated in their fourth case, hones their focus on the task in their fifth case by highlighting the horror at the unsolved murder of a ten-year-old child, and in their seventh case motivates them to continue against the express order of DC Bevan.

Inspirational motivation. In the UCOS team, *inspirational motivation* is closely tied to *idealized influence* behaviors. By the very act of seeking out and hiring Jack, and recruiting Brian and Gerry, Sandra provides inspiration. By showing on an ongoing basis that she believes in their abilities, Sandra brings meaning to their lives. On more than one occasion she strongly defends her team members (especially Gerry and Brian) against criticism from her boss, DAC Bevan. Bevan believes Brian to be unstable, has a personal vendetta against Gerry, and makes it clear that he believes Brian and Gerry are a PR risk. Her team is aware of Sandra's loyalty, and is inspired by her leadership. They, in turn, protect her from Bevan's ire, for example, keeping it a secret from Bevan when Sandra dates Sir Timothy, a suspect who turns out to be guilty of art theft and arson (Episode 2), and standing by her when Sandra insists on continuing with their seventh case after Bevan orders her to stop.

The team's contentious relationship with DAC Bevan provides Sandra with many opportunities for inspirational motivation. For example, in episode 2, Bevan suspends Gerry because of prior association with a suspect. Sandra uses the incident to motivate the other team members to work harder to solve the case—which they soon succeed in doing.

Intellectual stimulation. In the UCOS team, this characteristic of transformational leadership is also closely linked to *inspiration motivation* and *idealized influence*, as can be seen from the examples above. Sandra excels at providing her team with *intellectual encouragement*, allowing them to be *innovative*. One example is allowing them the creative choice of their next cold case. In episode 4, even though choice of cases is her prerogative, she does not withdraw the privilege even when it leads to the team's selection of a seemingly dead-end case, the suicide of a seventeen-year-old golfer after he was suspected of murdering a ten-year-old boy at their golf club. The team's reinvestigation of the case unearthed fresh evidence, which led to the exoneration of the dead suspect and dramatically changed many lives. Another instance of allowing the team initiative and stimulation occurred in episode 5, when Sandra allows Brian to reopen a missing person case that he failed to solve early in his career, thus giving him the motivation and stimulation to put extra effort into solving the case.

Sandra also gives her team wide scope for their *creativity*. Brian is the thinker and memory of their team, but he steps outside that box during an art investigation (Episode 2). When their seconded art expert cannot get key information, Brian creatively (and illegally) threatens a tax investigation to leverage release of the information to UCOS, information which eventually broke the case. Episode 3 sees another example of Brian's creative thinking, when he establishes common ground with a suspect/witness in an institution by revealing his own mental health issues, thus getting the witness to open up to him and provide vital information. Their work on this particular case demonstrated the entire team's intellectual creativity, as they worked out, individually and together, a complicated murder covered up the Secret Service.

Like Brian, Gerry is a creative thinker, encouraged by Sandra. He leverages his underworld contacts in episode 2, getting inside information on arson from a white supremacist and from a convicted arsonist. Gerry thinks and acts outside the box in ways that could jeopardize their investigations. In their first case, Gerry tapes suspects without their knowledge or permission, while in their fifth case he continues to investigate after being suspended by Bevan. Both times Gerry uncovers information crucial to solving the cases and is appreciated by Sandra even as she informs him firmly that what he has done is unacceptable as it endangers the validity of their results.

Individualized consideration. The examples above demonstrate Gerry and Brian's often unconventional behaviors and actions. But no matter how she feels about her team's behavior, Sandra always does them the credit of listening to them, valuing their contributions, and giving them the individual attention they warrant. She *actively listens and communicates* with the team the way she expects them to communicate with her—promptly and honestly. Brian and Gerry can be a challenge, often testing boundaries while on the job. For example, in their third case (Episode 2), Brian solves a case by removing evidence without a warrant, making it inadmissible and endangering their case. Sandra makes it clear to him that what he has done is wrong; then she praises him for "amazingly intuitive work." (Interestingly, this leads Brian to save Clarkie from a similar mistake in episode 5, talking Clark into discarding illegally obtained DNA evidence from a purloined cigarette butt.) Another example comes in their fifth case, when Gerry entraps a rapist by getting drunk with him in order to merit a blood/DNA test at a contrived traffic stop, Sandra is furious. But she does Gerry the credit of believing in his quest for justice, and privately thanks him, while publicly defending him from Bevan.

Team outcomes. The characteristics of transformational leadership exhibited by DS Sandra Pullman make the UCOS team stronger. Dionne et al. (2004) posit that a transformational leader can enhance such *team outcomes* as shared team commitment and cohesion, effective, open and prompt team communication, and functional and positive team conflict.

As a leader, Sandra has built a strong and cohesive team. *Team cohesion* is the degree to which team members are motivated to remain on the team. A transformational leader's idealized influence and inspirational motivation can promote team cohesion (Dionne, Yammarino, Atwater, and Spangler, 2004). Sandra's success as a team leader can be seen in the rapid cohesion of the UCOS team. When the team begins to work together, Sandra and Jack tend to team up on interviews while Brian and Gerry are thrown together by default. By the fourth case the partnerships in interviewing and investigating have become more mixed, with Gerry and Jack attending arson training, Brian and Gerry visiting a witness in the country, and Sandra interviewing a suspect with Gerry (Episode 3). By their fifth case, even Clarkie is included on an interview with a suspect (Episode 4), and by this time Sandra is finally completely comfortable with Gerry.

Another sign of team cohesion is social bonding, as it takes a cohesive team to spend time together outside work. At the outset (during their first case, the pilot episode), the three senior team members are seen at a pub—without Sandra or Clarkie. By their third case (Episode 2) Clarkie and Sandra have joined the group at the pub, while by their fifth case they all meet for dinner at Brian and Esther's home. The last case in season 1 (Episode 6) shows the whole team at a pub several times, indicating the strength of their cohesion.

Sandra's *individualized consideration* of her team members makes for a team with *effective, open and prompt team communication*. As Dionne and colleagues (2004) note, a considerate leader is open to communication, listens attentively, considers individual needs, and empowers team members. Sandra is an *active listener* and *an open communicator*. She *cares about her team members*, ensuring that Brian is taking his medication, that Gerry is not in trouble when he has to sells his beloved sports car, and that Jack is coping without his adored wife. The team members understand this, and are not afraid to share their opinions and speak their minds, whether it is concerning their confidence that she will not leave them even if granted a promotion (in Episode 6), or when it is on inappropriate topics such as Sandra's unsatisfactory love life (throughout Season 1).

The final outcome promoted a transformational leader is *positive and functional team conflict*. Interestingly, from the very outset there is little negative conflict in the UCOS team. Although Gerry's brash personality and Brian's obsessiveness do irritate Sandra at first, she is comfortable communicating to them when they step outside the bounds of acceptable behavior, and they are comfortable expressing their opinions of each other, and of her. Such open communication moves conflict in a positive direction.

An example of positive functional conflict in the team was mentioned previously. When Bevan suspends Gerry because of prior association with a suspect, Sandra uses the struggle between Bevan and Gerry to motivate the other team members to work harder to solve the case. Other examples can be seen during the third and sixth cases. During the third case, functional conflict develops within the team as they strongly oppose Sandra's communication with Special Services who never shares information. Sandra allows the team's criticism, but continues to flirt with Special Branch DI Johnson, successfully extracting hidden information that helps them solve the case. During their sixth case, the team uncovers two additional and unexpected murders, and is hindered by dead ends and confusion. There is functional disagreement within the team on which suspect should be the focus of suspicion, who should interview the chief suspect, and how to proceed in general. But the team eventually pulls together and solves the murder, giving the victim's mother peace, and reuniting her family.

A REVIEW OF PRACTICAL IMPLICATIONS

As can be seen in this chapter thus far, *New Tricks* provides an entertaining vehicle to study transformation leadership in teams, and adds to viewer's understanding of gender and leadership. On TV, male leaders are portrayed far more often that female leaders, so *New Tricks* emphasis on gender highlights the under-studied aspect of leadership in a male-dominated world.

Equally importantly, *New Tricks* provides an enjoyable illustration of how gendered leadership can contribute to successful team outcomes. Viewers can see that how a female leader can create strong team outcomes through the exercise of idealized influence, inspirational motivation, intellectual stimulation, and individualized consideration. Positive team outcomes lead to stronger team cohesion, motivating members to contribute to the team. DS Sandra Pullman's idealized influence and inspirational motivation as a transformational leader made her team cohesive, effective, and successful. Sandra's individualized consideration of her team members also makes for a team with effective, open, and prompt team communication and positive and functional team conflict.

Teams are an integral part of the workplace today, and a study of *New Tricks* adds to viewer's understanding of some of the complex factors affecting the dynamics of teams in the workplace. Such an understanding is important for individual career success. Similarly, *New Tricks* shows how a consideration of age diversity is increasingly important, given the aging of the workforce in the developed world. Students who better understand age as a factor in team functioning can be more successful when they work in teams, with reduced age stereotypes and less conflict.

CONCLUSION

This discussion of the first season of BBC One's *New Tricks* demonstrates Sandra Pullman as a transformational leader, with an age-diverse UCOS team that benefits from her leadership style. This chapter focuses only on series 1 of *New Tricks*, where Sandra Pullman's transformational leadership characteristics can be seen to transform the disparate personalities and varying experience of new UCOS team members into a highly functioning successful team. But if the TV show is new to the reader, I can recommend with confidence that the interested viewer watch not only series 1, but also the many series that follow. The ten seasons featuring Sandra, Jack, Gerry, and Brian continue to be entertaining, and further establish the effectiveness of team outcomes and demonstrated transformational leadership.

Appendix A   Character Guide, *New Tricks*

Character	Character description
A note on leadership structure In the City of London Police force, the leadership hierarchy is as follows: Chief Constable (at the very top), followed in descending order, by Assistant Commissioner, Deputy Assistant Commissioner, Chief Superintendent, Superintendent, Chief Inspector, Sargent and Constable.	
The leader: **Sandra Pullman** (Played by Amanda Redman in 84 episodes, 2003–2013)	Sandra Pullman is Detective Superintendent, Metropolitan Police and Head of the Unsolved Crime and Open Case (UCOS) Squad. She's (relatively) young, beautiful, successful, ambitious, and driven to the extent that has been 'fast-tracked" to her current elevated rank. Sandra is initially assigned to lead UCOS as a punishment for a bungled kidnap rescue, but her drive, talent and leadership skills make the unit a success. Sandra's focus on career leads to sacrifice of a personal life, and she enters she team divorced and ending an affair with a married man. Sandra expects her team to work as hard as she does, but works alongside them, providing motivation and rewards
The Team: Because few experienced personnel are available, Sandra Pullman is authorized to hire retired detectives. She recruits her former mentor Jack Halford, and interviews a number of unsuitable retired detectives before settling Brian Lane and Gerry Standing. A young Police Constable, Izzy Clark, is assigned to the team as administrative and IT support	

(Continued)

Appendix A (*Continued*)

Character	Character description
Jack Halford (Played by James Bolam in 69 episodes, 2003–2013)	Jack Halford is a retired Detective Chief Superintendent who returns to work with the new UCOS team. Jack is an intelligent, cultured man who retired when his wife Mary was killed in an unsolved hit and run. He remains haunted by her death, and her presence is a continuing factor in the show as Jack discusses his cases with her, sitting by her grave in his back yard. More than the other members of UCOS, Jack was pleased to return to the workplace, and specially a cold case team as he resents the fact that his wife's killer was never charged. Although a senior member of the Met, Jack has little time for bureaucracy and internal politics
Brian Lane (Played by Alun Armstrong for ten seasons, 2003–2013)	Brian Lane is a retired Detective Inspector, who was forced into retirement by a breakdown. Brian has mental health issues which lead to occasional erratic behavior, and is a recovering alcoholic. His exceptional, almost eidetic, memory makes him an invaluable team member. Brian obsesses about his work, which literally becomes his life. On the team, Brian serves as the researcher and team's 'recollection'. Brian is not comfortable with many aspects of modern life, for example not driving a car and bicycling to work. Brian is capable of bending the rules when he is focused on finding the truth, sometimes endangering the team's success by not following rules
Gerry Standing (Played by Dennis Waterman in 99 episodes, 2003–2015)	The lowest ranking member of the team pre-retirement, Gerry Standing is a retired Detective Sargent, whose policing style is not suited to the 21st century. He is genial and loves people, as happy to mix with the criminal classes as with the law-abiding. With his love of gambling and drink, women, music and food, Gerry is also a good natured and an honorable man. As he tells Sandra in Episode 4, he's a "naughty boy, not a bastard." Gerry gets the job done well but often bends the rules to do so. While his sexist language and his lifestyle often rub Sandra the wrong way, she unfailingly defends Gerry against their boss, DAC Bevan, who hates Gerry

Appendix A   (Continued)

Character	Character description
Donald Bevan (Played by Nicholas Day, Tim Woodward in the Pilot)	Deputy Assistant Commissioner of Metropolitan Police, Donald Bevan founded UCOS as a PR gesture, with no real intention that it be successful as a cold case unit. He is more focused on bureaucracy than results. Unsurprisingly, his role is defined by a combative relationship with the UCOS team who resent his bureaucratic ways and lack of support, and with Sandra, who resents being sidelined into what she sees as a "punishment" job. Bevan's relationship with Gerry is particularly hostile, leading from Gerry having broken his jaw in the past
Izzy Clark (played by Chike Okonwo)	Izzy Clark is a police constable, a rank below Detective Constable in the Metropolitan Police. Clark has been assigned to the team as administrative and IT support. His knowledge of modern policing makes him stand out among the older non-conforming team members, while his computer skills and knowledge of 'smart policing' make him essential to the team's success. Soon affectionately known as "Clarkie," he becomes a valued member of the team, using his tech skills to help them solve cases, and joining them at the pub after work
Esther Lane (Played by Susan Jameson in 54 episodes, 2003–2013)	Wife of Brian Lane, Esther is a peripheral but important character in the series. She grounds Brian as he works on cases, offering him counsel and advice. In Episode 1, Brian says that "without Esther I don't have a home." Esther also becomes a friend to the team, a quiet and steady presence

Appendix B   New Tricks - Episodes, Series 1

Episode Title and Date	Episode Description
The Chinese Job Pilot/Episode 0 27 March 2003	After an attempt to rescue a kidnap victim, DS Sandra Pullman is put in charge of UCOS, a new unit focusing on unsolved cases. She hires three retired detectives, including her old boss and mentor, Jack Halford. Together they interview a number of ex-detectives and settle on Brian Lane, a reformed alcoholic who retired after a prisoner in his custody died, and Gerry Standing, who seems to know the accused murderer. When a wrongfully accused man is released from prison twenty one years after a murder in a nightclub, the team works together to arrest the real murderer(s). The pilot introduces the characters and shows the development of relational dynamics as the team successfully solves their first case
ID Parade Episode 1 1 Apr. 2004	The team investigates the unsolved murder of a policewoman seventeen years ago. Sandra's connection to the murdered PC Daniels, her classmate at Hendon, drives the show as Sandra's relationship to the dead woman's boyfriend and her knowledge of other characters reveal secrets from her days at Hendon
Painting on Loan Episode 2 8 Apr. 2004	The team steps outside their charge, asked to investigate art theft and forgery at the request of Sir Timothy, Surveyor of the Queen's Pictures. This episode reveals the reason for Bevan's hatred of Gerry, and Sandra's penchant for unsuitable relationships continues, as she is pursued by Sir Timothy. Sandra's detecting and leadership skills are revealed as she discovered the mind behind the forgeries, and solves both the art thefts and an old arson fire that injured several immigrant women
1984 Episode 3 15 Apr. 2004	The team investigates the murder of a young peace protester, killed near a nuclear base in 1984. They must decide if it was a cover-up by Special Branch or the military. Once again Sandra is pursued by an unsuitable man, DI Jonathon of the Special Branch, but she uses the relationship to further the investigation (although she does go on to date him). This episode highlights the effective working of the team, as Brian, Jack, Gerry and Clarkie use their skills to individually obtain information that helps the team solve the murder

(Continued)

Appendix B   *(Continued)*

Episode Title and Date	Episode Description
Good Work **Rewarded** Episode 4 22 April 2004	The team investigates the unsolved murder of a ten year-old boy on a golf course, but face obstruction from a snobbish and sexist golf club committee, who use the media to obstruct the team by ostensibly protecting the memory of a Falklands war hero. The team pulls together to solve the murder, arrest a rapist, and openly oppose Bevan. The episode ends with Bevan congratulating them for the first time on their "good work"
Home Truths Episode 5 29 Apr. 2004	The team investigates the disappearance of an attractive young mother and her six-month old son in the 1970s. The complex case uncovers other related murders of two other young women, pits the team against Bevan again, and shows the team working increasingly smoothly together. The team has to submit to a physical and psychological assessment
Talking to the Dead Episode 6 6 May 2004	Jack starts the team on an investigation of a twenty year unsolved abduction and murder after he visits a psychic in the hope of communicating with his dead wife. The team knowingly entraps the real murderer, coming under fire by Bevan who realizes that they have opened themselves to a lawsuit. The season ends with the team's passing of the physical and psychological assessment, and a reaffirmation of the team's commitment to each other and to UCOS, but with the team's future in doubt

Note: This series continued for about ten years with many of these characters, excepting Bevan. Detectives were replaced, as was the female superintendent, but the show continued for 12 years. A complete episode list of all 12 Series can be found at *BBC One: New Tricks* http://www.bbc.co.uk/programmes/b006t0qx/episodes/guide.
Source: Adapted from http://www.bbc.co.uk/programmes/b006t0qx/episodes/guide.

REFERENCES

Anderson, J. S., & Ferris, S. P. (2016). Gender stereotyping and 'The Jersey Shore': A content analysis. *Kome Journal*, 4(1), 1–19.

Bass, B. M. (1990). From transactional to transformational leadership: Learning to share the vision. *Organizational Dynamics*, 18(3), 19–31.

Bass, B. M. (1999). Two decades of research and development in transformational leadership. *European Journal of Work and Organizational Psychology*, 8(1), 9–32.

Bass, B. M., & Riggio, R. (2006). *Transformational Leadership* (2nd ed). Mahwah, NJ: Lawrence Erlbaum.

BBC One. (nd). *New Tricks*. http://www.bbc.co.uk/programmes/b006t0qx

Burke, C.S., Stagl, K.C., Goodwin, G.F., Salas, E., & Halpin, S. (2006). What type of leadership behaviors are functional in teams? A meta-analysis. *The Leadership Quarterly*, 17(3), 288–307.

Burns, J. M. (1978). *Leadership*. New York: Harper Collins.

Cox, N. (2012). Kicking ass...with lip gloss: Mediating gender on TLC's 'Police Women of Broward County'. *Critical Studies in Media Communication*, 29(2), 149–163.

Dionne, S. D., Yammarino, F. J., Atwater, L. E., & Spangler, W. D. (2004). Transformational leadership and team performance. *Journal of Organizational Change Management*, 17(2), 177–193.

Ellwart, T., Bündgens, S., & Rack, O. (2013). Managing knowledge exchange and identification in age diverse teams. *Journal of Managerial Psychology*, 28(7/8), 950–972.

Ghasabeh, M. S., Soosay. C., & Reaiche, C. (2015). The emerging role of transformational leadership. *The Journal of Developing Areas*. 49(6). 459–467.

Hill Collins, P. (2000). *Black Feminist Thought: Knowledge, Consciousness, and the Politics of Empowerment* (2nd ed.). New York: Routledge.

Hooks, B. (1992). Black Looks: Race and Representation. Boston: South End Press.

Jackson, S. E., Joshi, A., & Zedeck, S. (Eds). (2011). *APA Handbook of Industrial and Organizational Psychology, Vol 1: Building and Developing the Organization*, pp. 651–686. Washington, DC: American Psychological Association.

Judge, T. A., & Piccolo, R. F. (2004). Transformational and transactional leadership: A meta-analytic test of their relative validity. *Journal of Applied Psychology*, 89(5), 755–768.

Küper, K., Rivkin, W., & Schmidt, K. H. (2017). Training interventions to increase innovation and productivity in age-diverse teams. In *Advances in Ergonomic Design of Systems, Products and Processes: Proceedings of the Annual Meeting of GfA 2016*, pp. 115–124. Available online http://dx.doi.org/10.1007/978-3-622-53305-5_8

Paustian-Underdahl, S. C., Walker, L. S., & Woehr, D. J. (2014). Gender and perceptions of leadership effectiveness: A meta-analysis of contextual moderators. *Journal of Applied Psychology*, 99(6), 1129–1145.

Pew Research Center. (January 14, 2015). *Women and Leadership*. Available online www.pewsocialtrends.org/2015/01/14/women-and-leadership

Part III

POWER OF OPPORTUNITY

Chapter 9

Television Transcendent

How the Electronic Church Constructs Charismatic Leadership as a Norm of American Religious Life

Mark Ward Sr.

Televangelists did not elect Donald Trump. But for the one in four adults in the United States who identify as evangelical Christians (Pew Research Center, 2015), of whom 81 percent voted for the 2016 Republican presidential candidate (Smith & Martinez, 2016), the electronic church has constructed charismatic leadership as a norm of the religious "workplace" in congregations nationwide. Religious media are consumed daily by one in five adults, and each month more people consume these media than attend church (Barna Group, 2005). Though the 1980s incarnation of religious television remains fixed in popular memory, the electronic church today is far larger. While its public profile is lower due to media proliferation and audience fragmentation (Ward, 2016a), "Christian media" remain a key institution of the evangelical subculture. Due to media deregulation, today's electronic church is dominated by evangelical media conglomerates (Ward, 2009a, 2012, 2013a) that deliver content via every digital platform. Evangelical television networks are carried by all major cable and satellite TV services to 100 million households and by streaming media to millions more (Ward, 2016b), while one-fifth of U.S. radio stations air a religious teaching/talk or music format (Rodrigues, Green, & Virshup, 2013). What draws audiences to evangelical media personalities, and causes them to heed these leaders over credentialed experts on issues from evolution to climate change, is a perception that these (mostly) men are "anointed" by God (Stephens & Giberson, 2011), even as media exposure aggrandizes their authority. As such, TV and radio preachers fit the definition of charismatic leaders: those perceived as possessing special gifts, repeatedly validated, to empower followers, and carry out a radical vision in a time of crisis (Trice & Beyer, 1993).

The electronic church has always constructed charismatic leaders, typified by Charles Fuller and the *Old Fashioned Revival Hour* in the 1930s and

1940s, Billy Graham and the *Hour of Decision* in the 1950s and 1960s, Jerry Falwell and the *Old Time Gospel Hour* in the 1970s and 1980s, Joel Osteen and *Joel Osteen Ministries* today. Audiences have formed intense parasocial relationships (Horton & Wohl, 1956) with these figures, who became totems for media rituals (Holmes, 2005) through which evangelicals have formed a stable interpretive community (Lindlof, 2002; Ward, 2014). Televangelists do not draw audiences through careful Bible exegesis but by "spouting their own opinions and lecturing people on a few narrow scripture verses" (Winzenburg, 2005). From the "first televangelist" of the 1950s, Fulton J. Sheen, to today's top-rated TV preacher, Joel Osteen, the properties of the medium—as McLuhan (1964) and Postman (1985) predicted—push preachers toward universal themes (Sleasman, 2016). Yet compared to the 1980s heyday of the New Christian Right, two new themes have emerged in the message of the electronic church. First, the culture-war rhetoric of American evangelicalism has changed from *attacking* to *being attacked* (Moen, 1994). The movement today draws its vitality from a shared identity as an "embattled" (Smith, 1998; see also Smidt, 2013) and "persecuted" (Duerringer, 2016) minority. Second, this bunker mentality has pushed many evangelicals into the comforting subculture of the megachurch where "worship is more a therapeutic means to personal fulfillment than submission to a higher authority" (Worthen, 2013, p. 256). An aspect of this retreat is the ascendance of "prosperity theology." Today, 31 percent of Christians believe God materially blesses those who give, and 43 percent believe faith produces health and wealth (Bowler, 2013).

To plumb the connection between screen and pew, studies in media and religion have recently taken a "pragmatic turn." Traditional approaches to the field, including technological determinism (religious media are necessarily colonized by the values of technology; e.g., Postman, 1985) and cultural studies (religious media are only symptoms of deeper structural processes within society; e.g., Hoover, 1988), seem inadequate to explain the intersection of religious experience and today's complex digital media environment. The question asked by the pragmatic perspective "is not merely 'What are the issues surrounding the electronic church?' but 'How do audiences *read* it in a cogent way?'" Rather than focus on technology or cultural trends, pragmatics "suggest ways to think about media and *community*" (Stout, 2016, p. xi, emphases in original). At issue is "mediatization" (Hjarvard, 2008; Lövheim, 2011) or the integration of media forms and daily life as "functions traditionally found in churches become dependent on media technologies" (Trammell, 2016, p. 226). This chapter will review how the rhetorical practices and media rituals of the electronic church construct charismatic leadership and, by linking this phenomenon to the author's fieldwork in evangelical churches, demonstrate how this leadership style has been normalized in the evangelical subculture.

A BRIEF HISTORY OF THE ELECTRONIC CHURCH

Though a workable electronic television system was demonstrated as early as 1923, at the time only broadcast radio was primed for rapid commercial development. Commercial television service debuted in 1939 and the Federal Communications Commission (FCC) enacted technical standards in 1941, but the new medium was put on hold by the outbreak of World War II. Even after the war ended in 1945, the technology to link local stations into national TV networks did not exist until the end of the decade. Meanwhile, radio enjoyed a golden age in the 1930s and 1940s. A number of network radio preachers attracted large Sunday audiences, including Charles Fuller whose *Old Fashioned Revival Hour* drew 20 million weekly listeners (Fuller, 1972). Another media preacher, Walter Maier, aired the first made-for-television religious program when he simulcast his weekly *Lutheran Hour* for New Year's Day 1948 over national radio and his hometown St. Louis TV station (Ward, 1994). A year later, popular radio evangelist Percy Crawford debuted *Youth on the March* as the first weekly network religious telecast (Crawford, 2010). Fuller followed in 1950 with his *Old Fashioned Camp Meeting* weekly program (Fuller, 1972). Yet Crawford and Fuller soon discovered that, since relatively few American cities had TV stations and few households owned sets, viewer donations could not cover production costs (Ward, 2017). While a few programs supported by national church bodies were popular in the 1950s—most notably *Life is Worth Living* with Catholic bishop Fulton J. Sheen—independent televangelists honed their media skills on local television.

Prospects for televangelism changed, however, in the 1960s. The major broadcast networks ended their historic bans on selling airtime for religious programs (Hangen, 2008; Ward, 2013a). The FCC ruled in 1960 that stations could meet their public service mandates by selling, not just donating, time for religious programs. In 1964, the agency decreed that all new TV sets must receive the entire spectrum of TV channels, including the upper part of the spectrum where most independent nonnetwork stations broadcast. The invention of broadcast-quality videotape, plus falling prices for editing equipment, allowed televangelists to easily produce their programs and ship copies to stations nationwide. Thus, by the late 1960s and early 1970s, televangelists Oral Roberts, Rex Humbard, and Jerry Falwell entered first-run syndication by each purchasing airtime on more than 300 local stations and attracting weekly audiences of between 1 million and 7 million viewers (Melton, Lucas & Stone, 1997). Meanwhile, the number of religious radio stations tripled during the 1970s to more than a thousand outlets (Ward, 2013a).

Televangelism boomed through the 1980s until, in 1987–88, a series of high-profile financial or sexual scandals brought down prominent televangelists Oral Roberts, Jim Bakker, and Jimmy Swaggart. Almost overnight, the televangelism genre lost three-fourths of its audience (Winzenburg, 2005). Arguably, however, the televangelism market was due for a correction. By the early 1990s, the cable revolution was in full swing. The audience share for traditional over-the-air television declined as households signed up for cable. With dozens of channels available, the national TV audience became "fragmented" and the business of televangelism became attracting a loyal niche audience (Ward, 2016a). Gradually, power shifted from the televangelists who produced the programs to the religious cable channels that controlled access to religious viewers. The last nail in the coffin for over-the-air religious TV came in 1996 when the FCC mandated that all stations must switch from analog to digital broadcasting within ten years. Since most independent local religious stations could not afford digital conversion (Schultz, 2000, 2005), many sold out. The FCC also eliminated most restrictions on how many local stations or cable systems a single operator could own. In radio, the result was the rise of national evangelical networks that now dominate the medium (Ward, 2009a, 2012, 2013a) and enable nationally syndicated radio preachers to be heard on up to 2,000 outlets. In television, media consolidation changed the cable industry from a hodgepodge of local franchises to a relative handful of large national cable operators and direct-broadcast satellite TV providers. Evangelical channels able to afford space on these systems can then offer to syndicated televangelists national coverage of up to 100 million households, provided the televangelists generate sufficient revenues to afford the airtime. Yet because the religious cable and satellite channels on which these televangelists appear exist in a fragmented media universe of more than 900 channels (NCTA, 2017), the key is cultivating a loyal viewer base.

If the electronic church of the twenty-first century is digitized and deregulated, it is also divided. During the 1970s and 1980s, the unity of the evangelical movement was built on a vaguely defined "biblical worldview" that conveniently submerged long-standing differences (Worthen, 2013). Some evangelical traditions emphasize propositional truth, while others emphasize experiential piety. Evangelicals in the "cessationist" tradition believe "sign gifts" such as speaking in tongues ceased with the apostles, while their Pentecostal and charismatic brethren believe these gifts continue to operate in the church. One commentator (Lindsay, 2007) also suggested that the evangelical movement is now divided between "cosmopolitans" who believe that rational apologetics will best win a hearing for the gospel in an increasingly post-Christian culture, and "populists" whose primary focus is catering to the evangelical subculture. In the electronic church, the divide is strikingly seen in the bifurcation of evangelical radio and television. All of the national teaching/talk radio networks and most of the nationally syndicated preachers are associated with cessationism and emphasize propositional truth, Bible exposition, and apologetics. By contrast, all but one of the national TV networks and most of the nationally syndicated televangelists associate with either Pentecostalism or the Charismatic Movement, emphasize experiential piety, and preach aspects of prosperity theology (Ward, 2016b). This division between Bible expositors and apologists on the one hand, and "health and wealth" preachers on the other, is a key to understanding how evangelical media personalities accrue charismatic authority and how their respective approaches furnish models that are broadly reproduced by local evangelical church pastors.

RHETORIC, POWER, AND LEADERSHIP

The most admired radio preachers are perceived as trusted expositors of the Bible. These include men who are each syndicated on more than 2,000 radio outlets: Chuck Swindoll, Charles Stanley, John MacArthur, David Jeremiah, Michael Youssef. Their daily half-hour programs typically exposit a particular Bible passage, while their programs over the course of several weeks pursue either "book studies" (expositing a particular book of the Bible) or "topical studies" (bringing Bible passages to bear on a particular topic such as marriage or finances). Typically, these programs are edited versions of sermon series that the speaker delivered at the church he pastors. Each series is also repackaged as a DVD collection, published book, or small-group Bible study and promoted via radio, often as a "premium" for donating to the program. Through their rhetorical practice of "expository preaching," these men accrue "expert power" (French & Raven, 1959). In turn, such expertise makes them "anointed" authorities who are specially gifted by God as teachers, thus accruing charismatic authority that is repeatedly validated through daily radio sermons and a steady stream of DVDs and popular books that fill the shelves of local religious bookstores and church libraries. Their vision of a divinely inspired Word and its timeless wisdom empowers followers to lead godly lives and defend the Bible in a time of cultural crisis.

In contrast, the most admired televangelists are perceived as prophets who urge believers to claim by faith the blessings that God has promised them. Among those in daily syndication on the highest rated evangelical TV networks are Jim Bakker, Kenneth Copeland, Creflo Dollar, John Hagee, Kenneth Hagin, Benny Hinn, T. D. Jakes, Joyce Meyer, Rod Parsley, Joseph Prince, Joel Osteen, James Robison, Kerry Shook, and Andrew Wommack. The emphases of their half-hour telecasts range across "hard prosperity" (typified by "Word of Faith" preachers Copeland and Hagin who exhort the faithful to "name it and claim it") to "soft prosperity" (typified by Osteen's bestselling book, *Live Your Best Life Now*). Sermons often forego verse-by-verse Bible exposition and instead begin with recitation of a Bible verse or passage as a "proof text" whose truth is then elaborated through stories, a rhetorical practice that has been called "narrative preaching" (Ward, 2009b). DVD collections and books are also rife but focus less on Bible exposition and more on mechanisms for attaining prosperity, whether material blessing or emotional healing. Thus do these televangelist accrue "referent power" (French & Raven, 1959) by modeling the prosperity—with their businesslike attire and lavish megachurches—to which their viewers aspire. God's evident blessing on their ministries affirms their status as "anointed" and specially gifted prophets. Their charismatic authority is repeatedly validated through daily telecasts, DVDs and books, all filled with stories of ordinary believers who testify to the effectiveness of the televangelists' prescriptions for prosperity. Their vision of Christian prosperity in the midst of cultural crisis empowers followers to have faith and believe.

EXPOSITORY AND NARRATIVE PREACHING

That the rhetorical practices of expository preaching and narrative preaching are broadly reproduced in local evangelical churches—and that these practices respectively generate expert power and referent power as the bases for pastors' charismatic leadership—was corroborated in a four-year field study in which I surveyed some 200 evangelical churches in 17 states across the Southeast, Mid-Atlantic, and Midwest regions of the United States. Between 2003 and 2007, I traveled weekends by motor coach with a gospel singing group and was a participant-observer in more than 250 worship services. My standpoint as an ethnographer may be understood through Gold's (1958) quadrilateral of fieldwork roles. The fieldworker either may assume the standing of a "complete observer" who observes but does not interact, an "observer as participant" who interacts only to collect predetermined types of data such as structured interviews, a "participant as observer" who interacts without an agenda in order to shadow culture members and master their ways, or a "complete participant" who is already a culture member. Having affiliated with evangelicalism for many years following a teenage conversion experience, I conducted my fieldwork as a complete participant. As such, I comprehended the subculture's unarticulated assumptions and elicited candid and spontaneous talk from churchgoers by my ability to speak their evangelical argot. According to Pike's (1971) methodology for emic fieldwork, the test of fieldworkers' analyses is whether or not they have mastered the speech and behavior of a culture to the point of eliciting normal and appropriate reactions from members. Four years on the road rapidly refreshed my mastery, while

I also took field notes and gathered artifacts ranging from weekly church bulletins and prayer sheets to religious tracts and periodicals.

A connection between preachers' rhetorical practices and leadership styles immediately emerged from my observations and figured prominently in the first report of my findings (Ward, 2009b). As I then noted, "the *form* of preaching drove community practice as much, if not more so, than the actual arguments themselves" (p. 9, emphasis in original). Through preaching, clergy drove the logics of their congregations and normalized their sources of persuasion—in itself, a significant source of power to lead. My conclusions on the connection between rhetoric and leadership were summarized thus:

> Expository preaching implicates knowledge discovered through texts, ideology affirmed through deliberation, and performance experienced through cognition. Narrative preaching implicates knowledge discovered through stories, ideology affirmed through identification, and performance experienced through affect. Leaders who practice expository preaching derive their power from the expert authority to delimit the logics of the community. Leaders who practice narrative preaching derive their power from the [referent] authority to validate the stories of the community. (p. 17)

In a subsequent report (Ward, 2010), I affirmed that expository preaching "strives to rationally tease out the meanings of the scriptures, [so that] … the expositor is vested with the expert authority to delimit what passes for rational inquiry." By contrast, narrative preaching "exhorts audiences to govern their self-identities through stories … whose truth is validated by the authority of a speaker vested with [referent power]." Either way, "the preacher is authoritative for setting community norms" and thereby accrues charismatic authority (pp. 120–121). As I reviewed my data, I also began working out an answer to the question addressed by this chapter: To what extent is the preaching practiced in local evangelical churches, and representations of preaching seen and heard by evangelicals in the electronic church, connected? My observations affirmed that the rhetorical practices of expository and narrative preaching, and the charismatic authority they each produce, dominate in local churches as they also do in the electronic church. But does the preaching of "anointed" evangelical media celebrities drive local rhetorical practices as clergy emulate these media representations? Or do media representations merely reflect local rhetorical practices accepted within the evangelical subculture?

EVANGELICALISM AS AN INTERPRETIVE COMMUNITY

After studying the evangelical subculture through its local congregational practices (Ward, 2009b, 2010, 2013b, 2015a, 2015b) and its media establishment (Ward, 1994, 2009a, 2012, 2013a, 2014, 2016a, 2016c, 2016d, 2017), I have come to believe that the respective phenomena of embodied and mediated evangelical experience are, as structuration theory (Giddens, 1984) holds, not a dualism but a duality. American evangelicalism is a system of human practices: Evangelicals structure their institutions, primarily their local churches and their mass media, through their own agency. But in turn, they reproduce those structures by acting within what the structures enable and constrain. Bowler (2013) began her recent study of the prosperity gospel movement with a story that captures this phenomenon:

> The pastor and first lady of the Victorious Faith Center agreed to meet. ... No, the pastor stated firmly, his teachings had no historical precedent; they were born from revelation. This was an independent, nondenominational church built on faith alone. ... [So I tried] a different line of questioning. Where did he go to school? Where did he turn for spiritual inspiration? What ministries did the church support? The hidden structures of the prosperity movement began to emerge. Pastor Walton had spent several years learning from the televangelist host of *Success-N-Life,* Robert Tilton, at his Bible school in Texas. He sustained the momentum of his ministry by reading prosperity publications and by taking intermittent trips to witness divine healer Benny Hinn's crusades. The local church "sows" money like seeds into the international ministries of celebrities like Creflo Dollar, Kenneth Hagin, and Joel Osteen. While Pastor Walton sees his insights and preaching bubbling up from the wellsprings of scripture and personal revelation, in song, sermon, and giving, his Sunday mornings at the Victorious Faith Center also closely resemble thousands of similar churches dotting the American religious landscape. (pp. 3–4)

The same phenomenon is at work in other evangelical traditions. I have observed "King James [Version] Only" fundamentalist churches that gravitate around a vibrant subculture of Bible conferences, Bible colleges, ministerial associations, and the *Sword of the Lord* newspaper. By contrast, a conservative evangelical church might show David Jeremiah preaching videos on Sunday nights to the congregation, Focus on the Family's apologetic "Truth Project" video series to the youth group, and radio preacher Chip Ingraham's *Culture Shock* series to the weekly women's home Bible study, while stocking the church library with books by James Dobson and the literature table with *Our Daily Bread* devotional booklets from RBC (formerly Radio Bible Class) Ministries. Then, too, I have seen televangelists Joyce Meyer and R. W. Schambach pack arenas with Pentecostal believers from scores of local churches who come to speak in tongues, be slain in the spirit, stand in the healing line, and fill shopping bags with books and DVDs from the merchandise table. Such networks may be understood, as I have argued (Ward, 2010), by seeing them as systems of macro, meso, and micro level practices (Figure 9.1).

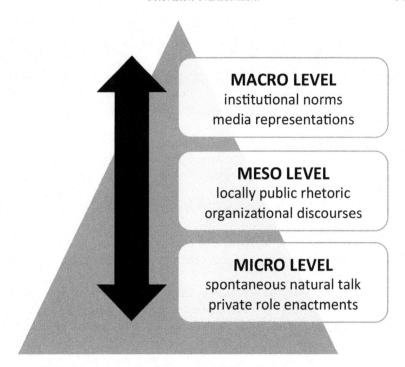

MACRO LEVEL
institutional norms
media representations

MESO LEVEL
locally public rhetoric
organizational discourses

MICRO LEVEL
spontaneous natural talk
private role enactments

Figure 9.1 American Evangelicalism as a Social System.

At the macro level is institutional evangelicalism and its media representations; at the meso level is the planned, locally public rhetoric of Sunday sermons and organizational discourses that transmit cultural norms and structure joint local action; at the micro level is the spontaneous natural talk and private role enactments by which laity reproduce evangelical culture.

Elsewhere I have shown that American evangelicalism may be productively analyzed not only as a historic movement but also as a mediated "interpretive community" (Ward, 2014). My argument begins by distinguishing between the traditional *social interaction* approach to media theory that "distinguishes media in terms of how close they come to the model of face-to-face interaction," and the *social integration* approach that "characterizes media not in terms of information, interaction, or dissemination, but in terms of ritual, or how people use media as a way of creating community" (Littlejohn & Foss, 2011, p. 340). To envision a medium not as a *conduit* but as an *environment* requires a shift in thinking from the modern to the postmodern. The conduit metaphor is grounded in the modern Western concept that messages are products of individual intention and media are instruments by which individuals cause their messages to be transmitted. By contrast, the environment metaphor is rooted in a "decentered" postmodern view in which individuals are seen not as self-contained agents whose intentions are conveyed via a medium; instead, individual subjectivity is seen as an *effect* of the media environment.

In broadcast media, noted Holmes (2005), "Audiences are specific to definite genres and times, and constitute a remarkably high degree of solidarity [that] ... is channeled totemically and ritually through ... the characters, the presenters, the hosts." In turn, "It is through these agents that individual members of a given audience 'interact' with each other" in ritual media occasions that "facilitate a sense of belonging, security and community, even if individuals are not directly interacting." Meanwhile, media presenters "are bestowed with charisma as a reflex of the [audience's] concentration of consciousness in their person" (pp. 147–148). In this way, not only does the rhetorical practices normalized by media preachers implicate a charismatic style of leadership, so does their very presence on television and radio as these celebrities become a ritual focus through which evangelical audiences create community.

A leading theory in the social integration approach to media studies is Lindlof's (1988) concept of interpretive communities, which he constructed from two streams of scholarship. From sociolinguistics, Lindlof took the concept of "speech communities" or groups of people who share common rules for interpreting speech (Hymes, 1962). From the literary theory of Reader Response Criticism, he took the idea that the meaning of a text resides not in the author but in the reader (Fish, 1980). Thus, as I have explained,

> The meaning of talk or of a text, however, is not a purely idiosyncratic, individual construction. Sociolinguistics and Reader Response Criticism both contend that people are situated in communities that share rules of interpretation; meanings are not just individual and thus indeterminate, but become concretized through communal validation. Lindlof's contribution was to import these concepts into media studies. (Ward, 2014, p. 118)

Interpretive communities of media usage, argued Lindlof (1988), "come into being with the typically ritualistic or rule-governed enactment of communicative events whose sense for interlocutors is the sharing of media technologies, content ... and occasions" (p. 92). Watching the nightly programs of a favorite televangelist from the living room sofa, or listening to sermons from an admired radio preacher on the daily commute home from work, is just such ritualistic and rule-governed enactment of communicative events shared by millions of evangelicals. The emergence of an evangelical interpretive community out of the genre audience for religious television and radio is a threefold process.

First, a community arises through its members' shared interpretation of the same media content; second, communal interpretations create a "text" whose intersubjectivity gives the reading historical validity and thus imparts a stabilizing and directing influence; and third, the validated reading becomes a referent for members' social actions within the interpretive community." (Ward, 2014, p. 118)

In this way, Pastor Walton of the Victorious Faith Center, his flock, and thousands of likeminded churches interpret the narrative preaching of televangelists Robert Tilton, Benny Hinn, Creflo Dollar, Kenneth Hagin, Joel Osteen, and others as helping believers attain faith to experience God's prosperity, an interpretation that is communally validated until this rhetorical practice becomes a referent for social action within the community. Similarly, conservative evangelical churches validate the interpretation that the expository preaching of radio's Chuck Swindoll, Charles Stanley, John MacArthur, David Jeremiah, Michael Youssef, and others is "true to the Word" because their sermons focus on propositional truths rather than experiential faith. In the end, institutional media representations of narrative and expository preaching are respectively validated as rhetorical norms of the evangelical subculture. Local pastors who then follow one practice or the other accrue either referent power or expert power that endows them with charismatic authority to lead their congregations.

SOCIAL EFFECTS OF CHARISMATIC LEADERSHIP

After plumbing the macro level of evangelical institutional norms and their media representations, and the meso level of church pastors' locally public rhetoric, the final link in the evangelical social system is the micro level of churchgoers' spontaneous natural talk and private role enactments. Do parishioners' micro practices reproduce the high power distance and sense of empowerment during a time of crisis that would be expected from the followers of charismatic leaders? An answer is suggested by my fieldwork which, like Lindlof's theory, is grounded in sociolinguistics and the concept of speech communities. While Lindlof applied sociolinguistics to mediated communities, its application to on-the-ground fieldwork is called the "ethnography of communication" (Hymes, 1974). Such ethnography elicits how a given speech community constructs a distinctive culture by patterning its talk around shared assumptions regarding the nature of persons, how they should be linked in social relations, and what symbolic actions are efficacious for establishing personhood as defined by the community (Philipsen, 1997).

High power distance in evangelical churches was reified, I observed, through forms of personal address which reflected a cultural assumption that people should be linked in divinely ordered, hierarchical social relations (Ward, 2009b, 2010). In the nearly 200 churches that I visited, the social order was reproduced as the leader was addressed by the honorific titles "Pastor" and "Preacher," men were often addressed as "Brother," and women were customarily addressed collectively as "the ladies." Many churches also interpreted "Body of Christ" as a root metaphor for organizing their congregations along hierarchical lines with the pastor as the "head" of the local church "body" and ordained to lead, and with laity ordained to lesser roles (Ward, 2015a). The divine ordering of relationships extended to a gender hierarchy governed by the rule of "male headship" with the pastor as charismatic paterfamilias, men as lay officers and teachers, and women cast in nurturing roles (Bartkowski, 2001; Bendroth, 1996; Brasher, 1998; Gallagher, 2003; Griffith, 1997; Ingersoll, 2003).

A sense of empowerment amidst crisis was constructed by churchgoers' metacommunication or the designations they gave to different categories of talk that they deemed appropriate for communicating with different categories of people (Ward, 2009b, 2010). "Having fellowship" was the strategy deemed appropriate for communicating with "believers" who are "saved" and thus truly "Christians," while "witnessing" was the strategy appropriate for communicating with "unbelievers" who are "unsaved" and thus "lost." By creating this binary distinction, evangelicals simultaneously empowered themselves as God's elect while implicating a crisis mission to "save" the "lost" before Christ's Second Coming and the imminent apocalypse that evangelicals call the "Great Tribulation." This double move was further reinforced through the rituals of "sharing my testimony" or personal conversion story at a worship service, and of "going witnessing" outside church through the use of highly prescribed methods for "leading people to Christ" and inducing converts to "say the sinner's prayer." These two rituals were powerful symbolic actions by which the faithful established their evangelical personhood.

CONCLUSIONS

Rhetorical practices that construct charismatic leadership are thus an institutional (macro) and local (meso) norm of American evangelicalism, while the social effects of such leadership are reproduced at the private (micro) level of practice. This discovery affirms Jasinski's (2001) observation that "rhetorical practice not only helps to produce judgments about specific issues, it also helps to produce or constitute a social world" (p. 192). This phenomenon operates *locally,* noted Jasinski, in four dimensions as rhetoric dynamically (re)constitutes a community's identity, temporal experience, political culture, and conceptual realm as expressed through language. The present study demonstrates that rhetorical practice also operates *systemically* as its institutional representation, local practice, and private reproduction dynamically interact across the macro, meso, and micro levels of a social system.

The implications of evangelical rhetorical practice and its construction of charismatic leadership as a norm of the subculture's religious life are profound for American civil discourse and its current polarization. In a 2010 survey, a majority (52%) of evangelicals agreed with the statement, "There is a natural conflict between being a religious person and living in modern society," as compared to 34 percent of mainline Protestants and 36 percent of Roman Catholics. A majority (54%) also agreed in a 2007 survey that "My values are threatened by Hollywood." Thus, "evangelicals do report higher levels of tension and conflict from living in contemporary American society" and "are the most likely of the religious traditions examined to report such tension and conflict with the broader culture of which they are a part" (Smidt, 2013, p. 161). A factor in this tension is arguably the charismatic style of evangelical leadership which draws its power by cultivating in followers a sense of crisis for which the charismatic leader's special gifts and radical vision, rather than any dialogue or compromise, are the solution. None, however, should dismiss televangelism (broadly construed) as a purely religious phenomenon. At this writing, Americans have elected their own "televangelist-in-chief" who claims special gifts and a vision for radical change to lead a country in crisis. Will such rhetorical practice gain traction in the nation's political and media institutions? Will it be normalized at the level of local politics? And, ultimately, will it produce in ordinary individuals the sense of societal tension and conflict needed for charismatic leadership to thrive?

REFERENCES

Barna Group (2005). *More people use Christian media than attend church.* Retrieved May 9, 2017, from https://www.barna.com/research/more-people-use-christian-media-than-attend-church/

Bartkowski, J. P. (2001). *Remaking the Godly Marriage: Gender Negotiation in Evangelical Families.* New Brunswick, NJ: Rutgers University Press.

Bendroth, M. L. (1996). *Fundamentalism and Gender, 1875 to the Present.* New Haven, CT: Yale University Press.

Bowler, K. (2013). *Blessed: A History of the American Prosperity Gospel.* New York: Oxford University Press.

Brasher, B. E. (1998). *Godly Women: Fundamentalism and Female Power.* New Brunswick, NJ: Rutgers University Press.

Crawford, D. D. (2010). *A Thirst for Souls: The Life of Evangelist Percy B. Crawford, 1902–1960*. Selinsgrove, PA: Susquehanna University Press.

Duerringer, C. M. (2016). The "war on Christianity" and the construction of identity in evangelical media. In M. Ward Sr. (Ed.), *The Electronic Church in the Digital Age: Cultural Impacts of Evangelical Mass Media, Vol. 2* (pp. 205–225). Santa Barbara, CA: Praeger.

Fish, S. (1980). *Is There a Text in This Class?* Cambridge, MA: Harvard University Press.

French, J. R. P., & Raven, B. (1959). The bases of social power. In D. Cartwright (Ed.), *Studies in Social Power* (pp. 150–167). Ann Arbor, MI: University of Michigan, Institute for Social Research.

Fuller, D. P. (1972). *Give the Winds a Mighty Voice: The Story of Charles E. Fuller*. Waco, TX: Word.

Gallagher, S. K. (2003). *Evangelical Identity and Gendered Family Life*. New Brunswick, NJ: Rutgers University Press.

Giddens, A. (1984). *The Constitution of Society: Outline of the Theory of Structuration*. Berkeley, CA: University of California Press.

Gold, R. L. (1958). Roles in sociological field observations. *Social Forces, 36,* 217–223.

Griffith, R. M. (1997). *God's Daughters: Evangelical Women and the Power of Submission*. Berkeley, CA: University of California Press.

Hangen, T. J. (2002). *Redeeming the Dial: Radio, Religion, and Popular Culture in America*. Chapel Hill, NC: University of North Carolina Press.

Hjarvard, S. (2008). The mediatization of society. *Nordicom Review, 29,* 105–134.

Holmes, D. (2005). *Communication theory: Media, Technology, and Society*. Thousand Oaks, CA: Sage.

Hoover, S. M. (1988). *Mass Media Religion: The Social Sources of the Electronic Church*. Newbury Park, CA: Sage.

Horton, D., & Wohl, R. (1956). Mass communication and para-social interaction: Observations on intimacy at a distance. *Psychiatry, 19,* 215–229.

Hymes, D. (1962). The ethnography of speaking. In T. Gladwin & W. C. Sturtevant (Eds.), *Anthropology and Human Behavior* (pp. 13–53). Washington, DC: Anthropological Society of Washington.

Hymes, D. (1974). *Foundations in Sociolinguistics: An Ethnographic Approach*. Philadelphia, PA: University of Pennsylvania Press.

Ingersoll, J. (2003). *Evangelical Christian Women: War Stories in the Gender Battles*. New York: New York University Press.

Jasinski, J. (2001). *Sourcebook on Rhetoric: Key Concepts in Contemporary Rhetorical Studies*. Thousand Oaks, CA: Sage.

Lindlof, T. R. (1988). Media audiences as interpretive communities. In J. A. Anderson (Ed.), *Communication Yearbook 11* (pp. 81–107). Newbury Park, CA: Sage.

Lindlof, T. R. (2002). Interpretive community: An approach to media and religion. *Journal of Media and Religion, 1,* 61–74.

Lindsay, D. M. (2007). *Faith in the Halls of Power: How Evangelicals Joined the American Elite*. New York: Oxford University Press.

Littlejohn, S. W., & Foss, K. A. (2011). *Theories of Human Communication* (10th ed.). Long Grove, IL: Waveland.

Lövheim, M. (2011). Mediatization of religion: A critical appraisal. *Culture and Religion, 12,* 153–166.

McLuhan, M. (1964). *Understanding Media: The Extensions of Man.* New York: McGraw-Hill.

Melton, J. G., Lucas, P. C., & Stone, J. R. (Eds.). (1997). *Prime-Time Religion: An Encyclopedia of Religious Broadcasting.* Phoenix, AZ: Oryx.

Moen, M. C. (1994). From revolution to evolution: The changing nature of the Christian right. *Sociology of Religion, 55,* 345–357.

NCTA: The Internet and Television Association (2017). *Industry data.* Retrieved May 9, 2017, from https://www.ncta.com/industry-data

Pew Research Center (2015). *America's changing religious landscape.* Retrieved May 9, 2017, from http://assets.pewresearch.org/wp-content/uploads/sites/11/2015/05/RLS-08-26-full-report.pdf

Philipsen, G. (1997). A theory of speech codes. In T. L. Albrecht & G. Philipsen (Eds.), *Developing Communication Theories* (pp. 119–156). Albany, NY: State University of New York Press.

Pike, K. L. (1971). *Language in Relation to a Unified Theory of the Structure of Human Behavior* (2nd rev. ed.). The Hague: Mouton.

Postman, N. (1985). *Amusing Ourselves to Death: Public Discourse in the Age of Show Business.* New York: Penguin.

Rodrigues, R., Green, J., & Virshup, L. (2013). *Radio Today: How America Listens to Radio, 2013 edition.* Columbia, MD: Arbitron.

Schultz, B. E. (2000). The effects of digital environments on religious television stations. *Journal of Communication and Religion, 23,* 50–71.

Schultz, B. E. (2005). The economic response of religious television stations to digital implementation. *Journal of Communication and Religion, 28,* 307–325.

Sleasman, B. C. (2016). The medium is the ministry: Televangelism and the electronic age church. In M. Ward Sr. (Ed.), *The Electronic Church in the Digital Age: Cultural Impacts of Evangelical Mass Media, Vol. 1* (pp. 127–149). Santa Barbara, CA: Praeger.

Smidt, C. (2013). *American Evangelicals Today.* Lanham, MD: Rowman & Littlefield.

Smith, C. (1998). *American Evangelicalism: Embattled and Thriving.* Chicago, IL: University of Chicago Press.

Smith, G. A., & Martinez, J. (2016). *How the faithful voted: A preliminary 2016 analysis.* Pew Research Center, November 9, 2016. Retrieved May 9, 2017, from http://www.pewresearch.org/fact-tank/2016/11/09/how-the-faithful-voted-a-preliminary-2016-analysis/

Stephens, R. J., & Giberson, K. (2011). *The Anointed: Evangelical Truth in a Secular Age.* Cambridge, MA: Harvard University Press.

Stout, D. A. (2016). Foreword. In M. Ward Sr. (Ed.), *The Electronic Church in the Digital Age: Cultural Impacts of Evangelical Mass Media, Vol. 1* (pp. ix–xiv). Santa Barbara, CA: Praeger.

Trammell, J. Y. (2016). Jesus? There's an app for that! Tablet media in the "new" electronic church. In M. Ward Sr. (Ed.), *The Electronic Church in the Digital Age: Cultural Impacts of Evangelical Mass Media, Vol. 1* (pp. 219–237). Santa Barbara, CA: Praeger.

Trice, H. M., & Beyer, J. M. (1993). *The Cultures of Work Organizations.* Englewood Cliffs, NJ: Prentice Hall.

Ward, M., Sr. (1994). *Air of Salvation: The Story of Christian Broadcasting.* Grand Rapids, MI: Baker.

Ward, M., Sr. (2009a). Dark preachers: The impact of radio consolidation on independent religious syndicators. *Journal of Media and Religion, 8,* 79–96.

Ward, M., Sr. (2009b). Fundamentalist differences: Using ethnography of rhetoric to analyze a community of practice. *Intercultural Communication Studies, 18,* 1–20.

Ward, M., Sr. (2010). "I was saved at an early age": An ethnography of fundamentalist speech and cultural performance. *Journal of Communication and Religion, 33,* 108–144.

Ward, M., Sr. (2012). Consolidating the gospel: The impact of the 1996 Telecommunications Act on religious radio ownership. *Journal of Media and Religion, 11,* 11–30.

Ward, M., Sr., (2013a). Air of the king: Evangelicals and radio. In R. H. Woods Jr. (Ed.), *Evangelical Christians and Popular Culture: Pop Goes the Gospel, Vol. 1* (pp. 101–118). Santa Barbara, CA: Praeger.

Ward, M., Sr. (2013b). Managing the anxiety and uncertainty of religious otherness: Interfaith dialogue as a problem of intercultural communication. In D. S. Brown Jr. (Ed.), *A Communication Perspective on Interfaith Dialogue* (pp. 23–43). Lanham, MD: Lexington.

Ward, M., Sr. (2014). Give the winds a mighty voice: Evangelical culture as radio ecology. *Journal of Radio and Audio Media, 21,* 115–133.

Ward, M., Sr. (2015a). Organization and religion: Ontological, epistemological, and axiological foundations for an emerging field. *Journal of Communication and Religion, 38,* 5–29.

Ward, M., Sr. (2015b). Cognition, culture, and charity: Sociolinguistics and "donor dissonance" in a Baptist denomination. *Voluntas: International Journal of Voluntary and Nonprofit Organizations, 26,* 574–603.

Ward, M., Sr. (2016a). Televangelism, audience fragmentation, and the changing coverage of scandal. In H. Mandell & G. M. Chen (Eds.), *Scandal in a Digital Age* (pp. 53–68). New York: Palgrave MacMillan.

Ward, M., Sr. (2016b). Major networks and personalities. In M. Ward Sr. (Ed.), *The Electronic Church in the Digital Age: Cultural Impacts of Evangelical Mass Media, Vol. 1* (pp. 255–284). Santa Barbara, CA: Praeger.

Ward, M., Sr. (Ed.). (2016c). *The Electronic Church in the Digital Age: Cultural Impacts of Evangelical Mass Media, Vol. 1: How Evangelical Media Shape Evangelical Culture.* Santa Barbara, CA: Praeger.

Ward, M., Sr. (Ed.). (2016d). *The Electronic Church in the Digital Age: Cultural Impacts of Evangelical Mass Media, Vol. 2: How Evangelical Media Engage American Culture.* Santa Barbara, CA: Praeger.

Ward, M., Sr. (2017). *The Lord's Radio: Gospel Music Broadcasting and the Making of Evangelical Culture, 1920–1960.* Jefferson, NC: McFarland.

Winzenburg, S. (2005). TV ministries use of air time, Fall 2004. Retrieved May 9, 2017, from http://faculty.grandview.edu/swinzenburg/tv_ministries_study.pdf

Worthen, M. (2013). *Apostles of Reason: The Crisis of Authority in American Evangelicalism.* New York: Oxford University Press.

Chapter 10

Self-disclosure and Leadership

An Examination of Workplace Privacy Rules and Boundaries for Leadership in Brooklyn Nine-Nine

Donna M. Elkins

Communication scholars have long pointed to self-disclosure as a key communicative behavior for building and maintaining both personal and professional relationships. Communication has been understood as the background by which we can understand human beings and the way they function in organizations. Some scholars have gone so far as to say that "management is communication" (Gibson & Hodgetts, 1985, p. 41). Leaders who reveal goals, motives, intentions, values, and even emotions can increase subordinates' liking. "There is considerable evidence that leaders who disclose their authentic selves to followers can build not only trust, but generate greater cooperation and teamwork as well" (Offermann & Rosh, 2012, p. 1). Self-disclosure can humanize a leader, increasing feelings of trust and intimacy and a readiness to work together collaboratively. However, there is long-standing uncertainty about the appropriate breadth and depth of that communication. Successful self-disclosure from leaders requires strategy. Used incorrectly, or without understanding of cultural norms in the workplace, self-disclosure can backfire. It is important to consider depth, breadth, and timing of self-disclosure with a clear "goal of furthering the collective task rather than furthering personal agendas" (Offermann & Rosh, 2012, p. 2). Intensely personal disclosures even when couched in metaphor or humor can be off-putting to subordinates, while too little disclosure may increase uncertainty and suspicion among coworkers or subordinates (Offermann & Rosh, 2012).

Social penetration theory posits that as members of a relationship disclose more in breadth of topics and depth of feeling, relationships increase in intimacy (Altman & Taylor, 1973; Hesse & Rauscher, 2013). One important element noted in this theory is that increased intimacy comes when disclosure includes emotion. Emotional disclosure has been found to be psychologically and physically healthy and improve relationships (Hesse & Rauscher, 2013).

However, in emotionally charged occupations such as law enforcement, health care, or firefighting, organizational members must not only manage their own emotional reactions, but monitor carefully how they disclose these emotions to clients and coworkers, frequently in the face of life-threatening events. These workers have "a particularly difficult charge as they labor to communicate with calmness and competence in emotionally-volatile circumstances that require precision, skillfulness, and speed" to manage their own emotions and those they serve (Scott & Myers, 2005, p. 68).

Disclosure in general can be motivated by a need for catharsis (Kennedy-Lightsey, Martin, Thompson, Himes, & Clingerman, 2012). Sharing personal information creates a bond between the discloser and recipient (Petronio, 2002), but relationships can also terminate over private information revealed outside of the relationship (Kennedy-Lightsey, et al., 2012). Despite its positive relational benefits, the act of disclosure is associated with numerous negative emotions such as fear of rejection, stress, and anxiety (Hesse & Rauscher, 2013), fear of creating a negative impression, losing autonomy and/or losing influence in a relationship (Kennedy-Lightsey, et al., 2012), and the impact of displaying feelings or thoughts upon the ability to deliver adequate service to clients in the workplace (Scott & Myers, 2005). In other words, risks can outweigh benefits, especially in new or limited relationships or in workplaces that require intense emotional management.

COMMUNICATION PRIVACY MANAGEMENT THEORY

As study of self-disclosure evolved from Altman and Taylor's (1973) model of social penetration (relationships become more intimate as partners disclose more breadth and depth of topics), one primary question became how individuals decide when to disclose and when to keep information private. Sandra Petronio's Communication Privacy Management Theory (CPM) is an excellent theoretical frame for examining self-disclosure in leadership positions. CPM conceptualizes disclosure as a dialectical tension wherein an individual is constantly struggling with decisions about what to reveal and conceal (Hesse & Rauscher, 2013). In CPM, disclosure is not defined as what is revealed but as "the process of telling" (Petronio, Helft, & Child, 2013, p. 176). In any relationship, disclosure of private information must be balanced against the perceived costs and benefits received from sharing, but for leaders this tension is even stronger when facing difficult decisions about when to share or allow others to co-own private information with them (Petronio, 2007, 2013; Petronio, et al., 2013).

Underpinning CPM is "the dialectical assumption that people need to be both social (through disclosing) and private (through protecting) simultaneously leading them to make choices about when to protect and when to tell" (Petronio, et al., 2013, p. 176). Fundamentally, CPM relies on an individual's belief that he or she owns private information, thus believing in the right to control the flow of this information to others, and therefore creating privacy rules to decide whether to open privacy boundaries for disclosure or close privacy boundaries for concealment. Once the information is revealed, he or she has made others "authorized co-owners" of this information and assumes these co-owners will follow existing privacy rules or openly negotiate different rules (Petronio, 2013, p. 10; Thompson, Petronio, & Braithwaite, 2012). If there is a disruption in the coordination of these privacy rules or when someone's privacy boundary is blatantly violated, the result is boundary turbulence such as "mistrust, anger, suspicion, or uncertainty about sharing private information" (Petronio, 2007, p. 219).

The goal of CPM is not only to offer a theoretical perspective for understanding the tension between revealing and concealing private information, but also to predict how privacy rules are created with the objective of providing solutions, solving problems, and creating a new way of processing when people face violations of privacy and trust (Petronio, 2007; Thompson, et al., 2012). Petronio, Helft, and Child (2013) define private information as "information that has the potential to yield vulnerabilities if shared with others" (p. 176). Everyone may have a different sense of what is private. Once people start to manage and regulate information for who can know, how much they can know, and how freely they can share the information with others, they are establishing privacy rules and this signals that the information is private for that individual because it carries potential vulnerability.

To build the privacy rules, individuals use decision criteria such as motivations to reveal or conceal, cultural values, the situation or context, gender norms, a risk-benefit ratio (Flaherty, 2006; Kennedy-Lightsey, et al., 2012; Thompson, et al., 2012), family teachings about the concept of privacy (Serewicz, 2013), individual privacy orientation traits, anticipated boundary turbulence, emotional competence (Hesse & Rauscher, 2013), cognitive fluency which is the level of ease or difficulty associated with processing information, environmental cues such as whether the venue seems private, prevailing laws that encourage disclosure (Alter & Oppenheimer, 2009), desire to keep a competitive edge by refusing to share useful information (Gibson & Hodgetts, 1985), and trust based on the previous relationship with the recipient (Hesse & Rauscher, 2013; Myers & Johnson, 2004). "Parents and family members are often the first teachers of the concept of privacy, in socializing children into societal expectations for privacy in terms of information ... bodily privacy ... and physical/environmental privacy" (Serewicz,

2013, p. 2). As they grow, children look to peers, friendships, school and mediated communication to grow their concept of privacy (Serewicz, 2013). Individual privacy orientations or general tendencies based on overall trust are developed from these influences and "through a combination of criteria including gender, cultural, context, motivations, and assessments of risks and benefits" (Hesse & Rauscher, 2013, p. 94).

A CASE STUDY OF CAPTAIN RAY HOLT IN *BROOKLYN NINE-NINE*

Analyzing a case study of a leader called upon to face the tensions related to sharing private information and navigate the rules of privacy in a challenging work setting is a productive way to examine privacy management in the workplace. Captain Raymond Jacob "Ray" Holt (portrayed by Andre Braugher) in the American police sitcom *Brooklyn Nine-Nine*[1] is such a case. As the show opens, Holt has just taken command of a police unit and as someone who has a heightened privacy orientation due to his past personal experiences on the police force, he is faced right away with tensions related to sharing private information with his new squad. Members of the squad, like those in most work settings, vary as to their interest in and desire to become recipients of the Captain's private information. As the series has developed over four seasons, the viewer can trace progression in the Captain's willingness to disclose and his ongoing navigation of privacy rules and boundary turbulence with subordinates as their relationships deepen.

Captain Holt's character is introduced in the first season as the new captain for the 99th Precinct and he attempts from the beginning to create a more structured, rule-bound atmosphere for the mad-cap group of police detectives on his force. Part of his method in creating the more formal working environment is selectively guarding his private life, his emotional state, and his history in the police department. Gradually over time, the detectives working for him discover more and more information about him, either through his self-disclosure or through their own detective skills. Some members of the team such as Detective Jake Peralta (Andy Samberg) and Detective Amy Santiago (Melissa Fumero) are determined to know him better and to discover private details about his life in part because of his reticence to share. Others like Sergeant Terry Jeffords (Terry Crews) and Detective Rosa Diaz (Stephanie Beatriz) admire him more because of his compartmentalization of his private life from his work and strive to maintain that distance, not only reluctant to be recipients of disclosure, but also closely guarding private information of their own.

NAVIGATING PRIVACY BOUNDARIES
FROM THE INITIAL INTERACTION

In the pilot episode of *Brooklyn Nine-Nine*, the viewers are introduced to the characters of the 99th Precinct and the new captain. Early in the episode, the scene is a morning briefing with all detectives present and the expectations for the new leader are heightened right away with inquiries directed at learning more about him. This leads to discussion among those in the precinct about what they expect the new leader to be like as they also recount what they liked or did not like about the previous captain. Detective Jake Peralta asserts, "The new one is going to be another washed-up pencil pusher concerned with following every rule in the patrol guide." He inserts robot noises and says, "Robot Captain engage." Without his knowledge, Captain Holt has come to stand right behind him during this display. The first words, the Captain speaks are, "Don't let me interrupt. You were describing what kind of Captain I'm going to be. I'd like you to finish."

Immediately the detectives note that their new Captain displays no emotions, no facial expression or vocal emphasis, even when in a situation where it is surmised that he is displeased.

"Everyone I'm your new commanding officer Ray Holt," he introduces himself.

"Speech!" Detective Amy Santiago chants.

"That was my speech," Holt replies and walks into his office.

Sergeant Terry Jeffords joins Holt in his office to orient him to the precinct. In an unusual bout of self-disclosure, Terry begins with an explanation of why he is now on desk duty and no longer goes into the field. He shares some depth of his feelings and anxieties, along with his psychological status, right away. Normally one might expect a statement of sympathy, an acknowledgment of the depth of this information, or the norm of reciprocity for personal disclosure to impact Holt's reaction, but it does not. He simply asks for a briefing about each of the detectives. To smooth over frustrations about having a new captain, Terry shares with the squad information he knows about Captain Holt solving a prominent case early in his career and arresting the Disco Strangler. While Jake and Amy are on a stakeout with the Captain later, Jake uses this information outside of the expected privacy rule boundaries to prompt Holt to share more about his past, asking why it took so long for him to get his first command after solving such a high-profile case.

"Because I'm gay," Holt responds promptly. The detectives laugh nervously and Jake says, "Seriously?"

"I'm surprised you didn't know," Holt says. "I don't try to hide it."

Amy asks when he came out. "About 25 years ago. The NYPD was not ready for an openly gay detective but then the old guard died out. Suddenly, they couldn't wait to show they had a highly ranking gay officer. I made Captain, but they put me in a public affairs unit. I was a good soldier. I helped recruitment. But all I ever wanted was my own command and now I finally got it and I'm not gonna screw it up," Holt replies.

WORKPLACE CULTURE AND SUBORDINATE NEEDS AS VARIABLES IN LEADER DISCLOSURE

Those in subordinate roles are likely to find relationships less satisfying and have higher levels of reluctance to receive information from those in a powerful or supervisory role (Sidelinger, Nyeste, Madlock, Pollak, & Wilkinson, 2015). Reluctant confidants receive information they find undesirable and/or are not prepared to manage (Petronio, 2002, 2007). Leaders therefore must consider not only their own need or desire to share information, but also the mindset and preparedness of their subordinates to co-own this information. The case for open, candid communication is strong, but open communication is not always possible or even desirable (Gibson & Hodgetts, 1985), especially in emotionally charged and dangerous occupations such as law enforcement or firefighting where members often "compartmentalize their emotions in order to prevent them from interfering with daily activities" (Scott & Myers, 2005, p. 73). Will the proposed self-disclosure enhance subordinates' workplace abilities, give them greater understanding of the goals or mission or individual personality of the leader, or instead simply confuse and perhaps create an atmosphere of lowered trust and productivity?

A recurring theme in the *Brooklyn Nine-Nine* workplace, where detectives' job is in part to encourage suspects and witnesses to talk, is an admiration for those who hold their tongues about private issues and a reluctance to share or receive personal information from coworkers. Both Terry and Rosa demonstrate this reluctance in multiple episodes. In season 4, episode 11, "The Fugitive Parts 1 & 2," Marshawn Lynch, a professional football player known for his unwillingness to talk to the media, makes a guest appearance. When Lynch is one of two witnesses to a prison van break, Rosa and Captain Holt must interview him to get information. Rosa is excited when she finds out he is one of the witnesses, "You're not getting anything out of him. He's always getting fined for refusing to talk to the press. He's one of my heroes," she tells the Captain with a large smile.

"It might be tough and it may take a while but I'm sure we'll get him to open up," Holt replies.

"Sir, there are some vaults you just can't open," Rosa says with admiration. But she is wrong. When they begin to interview Lynch he has nothing to say about the incident, but he prattles on about his lunch and childhood stories until Rosa begs him to stop and loses the respect she had for him.

In contrast to their reluctant confidant coworkers, Jake and Amy are determined to find out more about their boss. Jake finds an effective means of getting Holt to share things he normally would not by asking him questions when they are in times of high stress such as waiting to make arrests or go into dangerous situations. When Holt and Jake are alone on a stakeout at a railyard waiting for a suspect to appear, Jake quickly asks, "What cute little nickname do you call your husband?" Immediately Holt replies, "Kevin." Instead of chastising Jake for asking a personal question or refusing to answer as he usually would, Holt responds immediately because of the tense setting.

Again, in a squad car waiting to go and arrest a perpetrator (another high stress situation), Holt discloses his personal reasons for displaying an unusual amount of anger toward others at work. Holt admits he acted rashly in fighting off three muggers one morning on the street like he was a young man and realizes he could have been seriously hurt. Not only did he act rashly, but he lied to his husband about the whole incident. Though he took it out on the staff, he admits he truly was mad at himself. Rather than creating a rift between Jake and Holt, these interchanges that emerge in moments of stress seem to bring them into a closer relationship and deeper understanding of one another as predicted by Social Penetration Theory.

PRIVACY RULES AND BOUNDARY TURBULENCE IN WORKPLACE VS. PERSONAL RELATIONSHIPS

Boundary coordination often requires explicit and clear communication between individuals about who should or should not have access to the shared information. It allows individuals to satisfy the tensions they experience when wanting to protect risky information, but also desiring to receive the benefits of disclosure. Without a formal statement of the rules, however, the co-owner or recipient of the disclosure is left to make judgments of his or her own about when to share and how to use what they know. Those judgments will likely be based on previous experiences or personal criteria. As the risk level of the information increases, so do boundary coordination efforts, especially in longer friendships (Kennedy-Lightsey, et al., 2012). Boundary turbulence occurs when information is shared with others with whom the original discloser did not want to share. This can occur when the co-owner fails to follow the established or implied rules, an outsider breaches the boundary without permission (such as overhearing) or an outsider pressures the co-owner to reveal the information (Kennedy-Lightsey, et al., 2012).

Season 2 of *Brooklyn Nine-Nine* finds the coworkers becoming more familiar with each other and with their new leader. Episode 2, "Chocolate Milk," opens with detectives overhearing a private conversation Terry is having at his desk about scheduling an appointment. When pressed, he admits he is making an appointment to have a vasectomy after he and his wife had twin girls. The resultant puns and Jake's desperate attempts to keep him from having the operation are evidence of the turbulence arising from a boundary breach. Terry more than once points out that Jake is a work colleague and "not that kind of friend." "You and I are work friends, not 'friend' friends," he insists when Jake offers to drive him to the doctor's appointment. Jake's attempts to insert himself into Terry's personal medical decision are made in part to present himself as a "'friend' friend."

The episodes in the second season continue to offer more insight into the personal life of Raymond Holt even as this divide between professional work relationships and friendships is explored further. In episode 16, "The Wednesday Incident," Holt is uncharacteristically cold and dismissive at work, yelling at detectives to remove all personal items from their desks, turning their cases over to other departments, and cancelling overtime. Most of the office, even Terry, is reticent to ask what is wrong, but Jake approaches Holt to ask why he is in a bad mood and is immediately rebuffed.

"Have I not been bursting into song enough for you lately? Would you like me to click my heels together or skip like a school child?" Holt asks. When pressed further, Holt continues, "Peralta, I'm not going to discuss my home life with you. We're not friends, we're not family, you're not my husband."

Jake is determined to find out what is going on in the Captain's personal life so he can "fix" the unhappiness at work. He and Gina Linetti (Holt's assistant played by Chelsea Peretti) go to visit Holt's husband, Kevin, and find that Holt has been happy at home. Nothing has happened there. But they pinpoint the time and day that he began to show anger at work and decide, with Kevin, to retrace his steps that morning. They visit three locations and talk to people there about Holt's movements on the morning in question and at the final location, his fencing class, find out that he has been lying about going to the class three mornings a week. Kevin is visibly upset by this finding and leaves immediately.

Jake and Gina realize they have stepped over a boundary. "You meddled in his marriage with possible long-term repercussions," Gina tells Jake. Jake sees he is on dangerous ground but finds a sidewalk security camera along the route that Holt traveled that morning and can't resist watching the footage to see what actually happened. He sees that Holt was followed and pushed into an alley by three men. He assumes Holt was mugged and immediately goes to tell Kevin this news, again breaking a privacy boundary. While he is there, Holt returns home and catches him telling Kevin about the incident. In reality Holt was not mugged, he fought off all three attackers, but was "lightly stabbed" in the activity. Kevin is outraged that Holt hid this from him though Holt tries to explain it was because he didn't want to alarm his spouse. Jake again realizes he has inserted himself too deeply into the relationship.

"What you have done is beyond unprofessional. You cannot muck around in people's private lives. Get out of my house!" Holt tells him sternly. This creates an uncomfortable barrier between Holt and Jake at work. Jake feels he can't ask or say anything personal to Holt. He finally alleviates the discomfort and heals the relationship by finding one of the muggers and taking Holt with him to make the arrest.

The exploration of workplace versus personal relationships continues in yet a third episode in season 2, episode 12, "Beach House." This episode shines light on the relationship between coworkers and between coworkers and their leader in general. The detectives are going for a long weekend retreat vacation to one of the detective's beach houses; however, Jake feels sorry that Holt is not invited when Holt shares with him that he was never included in these types of getaways as a detective because of his race (African American) and sexual orientation and always wished he could go and "josh around." Without the knowledge or consent of his fellow detectives, Jake invites Holt to join them and the weekend of drunken games they had anticipated is ruined. The detectives are uncomfortable in bathing suits in front of the Captain, are forced to go on a long walk on the frigid beach at his request, and listen to his boring choice of music and old stories instead of having the drinking games they planned. Jake decides the best way to handle this is to have two parties in the same house, one fun loose one downstairs and another "boring" one with Holt at the same time. Holt realizes what is happening and apologizes for ruining their weekend. The solution they reach is to play a game poking fun at Holt and his stilted phrases, playing "Real Ray vs. Fake Ray." Jake reads a series of long formal phrases and the others decide if Holt said it or not. Holt joins in the fun, making great sport of himself and his stilted opinions.

DISFLUENCY AND LEADERS' EMOTIONAL DISCLOSING

Alter and Oppenheimer (2009) found that people are less willing to disclose potentially damaging information about themselves when they experience disfluency (unease or difficulty processing information). Alter and Oppenheimer found that disfluency did lead participants to hide their flaws and to think more readily about risk and concern. Disfluency leads individuals to have less confidence and heightened vigilance, in other words, increasing the perception of risk associated with sharing negative information (or information that is perceived as negative). Ironically, this disfluency might lead participants to more strongly desire social support, while in turn increasing caution when disclosing information in order to make a favorable impression (Alter & Oppenheimer, 2009).

Throughout the pilot episode Holt asks that Jake wear a tie. Jake reacts to this in all manner of passive-aggressive ways (such as wearing the tie tied around his stomach under his shirt or wearing a tie but no pants). When Holt asks the detectives if they understand why everyone wearing a tie is so important to him, they have no answer and he does not provide one. By the end of the episode, after Jake has prompted Holt's disclosure about his difficulty in rising to Captain because of his race and sexual orientation and the squad has come together to make an arrest of a dangerous criminal, Jake suddenly realizes why Holt cares so much about him wearing a tie. Jake shouts to the others that because Holt was kept off the team for so long, now he wants them all to wear the same team uniform as an outward visual of their connection. As a new leader, Holt could not communicate this clearly to his team right away but through a progression of disclosure about his background and shared activity, Holt and Jake processed this information together into a common conclusion.

Holt's background of denied inclusion and his need to be part of a team create disfluency as a theme in other episodes during the first season. In the Christmas episode, Jake becomes Holt's personal security guard after the Captain receives a series of death threats. Holt says that he chose Jake for this role because he assumed Jake would not follow the rules and would let him come and go as he pleased. He also cautions Jake sternly not to share the threats with anyone else in the precinct because he does not want to alarm the rest of the squad. However, Jake chastises him for not wanting to approach these very real threats as a team which he would if it was anyone else but himself in need.

"I don't need everyone's help ... I brought this situation on myself. No one should get hurt because of a mistake I made as a brash, young detective," Holt argues. But Jake calls him to remember that he is no longer required to do things alone as he did in the past, now that he has an expert team to help him and they want to help him.

In an episode titled "The Party," Jake uncovers that Holt's husband, Kevin, a professor at Columbia University, has a "no cop talk policy" in their home, not because he doesn't care about police work, but because he holds deep resentment against the NYPD for the years that Holt was shunned or pushed aside. In this episode, Kevin sends an invitation to the detectives of the *Nine-Nine* to attend Holt's birthday party. Initially, the detectives believe Holt doesn't want them to come because the invitation came from his husband. Being in Holt's home with a crowd of his friends (all high-class educated individuals), the detectives flounder into more personal facts about Holt. Amy takes pictures of his cabinets and appliances trying to find things they have in common. Jake lies about reading the *New Yorker* to impress Kevin and all hear how Kevin and Holt met during a phone interview for a research project in which Holt made Kevin laugh. Members of the crowd attest to how funny Holt is and the detectives struggle to see him in a light so different from their own experience of his emotionless responses. The true surprise about Holt comes as Jake, Amy, and Terry hide in his bedroom and overhear an argument between Holt and Kevin about how the detectives are affecting the party. Kevin says they are ruining the evening and Holt says Kevin is acting like a snob toward them. They also overhear that, despite what they had thought, Holt made his husband invite them.

"I made you invite them because I like them. They're good people," Holt says, although it is clear that he would never have given this acknowledgment if he had known they were present.

When Holt later calls off a trip to visit Kevin in Paris (Season 3, Episode 18, Cheddar) because his dog sitter cancelled and his home has no heat, Jake volunteers himself, Amy, and another detective to do the house sitting. But when the dog Cheddar runs away before Holt even gets on the plane, he comes home immediately to search for him. When they find Cheddar, Holt engages in perhaps the deepest emotional disclosure he has offered to date.

On his knees in the grass, petting Cheddar's head, Holt admits, "Kevin and I are having a hard time right now. Whenever we talk, we fight and I'm just afraid. I'm just afraid if I go to Paris and we fight, then" This emotional admission creates a visible discomfort in Jake and Amy who quickly try to deny the possible extent of the relational break and encourage Holt about the strength of his relationship. These examples demonstrate the type of struggles leaders face when experiencing disfluency and striving to balance the need for support with maintenance of a positive impression among their subordinates.

OUTCOMES OF BOUNDARY TURBULENCE

"Once information is shared with a friend, however, the original owner no longer has sole control over its dispersion. In an effort to maintain some degree of control over the information, friends develop privacy rules prior to an initial disclosure and coordinate boundaries with co-owners after an initial disclosure," Petronio has stated (as cited in Kennedy-Lightsey, et al., 2012, p. 666). Metaphorically, think of the private information as housed within a privacy boundary and others can only gain entrance if the boundary is opened to them. Once individuals have access behind the privacy boundary, there is an expectation that they will abide by the same privacy rules held by the owner, but recipients may not coordinate these rules with the original owner, might not be able to follow them, might choose not to follow them, or might make mistakes about what privacy rules are appropriate. In such cases, the result is privacy turbulence (Thompson, et al., 2012).

A former colleague and nemesis of Holt's, Madeline Wuntch (portrayed by Kyra Sedgewick) arrives in season 2 to evaluate the precinct. Amy assists Holt in preparing for the review, but when it becomes clear that Wuntch is not going to give them a positive review no matter what they do, Holt recounts his history with her to Amy, disclosing that he rebuffed her sexual advances years ago and told her he was gay. He is certain that she has been out to damage his career for that reason. Holt shares this information with Amy only because he sees it as required for them to do the evaluation work together. However, Amy uses that information to visit the NYPD records and find an old recommendation letter that Wuntch had written for him after the encounter between them. She discovers that Wuntch actually wrote a positive review about him and brings this forward in front of them both, forcing Holt and Wuntch into an uncomfortable personal discussion that includes a list of all of the things they hold against each other. Amy and Gina are present for this interchange and both are obviously embarrassed, looking down to avoid eye contact, and leaving the room as soon as possible. Though Holt does not chastise her for it, Amy has breeched his expected privacy boundaries by engaging with the information he shared in ways he did not intend. Though he does not require it, she apologizes for this breech of expectation in an attempt to maintain the relationship.

CONCLUSION

Privacy management is an ongoing negotiation between those in a relationship, especially in a workplace relationship between a leader and subordinates. Therefore, even a selection of disclosures between individuals over time does not capture the process in its entirety. Boundaries expand and contract, suggesting that over time, in different circumstances and with different relationships privacy management, boundaries may change (Kennedy-Lightsey, et al., 2012).

Stephanie Brody (2013), a practicing psychologist, wrote about the vulnerability she experienced and the reaction of patients to her disclosure of a personal medical event. Even though she did conceal many aspects of the event, she knew she could not conceal all because of evident physical changes.

> This is what I have come to know. Within our field, there is an absence. There are no rules for public disclosure; there is no framework within which to

understand and explore the source of a colleague's curiosity or fantasy, or a distortion rumor about another colleague. Once the information was out of my mouth, there could be no guarantees or assurances. (Brody, 2013, p. 56)

Likewise, leaders in many types of organizations navigate the difficult tensions between sharing private information and maintaining the trust of subordinates and colleagues as if balancing on a tightrope. Once the information is shared, they may lose most control over how privacy rules will be maintained by the recipient and how the information will be viewed or shared. If they refuse to share any private information, those who work for them may perceive them to be secretive or untrustworthy.

As the case of Captain Ray Holt, leader of the Brooklyn 99 police division portrays, leaders make difficult decisions about how much and when to disclose private information about their past and their emotional present to build effective working relationships with their subordinates. For Holt, his carefully balanced disclosures have led to a deeper intimacy and friendship with his subordinates. His example demonstrates that when faced with times of stress or duress, leaders may be more open to disclosing, especially if pressed by subordinates in the heat of the moment. However, subordinates must also be called to account if they mettle too deeply into leaders' personal lives or use private information shared with them to interfere in workplace decisions. One aspect of leadership that many leaders may not be prompted to consider deeply enough before taking on the mantle of leader is how to navigate the boundaries of disclosing enough to build trust among their workers and yet maintain the respect of those who serve with them. As CPM theorizes, the co-ownership and navigation of boundaries is often not discussed at all in a relationship until after a perceived violation of trust occurs. As relationships build and leaders become a true and active part of their team, the interactions they have with others become more collegial in nature and the hierarchy of leadership can be leveled or dismissed. This, then, is where oversharing private information becomes an even larger issue.

Captain Ray Holt is an African American homosexual male interacting with male and female subordinates who are all younger heterosexuals. Flaherty (2006) argues that female leaders face added layers of vulnerability that affect their comfort with disclosure. Holt also has added layers of vulnerability that are repeatedly portrayed in his relationship decisions with his subordinates. Questions remain about how gender, race, and sexual orientation influence leader disclosure and impact negotiation and breech of privacy boundaries.

In 1985 Gibson and Hodgetts asserted that "American corporate values" reinforce the manager's or leader's reluctance to self-disclose (p. 43). Has the workplace changed enough in the past three decades to counteract their assertion? This sense of the value of guarding one's private information seems to be in play in this television workplace even though an important part of the detectives' job is to ferret out information others (suspects and witnesses) want to keep private. Scott & Myers (2005) found that service workers in intense emotionally charged occupations face added emotional management and disclosure issues and argued that "formal training might counteract the reluctance of members to discuss openly emotion management concerns and techniques they find more or less helpful in particular situations" (p. 88). Does the culture of a police station workplace lead the workers and their leader to be even more cognizant of the importance of strategic self-disclosure and privacy management boundaries?

There are no easy or set rules about how leaders navigate privacy issues in their workplace, but understanding the predictions of CPM may encourage leaders to advance private information selectively and hold clear conversations with their subordinates about the boundaries and rules they have for how their shared private information is handled once it is co-owned. The impact of highly stressful moments and the reluctance or desire among subordinates for private information are other variables to consider in leadership self-disclosure. But a leader must also understand that if she or he has a strong personal privacy orientation, she or he may need to set that aside to share enough information with subordinates to establish trust and build a team mentality. As Captain Ray Holt said to Jake and Amy when he realized they tried to help him overcome a personal issue despite his reluctance to involve them, "I was too proud to admit I was lonely. You brought me back to the Nine-Nine and for that I'll always be grateful."

REFERENCES

Alter, A. L., & Oppenheimer, D. M. (2009). Suppressing secrecy through metacognitive ease: Cognitive fluency encourages self-disclosure. *Psychological Science, 20*(11), 1414–1420. doi: 10.1111/j.1467-9280.2009.02461.x

Altman, I., & Taylor, D. A. (1973). *Social Penetration: The Development of Interpersonal Relationships*. New York: Irvington.

Brody, S. R. (2013). Entering night country: Reflections on self-disclosure and vulnerability. *Psychoanalytic Dialogues, 23*, 45–58. doi: 10.1080/10481885.2013.752703

Brooklyn Nine-Nine: About the show. Retrieved from: http://www.fox.com/brooklyn-nine-nine/article/about-the-show-8

Flaherty, D. G. (2006). *Telling Our Stories: A Phenomenological Study of the Leader's Gendered Experience of Self-disclosing*. Yellow Springs, Ohio: Antioch University. http://rave.ohiolink.edu/etdc/view?acc_num=antioch1164899101

Gibson, J. W., & Hodgetts, R. M. (1985). Self-disclosure: A neglected management skill. *IEEE Transactions on Professional Communication, 28*(3), 41–45. doi:10.1109/TPC.1985.6448829

Goor, D., & Shur, M. (Writers), & Lord, P. & Miller, C. (Directors). (September 17, 2013). Pilot [Television series episode]. In Samberg, A. & Nodella, M. (Producers), *Brooklyn Nine-Nine*. Los Angeles, CA: CBS Studio Center.

Goor, D. (Writer), & Szymanski, J. (Director). (December 3, 2013). Christmas [Television series episode]. In Samberg, A. & Nodella, M. (Producers), *Brooklyn Nine-Nine*. Los Angeles, CA: CBS Studio Center.

Hesse, C., & Rauscher, E. A. (2013). Privacy tendencies and revealing/concealing: The moderating role of emotional competence. *Communication Quarterly, 61*(1), 91–112. doi: 10.1080/01463373.2012.720344

Kennedy-Lightsey, C. D., Martin, M. M., Thompson, M., Himes, K. L., & Clingerman, B. Z. (2012). Communication privacy management theory: Exploring coordination and ownership between friends. *Communication Quarterly, 60*(5), 665–680. doi: 10.1080/01463373.2012.725004

Kolb, C., Noble, J., & Polonsky, J. (Writers), & Asher, R. & Case, R. (Directors). (January 1, 2017). The Fugitive Part I and II [Television series episode]. In Samberg, A. & Nodella, M. (Producers), *Brooklyn Nine-Nine*. Los Angeles, CA: CBS Studio Center.

Liedman, G. (Writer), & Goss, F. (Director). (October 5, 2014). Chocolate Milk [Television series episode]. In Samberg, A. & Nodella, M. (Producers), *Brooklyn Nine-Nine*. Los Angeles, CA: CBS Studio Center.

Liedman, G. (Writer), & McDonald, M. (Director). (October 18, 2015). The Oolong Slayer [Television series episode]. In Samberg, A. & Nodella, M. (Producers), *Brooklyn Nine-Nine*. Los Angeles, CA: CBS Studio Center.

McCreary, L. (Writer), & Scanlon, C. (Director). (February 15, 2015). The Wednesday Incident [Television series episode]. In Samberg, A. & Nodella, M. (Producers), *Brooklyn Nine-Nine*. Los Angeles, CA: CBS Studio Center.

Myers, S. A., & Johnson, A. D. (2004). Perceived solidarity, self-disclosure, and trust in organizational peer relationships. *Communication Research Reports, 21*(1), 75–83.

Noble, J. (Writer), & Holland, D. (Director). (January 18, 2016). 9 Days [Television series episode]. In Samberg, A. & Nodella, M. (Producers), *Brooklyn Nine-Nine*. Los Angeles, CA: CBS Studio Center.

Offerman, L., & Rosh, L. (June 13, 2012). Building trust through skillful self-disclosure. *Harvard Business Review.* Retrieved from: https://hbr.org/2012/06/instantaneous-intimacy-skillfu

Ozeri, G. & Liedman, G. (Writers), & Engler, M. (Director). (February 4, 2014). The Party [Television series episode]. In Samberg, A. & Nodella, M. (Producers), *Brooklyn Nine-Nine*. Los Angeles, CA: CBS Studio Center.

Petronio, S. (2002). *Boundaries of Privacy: Dialectics of Discourse*. Albany, NY: State University of New York.

Petronio, S. (2007). Translational research endeavors and the practices of communication privacy management. *Journal of Applied Communication Research, 35*(3), 218–222. doi: 10.1080/00909880701422443

Petronio, S. (2013). Brief status report on communication privacy management theory. *Journal of Family Communication, 13*, 6–14. doi:10.1080/15267431.2013.743426

Petronio, S., Helft, P. R., & Child, J. T. (2013). A case of error disclosure: A communication privacy management analysis. *Journal of Public Health Research, 2*(30), 175–181. doi:10.4081/jphr.2013.e30

Phillips, D. & Sundaram, L. (Writers), & Kirkby, T. (Director). (January 4, 2015). Beach House [Television series episode]. In Samberg, A. & Nodella, M. (Producers), *Brooklyn Nine-Nine*. Los Angeles, CA: CBS Studio Center.

Polonsky, J. (Writer), & Reid, A. (Director). (February 29, 2016). Cheddar [Television series episode]. In Samberg, A. & Nodella, M. (Producers), *Brooklyn Nine-Nine*. Los Angeles, CA: CBS Studio Center.

Scott, C. & Myers, K. K. (2005). The socialization of emotion: Learning emotional management at the fire station. *Journal of Applied Communication Research, 33*(1), 67–92. doi: 10.1080/00909880420003185214

Serewicz, M. C. M. (2013). Introducing the special issue on communication privacy management theory and family privacy regulation. *Journal of Family Communication, 13*, 2–5. doi: 10.1080/15267431.2013.73424

Sidelinger, R. J., Nyseste, M. C., Madlock, P. E., Pollak, J., & Wilkinson, J. (2015). Instructor privacy management in the classroom: Exploring instructors' ineffective communication and student communication satisfaction. *Communication Studies, 66*(5), 569–589. doi: 10.1080.10510974.2015.1034875

Thompson, J., Petronio, S., & Braithwaite, D. O. (2012). An examination of privacy rules for academic advisors and college student-athletes: A communication privacy management perspective. *Communication Studies, 63*(1), 54–76. doi: 10.1080/10510974.2011.616569

Chapter 11

The Contextualized Workgroup

Examining the Presentation and Practice of Leader, Peer, and Team Relationships in Television

Leah Omilion-Hodges

Television informs our perceptions and expectations of leaders. Because of this, television programs offer a guide for understanding how we should communicate, act, and relate within our places of work. Thus, because of its pervasiveness and the impact it can have in influencing expectations of leadership and related behavior within organizational life, television serves as an important pedagogical tool. To that end, I draw from and compare two award-winning television programs—*Nurse Jackie* and *Parks and Recreation*—to exemplify the importance of leader-member relationships. Moreover, these two television programs are employed to illustrate how the pivotal leader-member relationship helps to shape the peer relationships we foster, and ultimately, how our leader and peer associations culminate to impact team relationships.

FEATURED TELEVISION PROGRAMS

In this comparative analysis, I draw from two popular and critically acclaimed television programs: *Nurse Jackie* and *Parks and Recreation*. Both of these shows feature strong female leads and both also include vibrant ensemble casts in complex, interdependent relationships which play out in workgroups, friendships, and romances. The female leads allow us to explore women who have successfully navigated paths to the top reiterating the newer metaphor of a labyrinth instead of the outdated glass ceiling imagery. In this sense, communication scholars suggest that the obstacles women face are more surmountable, yet it is not necessarily a direct or easy route to top leadership positions.

Nurse Jackie—a dark comedy, revolving around a drug-addicted nurse— focuses on the veteran nurse, Jackie Peyton, as she struggles to find a balance between the demands of her job and her personal affairs. As a senior nurse, she provides mentoring, direction, administrative tasks, and is the go to for nurse peers, physicians, and hospital administrators. In contrast, *Parks and Recreation* is a comedy that centers on the leadership and professional development of Leslie Knope as she progresses from the Deputy Director of the Department of Parks and Recreation to the implied president of the United States. Knope, a dedicated, optimistic, and ambitious government employee in a formal leadership position, provides an excellent foil to Jackie Peyton from *Nurse Jackie*. Like Peyton, Knope often goes above and beyond to assist her team and the community stakeholders she serves. However, unlike Peyton, Knope does not also have a fatal flaw that interferes with her ability to lead, or develop trusting, collaborative relationships or satisfactorily fulfill her duties. Both of these shows are introduced in detail before integrating communication theory to compare and contrast the leadership and organizational lessons culled from the programs.

Nurse Jackie

Nurse Jackie enjoyed a seven-season run from 2009–2015 on Showtime and primarily takes place within All Saints' Hospital in New York City. The show revolves around the seasoned emergency room (ER) nurse, Jackie Peyton, who regularly pushed back against bureaucratic policies and procedures if she could engineer a means to offer better care to a patient. Played by Edie Falco, Jackie virtually always provided outstanding medical care to her patients (though notable exceptions will be addressed) even though she was addicted to pain pills. Throughout the series, viewers watch an extremely competent and compassionate medical profession struggle with addiction, bouts of sobriety, the development and loss of several romantic, personal, and professional relationships, and a fall from grace in terms of trust, respect, and leadership within the ER. While it appears that Jackie cares for her two daughters, Grace and Fiona, the true loves of her life are pills and her role/ identity as a nurse.

In early seasons of *Nurse Jackie*, the title character is a formal and informal mentor to other R.N.s, Zoey Barkow and Thor Lundgren, who work alongside her. Zoey, a student nurse, shadows Jackie. Impressionable and highly passionate, Zoey idolizes Jackie for several seasons basking in the glow of learning from the seemingly unshakable, assertive, fast-thinking, competent nurse. Though Jackie was not in a formal leadership position, she was Zoey's mentor in professional and personal matters. Others too looked to Jackie for informal leadership. The nurse administrator, Gloria Akalitus, trusts Jackie enough to ask her to watch a physician who is returning to the floor after a probationary period. Similarly, Jackie's credibility as a medical professional is immediately established in the pilot episode when she tells the attending physician, Dr. Fitch Cooper, that she suspects a patient has a brain hemorrhage. Dr. Cooper dismisses her advice and the young patient dies from the untreated bleed.

In addition to her professional relationships, Jackie spent the early seasons of the show married to Kevin and residing with their two daughters. However, simultaneously, Jackie managed to maintain a long-running affair with hospital pharmacist, Eddie Walzer. Unaware of her family life, Eddie engages in a physical and emotional relationship with Jackie during work hours, also often providing her pain pills for her supposed bad back. Eventually the truth of her relationship with Eddie emerges and she and Kevin divorce, and ultimately she becomes engaged to Eddie. While Jackie has other romantic interests and interludes throughout the show's run, Kevin and Eddie serve as the most lasting and impactful partners.

Taken together, *Nurse Jackie* centers on the professional life of Jackie Peyton and her work peers and superiors as she strives to provide care,

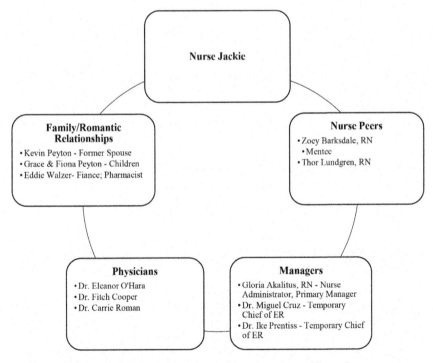

Figure 11.1 Primary characters in *Nurse Jackie*. Figure created by author.

comfort, and compassion while fighting an unending emotional and physical battle with her dependence on prescription drugs. However, because of the complexity of her work environment—an emergency room—and the inter-personal relationships she has built with others born out of her expertise, friendship, and romantic compatibility, we see how this untraditional work-group is simultaneously poised for success and failure.

Parks and Recreation

Revolving around the passionate and driven Leslie Knope, *Parks and Recreation*, follows the antics and endeavors of her team and their friends through six seasons. Throughout the series, Leslie spearheads countless community pursuits for Pawnee, Indiana from engendering community engagement through creation of a time capsule to planning and facilitating the Pawnee Harvest Festival and transforming a dangerous pit into Pawnee Commons.

Knope begins the series as a very proud deputy director of the Pawnee Parks and Recreation department. Her immediate supervisor, Ron Swanson, is the director and they are both under the leadership of Chris Traeger, Paw-nee City Manager. The Parks and Recreation department is also composed of Tom Haverford, Donna Meagle, Jerry Gergich, April Ludgate, and Andy Dwyer. Knopp's best friend, Ann Perkins, and her boyfriend turn spouse, Ben Wyatt, also work within Pawnee government in various roles.

Within the Parks and Recreation Department, Ron Swanson, Leslie's lib-ertarian-boss, believes that all government should be privatized and relishes in a brief government shut down. Despite his overly masculine image, Ron repeatedly goes out of his way for his colleagues from giving them pep talks to assisting with home improvement. Ron employs April Ludgate to ensure that he does as little work and interacting with citizens as possible. Eventu-ally April marries Andy Dwyer who viewers follow from unemployed mooch to shoeshine operator and eventually Leslie's assistant and a knighted talk show host. Tom Haverford serves as Leslie's sarcastic and somewhat under-achieving right hand man. Tom indulges an entrepreneurial spirit through his partial ownership of the Snake Lounge or developing corporations such as Entertainment 720, Rent-A-Swag, and Tom's Bistro. Rounding out the Parks and Recreation Department, are Donna Meagle and Jerry Gergich. Donna is known for her sassy personality and love for her Mercedes-Benz whereas Jerry is virtually always the butt of jokes though they are not generally war-ranted. However, it is clear that he is teased in good fun, where his peers and managers defend him when necessary—such as when he concocted a story about being mugged to conceal the fact that he hurt his arm attempting to fish a sandwich out of a pond. Finally, Leslie's love interest and fellow government employee (from Pawnee, IN to president of the United States),

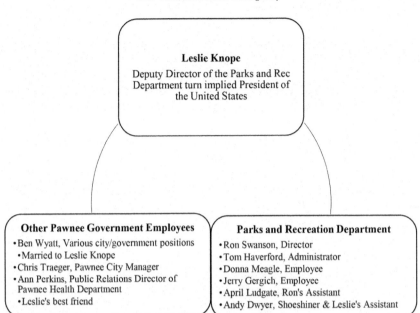

Leslie Knope
Deputy Director of the Parks and Rec
Department turn implied President of
the United States

Other Pawnee Government Employees
• Ben Wyatt, Various city/government positions
• Married to Leslie Knope
• Chris Traeger, Pawnee City Manager
• Ann Perkins, Public Relations Director of
Pawnee Health Department
• Leslie's best friend

Parks and Recreation Department
• Ron Swanson, Director
• Tom Haverford, Administrator
• Donna Meagle, Employee
• Jerry Gergich, Employee
• April Ludgate, Ron's Assistant
• Andy Dwyer, Shoeshiner & Leslie's Assistant

Figure 11.2   Primary characters in *Parks and Recreation*. Figure created by author.

Ben Wyatt shares her love for striving to provide citizens with everyday services and amenities and provides her with unwavering support.

At first blush it may seem like the cast of *Parks and Recreation*, is similar to the ER workgroup in *Nurse Jackie*. There are similarities in terms of their propensity to solicit professional and personal advice from coworkers and to even engage in workplace romances—however, due in large part to the overwhelmingly positive traits Leslie Knope brings to her work and her friendships, the Parks and Recreation Department fares better in terms of trusting, two-way communicative relationships. The emergency room staff at All Saints' Hospital, ride a rollercoaster of emotions in terms of trying to help Jackie kick her addiction, to realizing that she's virtually always lying and manipulating them, to recognizing that she's best kept at a distance. Considering these diverse female leaders and similarly rich workgroups, we now turn our attention to relevant leadership theory—the contextualized workgroup (Omilion-Hodges & Baker, 2017; Omilion-Hodges, Ptacek, & Zerilli, 2016).

THE CONTEXTUALIZED WORKGROUP

While some have suggested that two ingredients, people and tasks, makeup leadership, this rudimentary view obscures the complex and interdependent nature of leader-member relationships. Moreover, this dichotomous examination of leadership squelches the prominent role that communication plays in leading, following, relating, and organizing. For example, focusing only on people and tasks conceals the way in which organizational actors communicate to establish and maintain boundaries, navigate social interactions, and set and complete individual and group goals (Mathieu, Maynard, Rapp, & Gilson, 2008). Therefore, instead of focusing solely on formal leaders, employing a communicative view allows for a more comprehensive examination and understanding of workgroup dynamics inclusive of leader-member, peer, and team relationships (Omilion-Hodges et al., 2016).

Communication scholars (i.e., Omilion-Hodges et al., 2017; Omilion-Hodges & Baker, 2017; Sheer, 2014) in particular, continue to emphasize the importance of examining leadership within the milieu of the workgroup as a means to flesh out the messiness, meaningful dialogues, and the physical and social environment that is produced from a collection of varied leader-member relationships (Denis, Langley, & Rouleau, 2010; Lident & Antonakis, 2009). That is, because leaders develop relationships of varying quality with each member, workgroups become exceedingly complex relational sites where research has indicated that members are savvy observers of managerial behavior (Hooper & Martin, 2008). Considering this, it has been suggested that instead of utilizing traditional, insular approaches to study leadership, examination of the contextualized workgroup includes leader-member (LMX; Dansereau, Graen, & Haga, 1975), coworker (CWX; Sherony & Green, 2002), and team (TMX; Seers, 1989) relationships.

Though often studied in isolation, the aggregation of these relationships forge an employee's communicative and relational work experience. Thus in place of considering workplace relationships as points of a triangle, I suggest that the stakes of a teepee offer a more apt illustration. When examined individually, leader, coworker, and team relationships may be represented as the points on the larger triangle of workplace relationships. Although connected as parts of the same structure, the triangle approach does little to suggest how these relationships interact and are dependent on one another. Rather, a more accurate illustration of these relationships may be as the foundations of a teepee, each relationship representing a different stake and offering a three-dimensional view of workgroup complexity. The more relationships and perspectives considered, the more support the overall structure has—however, at its very core, the argument must consider multiple perspectives in order to stand alone and to give an increasingly precise depiction of how these relationships are interdependent. Research that considers multilevel effects of myriad relationships in tandem, or contextualized research, is what binds the teepee together. Put simply, contextualized research accounts for the dynamic and complex entanglement of leader, coworker, and team associations, holistically considering how these pivotal relationships may impact organizational life for any individual employee, but also how an employee's associations may subsequently impact others' leader, coworker, and team relationships. Considering this, we now focus on illustrations of the contextualized workgroup from *Nurse Jackie* and *Parks and Recreation*.

Leader-Member Exchange

Leader-member exchange (LMX; Dansereau, Graen, & Haga, 1975) is a communication-based theory of leadership that details the relational exchanges between an employee and their direct manager. LMX suggests that leaders develop different exchange relationships with each of their followers, meaning they may develop more trusting relationships with some employees or like some associates less than others. Because relationships develop and are maintained through communication, some scholars have argued that work and social communication are the most important aspects of the leader-member relationship (Sheer, 2014).

There are a number of factors that can impact the quality of leader-member relationships including employee competence, gender, trustworthiness, accountability, and personality factors like the use of humor, discretion, and overall communication competence. Moreover, employees who have high-quality leader-member relationships—commonly referred to as high LMX—enjoy increased latitude, more frequent promotions, and higher social standing than their low LMX counterparts. Typically, an employee's LMX tends to remain fairly stable once developed, however, in extenuating circumstances their LMX level may change. *Nurse Jackie* offers plentiful examples of Jackie as a high LMX employee, a trusted leader within the ER, a veteran nurse who teaches students, and can step in and manage physicians when necessary. By illustration, a young woman was readmitted to the ER complaining of back pain. Since she was in the emergency room the previous day for a car crash, the attending physician, Dr. Carrie Roman, suspected the patient of seeking additional drugs. After reviewing an X-ray, Dr. Roman ordered an immediate discharge though the patient continued to complain of back pain. Suspecting other underlying causes, Jackie orders lab work to show the patient has sepsis and was admitted to the ICU. In this example, Jackie relies on her medical expertise and experience, disregards the physician's order, and even orders lab work without a physicians' approval. However, because she was right and was seen as a highly competent nurse, she was merely talked to by the chief of the ER, Dr. Prentiss, rather than formally written up.

While Jackie enjoyed a number benefits associated with high LMX, viewers also watch Jackie's relationships with her nurse administrator and ER chiefs, plummet as her drug use increases. Akalitus first does not allow Jackie to administer pills, "not even an aspirin," she is warned, to having to enter a diversion program in order to maintain her nursing license. Jackie is stripped of her nursing blue scrubs, must wear orderly whites, and maintains no contact with patients. Generally, she changes bed sheets and must take daily drug tests that are monitored by Zoey, her former protégé.

A more typical view of leader-member exchange is the high LMX that Leslie Knope maintains throughout the series. Perhaps because they are polar opposites, Leslie and her manager, Ron Swanson, have a relationship that evolves from professional respect and accountability, to a lasting, trusting, friendship. Initially Ron is presented with the Indiana Organization of Women Woman of the Year award, much to the chagrin of Leslie who has long coveted the recognition. While he does not immediately inform Leslie of his plan because he feels she cares too deeply about external recognition, at the awards banquette Ron suggests that Leslie is the most deserving recipient and presents it to her. Ron also provides Leslie with emotional support when it appears she may lose a city council position telling her "You had a dream and we wanted to support your dream. That's what you do when you care about someone. You support them: win, lose or draw." Finally, because their leader-member relationship flourished into a deep friendship, Ron walked Leslie down the aisle at her wedding and the two were able to honestly and respectfully address tensions that threatened to damage the relationship in later seasons.

Coworker Exchange

Similar to LMX, coworker exchange (CWX) describes the relationship between two coworkers who report to the same leader (Sherony & Green, 2002). Research in this area suggests that when you have two coworkers who have a similar relationship with their leader, whether they both have low-, moderate-, or high-quality LMXs, they are more likely to share a strong peer relationship. Peer relationships are especially important sources of social support and are positively associated with job satisfaction and involvement and organizational commitment (Chiaburu & Harrison, 2008). Both, *Nurse Jackie* and *Parks and Recreation*, offer poignant examples of the power of coworker exchange.

The most impactful coworker exchange relationship in *Nurse Jackie* is that between Jackie and her trainee turned friend, Zoey. In early seasons, Zoey follows Jackie around recording her actions with a pen and paper in an attempt to learn all she could from her mentor. In many ways, Zoey looked up to Jackie as a nontraditional mother figure and friend, going to her for both professional and personal advice. The notoriously private Jackie even takes Zoey in when she is between places after a breakup. However, the relationship is not one-sided, where Zoey routinely stands up for Jackie when others question her sobriety and advises her on how to handle her teenage daughter. Yet as the series progresses, Zoey begins to realize that despite Jackie's best intentions to become and maintain her sobriety, she cannot trust her. This becomes exceedingly clear when Jackie, high on Oxy, inadvertently administers 100 times the ordered dose of insulin to a patient who immediately becomes unconscious. Zoey is able to rush in and rectify the mistake, but then tells the nurse administrator that she's "worried about her [Jackie], and I'm worried about us [All Saint's Hospital]." This coworker exchange relationship acts like a pendulum, alternating between a trusting, two-way relationship and one marked by suspicion, lies, and betrayal. Again, while CWXs may change in status, traditionally and similar to LMX, once established these relationships remain fairly stable unless there is a pivotal event or series of events that causes one party to rethink and renegotiate the relationship. For this reason, *Nurse Jackie* serves as an excellent exemplar to explore a more anomalous peer relationship.

Leslie Knope, due in part to her gregarious, warm, and honest nature, has high CWX relationships with each of her peers. Her work relationship with Tom, a *Parks and Recreation* administrator, is a particular strong example to draw from. While Tom and Leslie work closely together on a number of government projects from serving on a special task force to catch a possum at a golf course, the episode entitled "Meet N Greet," illustrates several important aspects of high-quality coworker exchange relationship. As a means of networking with prominent Pawnee city figures, Leslie hires Tom's company Entertainment 720 to organize a meet and greet before her upcoming city council race. Throughout the evening, Leslie becomes increasingly angered to realize that the event appears to only be promoting Tom's company rather than her bid for city council. Tom's face is on all of the promotional materials, he highjacks Leslie's conversation with the president of the chamber of commerce, and then interrupts her formal presentation with an elaborate multimedia pitch for his organization. Understandably Leslie is upset, especially when all of the attendees begin to leave because of the flagrant sales nature of the presentation. However, afterward and due in part to the high-quality exchange relationship Leslie and Tom share, the two were able to resolve their differences. Tom disclosed that his company was bankrupt and the stunt was a last ditched effort to drum up business and then he showed Leslie a video biography of her life that he has created and originally intended to show at the event. Additionally, Tom also secured a future meeting for Leslie with the chamber of commerce president. In this sense, we can see how in the presence of a well-developed and trusting coworker exchange relationship, peers can come together to reach higher levels of productivity and cultivate and maintain supportive interpersonal relationships.

Team-Member Exchange

Team-member exchange (TMX) explicates the social exchange relationships between a member and the sum of his/her team, and "refers to the extent to which information, help, and recognition between a member and other members of the workgroup is reciprocal" (Bakar & Sheer, 2013, p. 445). Unlike LMX and CWX, TMX encompasses all workgroup relationships and therefore is not dyadic in nature. Since team effectiveness relies on the quality of exchange between team members, interpersonal relationships are an integral element (Tse, Dasborough, & Ashkanasy, 2008) and each exchange relationship is unique from those of other members, as the individual member decides how he or she will interact with workgroup peers (Bakar & Sheer, 2013; Omilion-Hodges et al., 2016). Team-member exchange has gained recent attention due to the increased focus on team collaboration and performance within organizations.

A shining example of TMX in *Nurse Jackie* occurs when the then chief of the ER, Dr. Cruz, fires Jackie because he finds that she has disobeyed his wishes and has authorized the hire of temporary nurses. As a means to showcase his legitimate authority, he publically fires her for insubordination. As a sign of support to Jackie, her fellow nurses and attending physicians who stepped up and assumed responsibility for the successful running of the ER in the absence of formal leaders, stood up and started clapping for Jackie. This was an illustration of support for her, a means of opposing Dr. Cruz, and a way to illustrate the collective strength of the team. In this situation, Jackie demonstrates the impact of informal leadership on a team. Communication scholars (e.g., Fairhurst, 2007; Fairhurst & Connaughton, 2014) do not necessarily see those in formal leadership positions (i.e., manager, director) as the only organizational actors who are leaders, but rather that leadership is a process ascribed by followers suggesting that communication itself constitutes these relationships and is the basis of these perceptions.

The Pawnee Harvest Festival also offers a shining example of team-member exchange in addition to formal leadership. As the Parks and Recreations Department toils to put the finishing touches on the Harvest Festival—a highly visible and high stake event—a number of exchanges occur that produce team conflict. The team was thrilled to secure the presence of Li'L Sebastian, Pawnee's famous and beloved mini-horse. While Li'L Sebastian is entrusted to Jerry, he asks Tom to watch the mini-horse while he takes a break. Tom forgets to close the gate and Li'L Sebastian goes missing. Though aware that he is at fault, Tom continues to place the blame on Jerry. While the team assembles to find Li'L Sebastian, April tells Andy that she loves him to which he replies "Dude, shut up! That is awesomesauce!" April is angry and hurt by the response and will no longer talk to Andy or work with him to find Li'L Sebastian. Ron, the team's formal leader, becomes fed up with the in-group bickering and rectifies the situation by acknowledging that everyone knows that Tom is responsible for the lost mini-horse and explaining to Andy that April is angry that he did not respond traditionally to April's confession of love. Ron's ability to communicate clearly leads to Andy telling April that he also loves her and Tom apologizing to Jerry. Shortly thereafter, the team locates Li'L Sebastian in the adjacent corn maze. This offers a powerful example of how workgroups can be both sites for relationships and tasks, and that more often than not, it is impossible to disentangle one from the other. Moreover, in high TMX groups, it can be healthiest to integrate one's personal and professional life because of the breadth of trusted interpersonal relationships.

DISCUSSION

One cannot tease out only task aspects or relational aspects of leadership because these elements are communicatively interwoven (Omilion-Hodges & Wieland, 2016). Throughout this chapter, I have shown through illustrations from *Nurse Jackie* and *Parks and Recreation*, how communication can be employed to create, maintain, or destroy leader-member, peer, and team relationships within the contexts of organizational workgroups. By focusing on the role of communication in leading, students can become more self-reflective of their own competencies and about the implications of their words and actions within groups and work contexts. Similarly, a resolute focus on communication will equip students to ebb and flow between leader and follower roles and personal and professional relationships with colleagues. Communicatively rooted theoretical implications and practical takeaways are discussed below.

Theoretical Implications

Leadership research continues to reiterate the importance of high-quality leader, peer, and team relationships. This becomes even more important with the 50 percent increase in the amount of time managers and their members spend interacting to achieve organizational goals over the past two decades (Cross, Rebele, & Grant, 2016). This also suggests that employees are even better equipped to engage in relational comparisons between themselves and their peers. As a result, if leaders value the collective performance of their workgroups, they must manage individual and group resources, manage relationships, and manage follower perceptions of the individual and collective set of relationships (Omilion-Hodges & Baker, 2013). Thus, because leaders can enact a variety of behaviors in connecting to, coaching, and or disciplining employees, they need to be cognizant of how these various interpersonal exchange behaviors may influence the collective functioning of the group (Bakar & Sheer, 2013). And again, with the rise of team-based work, a leader's true success may lie in increased mindfulness of their communication practices and the resulting impact on workgroup relationships. Considering this, a communication view of leader-member relationships underscores the importance of social interactions within workgroups, highlighting how a series of incremental communicative exchanges induce these pivotal associations.

While the leader-member relationship continues to be prized for its importance and is often framed as a springboard for an employee's future success, recent research has shown that there may be some disadvantages of close-leader-member couplings, particularly in terms of group functioning. Omilion-Hodges and Baker (2017), for example, found that employees consciously withhold information from peers who have a different LMX status. In other words, if an employee with a high-quality relationship with their manager had access to information that would help a peer with a low quality relationship with the same manager, they would be hesitant to share it. Certainly, there may have been an incident or series of incidents that prompted an employee to decide to withhold information from a peer—such as when Zoey recognizes that Jackie is working in a compromised state. However, other concerns may be the fear of potential social ramifications of interacting with a lower status actor as is often seen in the ways the Parks and Recreation Department withholds or alters information designed for Jerry.

Omilion-Hodges & Baker (2017) also found that participants across three studies disclosed the same pattern: higher quality leader-member couplings engage in more frequent and more diverse communication behaviors. If we consider Ron and Leslie, for example, as the series progresses they go from task focused communication to Ron walking Leslie down the aisle. However, this finding can be particularly problematic in that it continues to promote relational discrepancies within workgroups. A more effective leadership approach would be to develop a high-quality communicative relationship with a member, and once the member was able to demonstrate self-leadership, the manager could turn his or her attention to increasing their communicative relationship with other members. In this sense, leaders would not shirk the responsibility of developing high-quality communicative relationships with all members, but would rather work to do so systematically.

One additional theoretical implication of this chapter is the importance of formal and informal leaders within workgroups. As the name suggests, formal leaders are those who are in management positions, and as such have access to position power such as the ability to hire, fire, and assign raises. Though essential to overall organizational health, as we saw in the *Nurse Jackie* TMX example, there are times when informal leaders are more impactful. While they may not have access to the same sources of power that formal leaders do, because of their expertise and the relationships they share with other workgroup members, informal leaders are seen as important referents (French & Raven, 1959). Moreover, those with referent power are often admired and respected which is often met with loyalty and friendship. Therefore, it is important to remember that even if you are not in a formal leadership position, there are still opportunities to guide, support, and influence others.

Practical Takeaways

In addition to enhancing theoretical knowledge of leadership communication, this chapter offers four primary practical takeaways: Workgroup relationships are incredibly important, mentors are essential, the gender leadership gap is closing and so is the transformative power of self-leadership.

Importance of workgroup relationships. Composed of leader-member, peer, and team associations, the contextualized workgroup encapsulates an employee's most pivotal organizational relationships. Workgroups can be thought of as a web, where despite a researcher's best intentions it is impossible to disentangle the influence of one relationship from the remainder (Liden & Antonakis, 2009). Likewise, workgroups are in a constant state of flux (Omilion-Hodges & Baker, 2013) where the quality of one's associations influences employees' other associations. This may lead to increased access to resources such as praise, promotion, and latitude, or it may lead to relative isolation. Therefore, the importance of working to cultivate a strong leader-member relationship is likely to spur trusting peer associations as well. This can be key to professional growth, but also personal support and guidance. Before the relationship became toxic, Jackie, a competent, trusted, veteran nurse, helped socialize Zoey into the profession by demonstrating basics such as starting an IV and how to deal with a difficult patient. However, with time the leader-member relationship blossomed into a trusted friendship where the two parties were able to trust and confide in each other, which acted as a buffer against professional and personal stressors. The Parks and Recreation Department too offers a wealth of examples of the many benefits of highly developed workgroup relationships. When Tom's Entertainment 720 eventually folds, Ron will literally not accept no for an answer in providing him his old job back after seeing him work as a perfume spritzer at Macy's. Similarly, when Ben is clearly depressed, Tom and Donna invite him to their annual Treat Yo Self Day, where they indulge any whim. Though Tom and Donna are quite different from Ben and it takes a while to find satisfaction in

Treat Yo Self Day, because of the trusted work association, they offered him necessarily social support.

The gender leadership gap. Eagly and Carli proposed a new metaphor, a labyrinth, to replace the outmoded glass ceiling imagery. While women are holding more leadership positions than they ever have historically, there are still large discrepancies in the ratio of men and women in the C-suite suggesting that a gap persists. Thus while there isn't necessarily an invisible barrier as forceful as a ceiling anymore, Eagly and Carli are quick to point out that it's not necessarily a linear path for women in securing leadership roles. One of the most efficient means of narrowing the gap is through assertive and mindful communication. While *Parks and Recreation* takes a tongue-in-cheek approach to illustrating the power of a woman using direct communication, it is nonetheless effective. Councilman Milton said, "I believe one problem with hiring women is that they're frail and breakable," to which Leslie responded with "Is it possible you're thinking about lightbulbs? Or your hip?" Similarly, women should also focus on relationship building and status/agency simultaneously in workplace interactions. In this sense, women can establish trusting two-way relationships, while still demonstrating their expertise and experiences. The resolute focus on relationships and status will help women to form social capital, increasing their networks and their reputations.

Mentors are essential. Mentoring offers benefits to mentees, mentors, and their organizations. Mentees benefit from boasts to their skills and self-confidence and increased access to new network contacts whereas mentors are able to give back, often reporting feeling a reenergizing of their career. Formal and informal mentoring often promotes employee loyalty, increases organizational citizenship behavior, and often results in enhanced productivity. Scholars' examination of mentors suggests that both leaders and coworkers are better at achieving goal outcomes than formal mentors (Raabe & Beehr, 2003). That is, mentor and leader relationships naturally forged by employees may be equally or more influential than formal mentoring relationships set up through organizational means. This suggests that although the organizational setting may have a significant influence on the nature of the coworker relationship, the communication that occurs between employees can allow for a more intricate relationship than is generally acknowledged.

The transformative power of self-leadership. Self-leadership, in many ways, details how the choices we make for ourselves position us for success or for failure. Inherently communicative, self-leadership describes the ways in which we influence ourselves to grow and move toward our objectives or allow ourselves to engage in behavior that detracts from our goals. Leslie Knope is a prime example of self-leadership from the framed pictures of respected world leaders in her office to her thorough and often over-prepared approach to work. She consistently makes choices that allow her to grow and move toward her goal of an elected official. Jackie Peyton, conversely, crumbles as the series continues. We see her lose her twenty-year marriage, custody of her children, spend time in jail, lose trusted friendships and work relationships, and her ability to provide patient care for some time. Addiction is a disease and *Nurse Jackie* is responsible in showing that, however, throughout the show Jackie got and maintained sobriety for varying lengths of time. In these brief interludes, we see her familial, romantic, and work relationships flourishing but we also see her stubbornly refuse to regularly attend meetings or honestly work with sponsors. More frequently, Jackie continued to lie and manipulate people and situations to shift the blame. These two extremely competent and assertive female leads powerfully demonstrate clear and varied consequences in terms of self-leadership.

REFERENCES

Bakar, H. A., & Sheer, V. C. (2013). The mediating role of perceived cooperative communication in the relationship between interpersonal exchange relationships and perceived group cohesion. *Management Communication Quarterly, 27*, 443–465. doi: 10.1177/0893318913492564.

Baker, C. R., & Omilion-Hodges, L. M. (2013). Examining the influence of workplace relationships on behavioral tendencies. *Communication Research Reports, 30*, 313–322.

Chiaburu, D. S., & Harrison, D. A. (2008). Do peers make the place? Conceptual synthesis and meta-analysis of coworker effects on perceptions, attitudes, OCBs, and performance. *Journal of Applied Psychology, 93*, 1082–1103. doi: 10.1037/0021-9010.93.5.1082.

Cross, R., Rebele, R., & Grant, A. (2016). Collaborative overload. *The Harvard Business Review, 94*(1–2), 74–79.

Dansereau, F., Graen, G., & Haga, W. J. (1975). A vertical dyad linkage approach to leadership within formal organizations: A longitudinal investigation of the role making process. *Organizational Behavior and Human Performance, 13*, 46–78. doi: 10.1016/0030-5073(75)90005-7.

Denis, J., Langley, A., & Rouleau, L. (2010). The practice of leadership in the messy world of organizations. *Leadership, 6*, 67–88. doi: 10.1177/1742715009354233.

Eagly, A. H. and Carli, L. L. (2007). "Women and the labyrinth of leadership", Harvard Business Review, September, 63–71.

Fairhurst, G. T. (2007). *Discursive Leadership: In Conversation with Leadership Psychology*. Thousand Oaks, CA: Sage.

Fairhurst, G. T., & Connaughton, S. L. (2014). Leadership: A communicative perspective. *Leadership, 10*, 7–35. doi: 10.1177/1742715013509396.

French, J., & Raven, B. (1959). The basis of social power. In D. Cartwright (Ed.), *Studies in Social Power* (150–167). Ann Arbor: University of Michigan.

Hooper, D. T., & Martin, R. (2008). Beyond personal leader-member exchange (LMX) quality: The effects of perceived LMX variability on employee reactions. *The Leadership Quarterly, 19,* 20–30. doi: 10.1016/j.leaqua.2007.12.002.

Kram, K., & Isabella, L. A. (1985). Mentoring alternatives: The role of peer relationships in career development. *Academy of Management Journal, 28,* 110–132. doi: 10.2307/256064.

Liden, R. C., & Antonakis, J. (2009). Considering context in psychological leadership research. *Human Relations, 62,* 1587–1605. doi: 10.1177/0018726709346374.

Mathieu, J. E., Maynard, M. T., Rapp, T., & Gilson, L. (2008). Team effectiveness 1997–2007: A review of recent advancements and a glimpse into the future. *Journal of Management, 34,* 410–476. doi: 10.1177/0149206308316061.

Omilion-Hodges, L. M., & Wieland, S. M. B. (2016). Unraveling the leadership dichotomy by rethinking leadership communication. *Journal of Leadership Education, 15*(1), 110–128.

Omilion-Hodges, L. M., & Baker, C. R. (2013). Contextualizing LMX within the workgroup: The effects of LMX and justice on relationship quality and resource sharing among peers. *The Leadership Quarterly, 24,* 935–951.

Omilion-Hodges, L. M. & Baker, C. R. (2017). Communicating leader-member relationship quality: Relationship building and maintenance through the exchange of communication-based goods. *International Journal of Business Communication.* Advanced online publication. doi: 10.1177/2329488416687052.

Omilion-Hodges, L. M., Ptacek, J. K., & Zerilli, D. H. (2016). A comprehensive review and communication research agenda of the contextualized workgroup: The evolution and future of leader-member exchange, coworker exchange, and team-member exchange. In E. L. Cohen (Ed.), *Communication Yearbook, 40,* 343–377. New York: Routledge.

Raabe, B., & Beehr, T. A. (2003). Formal mentoring versus supervisor and coworker relationships: Differences in perceptions and impact. *Journal of Organizational Behavior, 24,* 271–293. doi: 10.1002/job.193.

Seers, A. (1989). Team-member exchange quality: A new construct for role-making research. *Organizational Behavior and Human Decision Processes, 43,* 118–135. doi:10.1016/0749-5978(89)90060-5.

Sheer, V. C. (2014). "Exchange lost" in leader–member exchange theory and research: A critique and a reconceptualization. *Leadership, 11,* 1–17. doi:10.1177/1742715014530935.

Sherony, K. M., & Green, S. G. (2002). Coworker exchange: Relationships between coworkers, leader-member exchange, and work attitudes. *Journal of Applied Psychology, 87,* 542–548. doi: 10.1037//0021-9010.87.3.542.

Tse, H. H., Dasborough, M. T., & Ashkanasy, N. M. (2008). A multi-level analysis of team climate and interpersonal exchange relationships at work. *The Leadership Quarterly, 19,* 195–211. doi: 10.1016/j.leaqua.2008.01.005.

Index

About the Editor

Creshema R. Murray (PhD, University of Alabama) is an assistant professor of corporate communication at the University of Houston-Downtown. Dr. Murray teaches courses in leadership, organizational training and development, and destructive organizational communication. Dr. Murray is engaged in two areas of communication research. Her first area of research focuses on the lived experiences of women of color in workplace organizations. The second area focuses on the manner in which organizations foster destructive workplace practices with employees. In addition to her role at the University of Houston-Downtown, Dr. Murray engages in overseeing the creation and implementation of a multitude of strategically focused communication campaigns. Her most recent research was published in *Critical examinations of women of color navigating mentoring relationships, Contexts of the Dark Side of Communication,* and *Peer Review.*

About the Authors

Mia L. Anderson (PhD, University of Alabama) is an assistant professor of communication at the University of South Alabama. Her research interests include minority images in the media, image repair in sports, and magazine history. Her research has been published in the *Journal of Sports Media*, the *Journal of African American Studies, The Media in America: A History (9th ed.)*, and *Social Media: Usage and Impact.*

Raymond Blanton is an assistant professor of communication arts in the School of Media and Design at the University of the Incarnate Word in San Antonio, TX. His research is primarily concerned with the civic dimensions of rhetoric, communication, and media in intellectual history and American culture, particularly in the itinerant fieldwork of Alan Lomax, the Delta blues, the marches of the American civil rights movement, and in the Samaritan ethic of Martin Luther King, Jr.'s sermonic discourse. Additional interests include critical pedagogy, working-class, first-generation, and millennial cultures, cinema, sacred rhetoric and theology, and public memory.

Kristen L. Cole is an assistant professor in communication at Indiana University-Purdue University in Columbus, IN. She received her PhD from the University of New Mexico in 2013 and her MA from Colorado State University in 2009. Her research investigates representations of identity and pathology; specifically the ways discourses of gender, race, sexuality, and disability construct and disrupt normative assumptions and ways of knowing.

Loren Saxton Coleman conducts research on social justice in various forms of media, including community media, social media, television, and the Black press. More specifically, Dr. Coleman explores practices of contingent agency in various media forms to explore how marginalized communities engage in acts of resistance and practices of community uplift. She is particularly interested in how structures of race, gender, class, and space (social and physical infrastructures) condition ways in which black women exercise agency via media. Dr. Coleman earned her doctorate and master's degrees in mass communication from the Grady College of Journalism and Mass Communication at the University of Georgia. She earned her BA in communication at North Carolina State University. Dr. Coleman is originally from Washington, D.C.

Joseph M. Deye is a master's student at the University of Cincinnati. His research interests include leadership communication, organizational communication, and rhetoric. He also serves as a speech instructor and as a graduate teaching assistant for the Department of Communication at the University of Cincinnati.

Donna M. Elkins (PhD, University of Kentucky) is a professor in the School of Communication at Spalding University in Louisville, Ky. Elkins' current primary area of research interest is in the balancing of self-disclosure and privacy when seeking out social support. She has explored these issues in the context of organizational newcomers and cancer survivors. In 2016 she was chosen as a University of Alabama Plank Center for Leadership in Public Relations Educator Fellow. She teaches a variety of undergraduate courses in interpersonal and organizational communication, as well as graduate courses focused on interpersonal communication in the workplace.

Gail T. Fairhurst is a distinguished university research professor of organizational communication at the University of Cincinnati. She specializes in leadership processes, including problem-centered leadership and framing. She has published over 80 articles and chapters in communication and management journals and books. She is the author of three books, including *The Power of Framing: Challenging the Language of Leadership*. She is a fellow of the International Communication Association, a distinguished scholar of the National Communication Association, and a Fulbright Scholar.

Sharmila Pixy Ferris (PhD Penn State) is a professor in the Department of Communication at William Paterson University and Coordinator of the Social Justice Project. Her research brings an interdisciplinary focus to computer-mediated communication and online learning. She has published many articles and several books in the areas of technology, teaching, and learning including *Unplugging From the Classroom* (2017), *The Plugged-In Professor* (2013). *Teaching, Learning and the Net Generation* (2011), *Online*

Instructional Modeling (2008), *Teaching and learning with virtual teams* (2005), *Virtual and collaborative teams* (2004), and *Beyond survival in the academy: A practical guide for beginning academics* (2003).

Maxine Gesualdi is an assistant professor in the Department of Communication Studies at West Chester University of Pennsylvania. Her primary research focuses on the effects of shared resources on organizational role enactment. Her recent work examines how public relations and marketing professionals navigate their roles when responsibilities and goals encroach across department boundaries. Bringing over 15 years of professional corporate communications expertise to the classroom, Dr. Gesualdi strives to connect established theories and her own research with students' everyday experiences. She earned her PhD in media and communication from Temple University in Philadelphia, Pa., her MA in communication studies from West Chester University of Pa., and a BS in journalism from West Virginia University.

Creshema R. Murray (PhD, University of Alabama) is an assistant professor of corporate communication at the University of Houston-Downtown. Dr. Murray teaches courses in leadership, organizational training and development, and destructive organizational communication. Dr. Murray is engaged in two areas of communication research. Her first area of research focuses on the lived experiences of women of color in workplace organizations. The second area focuses on the manner in which organizations foster destructive workplace practices with employees. In addition to her role at the University of Houston-Downtown, Dr. Murray engages in overseeing the creation and implementation of a multitude of strategically focused communication campaigns. Her most recent research was published in *Critical examinations of women of color navigating mentoring relationships, Contexts of the Dark Side of Communication* and *Peer Review.*

Leah M. Omilion-Hodges (PhD. Wayne State University) is an associate professor in the School of Communication at Western Michigan University. Her research focuses on leadership and health communication within the larger context of organizational communication. Her work explores workgroup dynamics within applied settings to examine the influence of leader-member, peer, and team associations on relationship development, status distinctions, and the sharing of resources. Her work has been featured in venues such as *Communication Yearbook, the International Journal of Business Communication, the Leadership Quarterly, the Journal of Leadership Education, Health Communication,* and *Computers in Human Behavior* among others.

Alexis Pulos is an assistant professor at Northern Kentucky University where he teaches courses in game design, communication theory, and media studies. He received his PhD from the University of New Mexico in 2013 and his MA from Colorado State University in 2009. His current work focuses on the ways agency and meaning are structured and produced through the design and social regulation of information systems.

Mark Ward Sr. (PhD, Clemson University) is an associate professor of communication at the University of Houston-Victoria, Texas, United States. He is editor of the multivolume series, *The Electronic Church in the Digital Age: Cultural Impacts of Evangelical Mass Media* (2016), and author of two histories of religious broadcasting, *The Lord's Radio* (2017) and *Air of Salvation* (1994). His ethnographic research on the evangelical subculture and its congregational life and popular media has appeared in numerous edited volumes and scholarly journals, including the Journal of Communication and Religion, Journal of Media and Religion, Journal of Religion, Media and Digital Culture, Journal of Radio and Audio Media, Intercultural Communication Studies, and Voluntas. He serves on the boards of the Journal of Communication and Religion and the Religious Communication Association, which named his ethnography of evangelical media its 2014 Article of the Year. His research in organizational studies has also been published in the book Deadly Documents (2014), which explores the organizational culture of the Holocaust through ethnographic analyses of everyday Nazi bureaucratic documents, and the coauthored textbook *Organizational Communication: Theory, Research, and Practice* (2015). Before entering academia he served as communications director for several national nonprofits and industry trade associations and worked as a broadcaster in roles ranging from local announcer to national syndication.

9 781498 561518